Gifted Children and Teachers in the Primary School

Florence Maltby

 The Falmer Press

A member of the Taylor & Francis Group
London and Philadelphia

UK	The Falmer Press, Falmer House, Barcombe, Lewes, East Sussex, BN8 5DL
USA	The Falmer Press, Taylor & Francis Inc., 242 Cherry Street, Philadelphia, PA 19106-1906

First published in 1984

Library of Congress Cataloging in Publication Data

Maltby, Florence.
  Gifted children and teachers in the primary school.

  Revision of thesis (doctoral)—University of Sussex, 1983.
    Bibliography: p.
    1. Gifted children—Education (Elementary)—Great Britain. I. Title.
  LC3997.G7M34 1984   371.9   84-4040
  ISBN 1-85000-003-4
  ISBN 1-85000-002-6 (pbk.)

Typeset in 9½/12 Palatino by
Imago Publishing Ltd, Thame, Oxon

Jacket design by Leonard Williams

Printed in Great Britain by Taylor & Francis (Printers) Ltd, Basingstoke

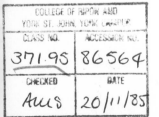

Contents

ACKNOWLEDGEMENTS vi

FRONTISPIECE vii

Introduction 1

1 Research Perspectives of Giftedness 5

2 The Categorization of Children as Gifted 17

3 Labelling and Giftedness 53

4 Educational Provision for Gifted Children 87

5 Gifted Children in the Classroom 135

6 Gifted Children and their Peers 171

7 Conclusions 205

APPENDIX 213

BIBLIOGRAPHY 235

INDEX 245

Acknowledgements

This book is based upon my DPhil. thesis completed at the University of Sussex in 1983. I would like to thank the staff and pupils of the thirteen schools that took part in this research. Without their generous cooperation this study would not have been possible.

I am greatly indebted to my two supervisors Dr. Stephen Ball and Dr. Peter Kutnick. I would also like to acknowledge the help of Stephen Steadman, John Hughes, Dr. Barry Cooper, Dr. Eric Ogilvie and Prof. Colin Lacey, who read and advised me on various chapters and drafts of this study. Dr. David Hitchin's advice about statistics was invaluable, and his computer saved me a great deal of time and effort.

Finally, though by no means least, I must thank my husband, Malcolm, and my children, Alexandra and Nicholas, for their patience and encouragement.

Frontispiece

A Staffroom Conversation in a First School

First teacher – 'To be gifted they have to be gifted all round.'
Second teacher – 'Einstein wasn't.'
First teacher – 'Was Einstein gifted?'
Third teacher – 'That depends on whether you are talking about creative giftedness.'

Introduction

In 1959 an article was published in America by Pegnato and Birch. Their research had a profound effect on American research concerning gifted children during the years that followed. The purpose of Pegnato and Birch's study was to assess the effectiveness and efficiency of a variety of methods of screening children for giftedness, including teacher judgment; honor roll listing; creative ability in art and music; student council membership; superiority in mathematics; group intelligence test scores; and group achievement test scores. They adopted as their criterion for giftedness a Stanford Binet Intelligence Quotient (IQ) cut-off point of 136, and compared each method of assessment with IQ. The effectiveness of each method was defined as the number of gifted children correctly identified, and the definition of efficiency was the number of confirmed gifted children identified by each screening procedure. Pegnato and Birch concluded that group intelligence tests were the most efficient and effective screening method. This is not surprising as group intelligence tests and the individual intelligence test used as the reference criterion are similar measuring devices. They also stated that 'Teachers do not locate gifted children effectively or efficiently enough to place much reliance on them for screening' (Pegnato and Birch, 1959). This conclusion has since been quoted extensively in both the US and England.

Subsequently there has been considerable research effort in the US concerning the inaccuracy of teacher-judged giftedness in children (Baldwin, 1962; Cornish, 1968; Henderson, 1981; Jacobs, 1971; Pohl, 1970; Shertzer, 1960; Walton, 1961; and Wilson, 1963). Efforts were also made to train teachers in order to improve their identification skills (Gear, 1975 and 1978; Post, 1980; and Smith, 1980).

In England, only two studies, those of Lowenstein and Painter, have been particularly concerned with teacher effectiveness in screening for giftedness as compared with identification by using tests (Lowenstein, 1982; and Painter, 1982). Two further studies, those of Tempest and Ogilvie also referred in passing to the subject of teacher effectiveness in the identification of gifted

1

children (Ogilvie, 1973; and Tempest, 1974). The findings of these four studies will be discussed in turn.

Lowenstein IQ tested 108 primary and secondary school children categorized as gifted by their headteachers or teachers using the Wechsler Intelligence Scale for Children (WISC). He then went on to discuss the accuracy and inaccuracy of teachers, as compared with the WISC test, in assessing the children. His conclusions were that,

> This short investigation indicates that teachers although they are able to identify a certain number of able children do in fact under-rate and over-rate the performance of children generally on the basis of academic achievement. This indicates that many gifted children under-achieve and some in fact 'over-achieve' and are therefore not gifted, in terms of having an IQ of over 135 (Lowenstein, 1982, page 35).

Painter used intelligence and creativity tests to screen 5079 comprehensive school pupils for giftedness. She found that teachers failed to recognize as gifted two-thirds of the children identified as such by tests. Conversely, one-third of those children identified by the teachers were not similarly identified by the tests. Painter then compared two groups of children, those who were identified as gifted by the teachers with those who were unrecognized by the teachers but were identified as gifted by the tests. The former group had lower mean scores on Group Tests of Mental Abilities; preferred mathematics and science to other subjects on the curriculum; liked reading and were inclined to study in their spare time; were interested in sport but less so than the other group; were less likely to opt for watching television; and had higher educational and career aspirations (Painter, *op cit.*).

There are several possible alternative conclusions which may be reached concerning Lowenstein's and Painter's studies.[1] That the teachers identified as gifted those children who showed their 'gifts' in their attitude, motivation and achievement within the class. Those children who were not identified by the teachers may have been less well motivated towards school work and therefore may not have appeared as particularly able to the teacher in the classroom environment. This may be interpreted as either failure by teachers to recognize potential, or as inadequacy by tests to reflect academic ability.

Tempest screened 1000 seven year old children in order to form a special class of gifted children for research purposes. He found that one-third of the children nominated as gifted by their teachers had IQs of above 127 on the Young's Non Reader Intelligence Test. Furthermore, approximately one-half of those who were selected by the Wechsler Intelligence Scale for Children (WISC) as having IQs of over 130, had been nominated as gifted by their teachers (Tempest, op cit). In other words, many children nominated by teachers were not confirmed as gifted according to test results; and teachers failed to nominate many children who were identified as gifted by the tests. Based on Tempest's results, Ogilvie examined case studies of individual schools and children. He concluded that 'the recognition of gifted children by teachers may not always be as efficient as might be hoped and expected' (Ogilvie, op cit, page 61).

The correctness of teacher identification of gifted children was assessed by a comparison with childrens' IQ scores. However, the dominance of IQ as a measure of giftedness has been challenged. Three recent American unpublished doctoral dissertations questioned the dependence on IQ as a criterion for giftedness. Monahan concluded from his study that early identification of children as gifted, using the Stanford-Binet Intelligence Test, may be misleading as a significant number of children classified as gifted at kindergarten and first grade were not similarly identified when retested at grade five (Monahan, 1980). Haznedar claimed that the use of the Stanford-Binet Intelligence Test was a questionable procedure for identifying disadvantaged gifted students (Haznedar, 1981). Whitson suggested that individual performances on intelligence tests varied greatly. A child selected as gifted on one test may not be selected on another (Whitson, 1981). The latter point was supported by Freeman (1981). The situation in these studies had been reversed, whereby the accuracy of IQ tests, rather than of teachers, in identifying giftedness had been questioned.

A great part of the differences that occurred in the identification of gifted children between teachers and researchers may be attributed to the use of different criteria and different perceptions of what constituted giftedness in children. Rather than being inaccurate in screening for gifted children identified by IQ tests, the teachers may have been basing their judgement on other more immediate criteria, such as academic ability as revealed in the classroom. Confirmation for this supposition was provided for the author when interviewing headteachers and teachers about their perceptions of gifted children (Maltby, 1979). During these interviews it became apparent that some children, who had been categorized as gifted by educational psychologists using individual IQ tests, were not regarded as gifted by their teachers. Ogilvie requested teachers to tick characteristics which they found to be reliable indicators of giftedness from a list of nineteen items. Fifty-three per cent of the teachers ticked high intelligence test scores (Ogilvie, *op cit*, page 70). This is some indication that IQ tests were not considered an important criterion by almost half of the teachers.

One of the intentions of this book is to understand giftedness from the perspective of the teachers of gifted children without superimposing a researcher-defined criterion of giftedness. It is intended to study those children categorized as gifted by teachers. This appears to be essential as the assumption can then be made that they are the children who are perceived, and therefore treated, as gifted.

Note

1. Painter's study has as yet only been published in a very shortened form, which does not allow for assessment of the methodology that was used.

1   Research Perspectives of Giftedness

The aim of the present chapter is to present the more important literature concerning gifted children in an historical context enveloping philosophical arguments, changes in psychometric testing and social circumstances, such as alterations in the educational system and/or the availability of economic resources. An attempt will be made, during the historical analysis, to account for the alterations during the course of this century in definitions and attitudes to the concept of giftedness.

Despite the differences that exist in educational provision between England and America, tentacles of theory have crossed and recrossed the Atlantic, so that an historical exploration of giftedness should include literature from both countries. The concentration in this research will be on first and middle schools in Britain, and therefore British research will predominate.[1]

The Conservative/Liberal Continuum of Categorization

Renzulli suggested that variations in categorization for giftedness could be analyzed along a continuum ranging from *conservative* to *liberal* according to the degree of restrictiveness of the definition (Renzulli, 1978). The argument is put forward here that there has been an historical progression along this continuum in the expansion of criteria for giftedness, definitions becoming *inclusive* rather than *exclusive*. Initially the criterion of giftedness was in terms of a measure of intelligence, or intelligence quotient (IQ). As interest in creativity and creativity testing developed, so criteria for giftedness tended to encompass both high IQ and creativity. More recently, criteria for giftedness have tended to become still more inclusive. At the same time there has been a further tendency for the minimum IQ demanded to be reduced.[2] This expansion of criteria and progression to the liberal and inclusive end of Renzulli's continuum will be discussed in more detail with reference to some prominent literature in the field of giftedness.

The conservative end of the continuum is well illustrated by the comprehensive and outstanding work of Terman in California which started in 1920 and was a longitudinal study of between 600 and 1500 gifted children. The study is still being continued by Terman's co-workers today. The children were originally nominated by their teachers and then tested with the then new Binet test. The intention was to screen for the highest one per cent of the school population, an arbitrary standard being set as those with IQs of over 140, though a few children scored as low as 135. The children were rated on various character and personality scales by their parents and teachers, and assessments made of their home and school environments. The work of Terman and his followers, though not a Bible to researchers on giftedness, could certainly be regarded as a concise dictionary, new findings being constantly compared with those of Terman (Terman, 1925). More recently, in England, Shields repeated much of Terman's methodology, and obtained many similar results (Shields, 1975).

Many of the American studies which used IQ as a criterion for giftedness were discussed in the Introduction. In America during the 1950s a strong interest in creativity as a basis for giftedness developed. It was considered that the ability to be creative, or think in a divergent, unusual and original manner was not necessarily reflected by high IQ scores. The suggestion was that high IQ, which reflected convergent and restricted thinking did not necessarily correlate with academic success, whereas high creativity scorers were more likely to be the inventors of the future. Many tests of creativity were developed (Getzels and Jackson, 1962; Torrance, 1962; and Wallach and Kogan, 1965). Several researchers turned their attention to creativity, and unsuccessful attempts were made to show a correlation between high scores on creativity tests and the subjective assessment of adult creativity (Barron, 1969; MacKinnon, 1962; and Roe, 1952). Furthermore, creativity and IQ were not necessarily independent factors (Hitchfield, 1973). Vernon et al suggested that below a certain level of IQ children may not be able to verbalize creative or original ideas (Vernon et al, 1977). Hoyle and Wilks stated that,

> ... there is probably a threshold point on the IQ scale, perhaps at about 120 points, below which intelligence score is the best predictor of academic achievement, but above this point measures of creativity become more significant for the prediction of achievement of some children (Hoyle and Wilks, 1974, page 10).

Tempest's method of selecting gifted children would be an example of the extension of criteria of giftedness to include creativity. Tempest selected from 1000 seven year old children using a group IQ test (Young's Non Reader Intelligence Test), teacher nomination followed by an individual test (WISC), and a number of items indicating divergency or creativity. His resulting class of fifteen children had IQs of 130 plus (Tempest, 1974). Hitchfield's criteria for giftedness were also broader. She used the Goodenough Draw-a-man test at age seven, school attainment in reading and arithmetic as assessed by teachers and tested when the children were aged seven plus, parental identification sought for through the BBC and advertisements in magazines and newspapers. The children were then given a battery of tests including a shortened version of WISC and divergent thinking tests. The mean IQ for boys was 131, 58 per cent being over 130; and the mean IQ for girls was 126, 36 per cent being over 130 (Hitchfield, 1973).[3]

The recent trend has been towards the inclusive end of the continuum. This trend is reflected in the definitions used by three respected sources of influence in education, the Department of Education and Science (Hoyle and Wilks, G.B., DES, 1974). Her Majesty's Inspectorate (G.B., DES, 1977), and the Schools Council (Ogilvie, 1973). The definition of giftedness given by the HMIs in their report included superiority in intellectual, academic and/or aesthetic areas, as follows,

> Children ... who are generally recognised by their schools as being of superior all-round intellectual ability, confirmed where possible by a reliable individual test giving an IQ of 130 or more;

> or

> who exhibit a markedly superior developmental level of performance and achievement which has been reasonably consistent from earlier years;

> or

> of whom fairly confident predictions are being made as to continual rapid progress towards outstanding achievement, either in academic areas or in music, sport, dance or art; and whose abilities are not primarily attributable to purely physical development (G.B., DES, 1977, pages 4–5).

The desire was to include talents in all areas of the curriculum including craft and constructional work, games and athletics, movement, drama, and spoken or written language. This is also reflected in Ogilvie's definition,

> The term gifted is used to indicate any child who is outstanding in either a general or specific ability, in a relatively broad or narrow field of endeavour ... Where generally recognised tests exist as (say) in the case of intelligence then giftedness would be defined by test scores. Where no recognised tests exist it can be assumed that the subjective opinions of experts in the various fields on the creative qualities of originality and imagination displayed would be the criteria we have in mind (Ogilvie, 1973, page 6).

Thus, selection was intended to include the top five per cent of gifted children in all areas, which allowed for a broad band of the population to be categorized as gifted.

The Ideologies of Educational Equality and Justice

So far, changes in definitions of, and categorization for, giftedness have been put within a psychological context. However, attitudes to giftedness need to be considered in terms of political and philosophical ideologies. There are two concepts which are particularly important when considering giftedness and educational provision for gifted children. These are educational equality and justice. The concern with educational equality has dominated educational philosophy for many years. The attempt to be just is assumed of those who make judgments concerning provision within the educational system. Warnock implied that justice demands that rules governing people's behaviour, such as in the distribution of goods, should be applied universally (Warnock, 1977). On the other hand, Baldwin suggested that there is some argument for treating unequals unequally if the differential treatment is based on objective and morally relevant situational differences (Baldwin, 1966). In the description of the history of educational equality in England which follows, it will be seen that there was a gradual move from provision for the elite to universal provision (as per Warnock) followed by a period of differential treatment (as per Baldwin).

At the beginning of this century the predominant ideology was that of *elitism*. Status positions and their resultant privileges were normally ascribed rather than competed for. Intelligence was considered to be the result of parenthood and was discriminated for in both England and America. Gradually it was realized that there were some bright children in working-class families. At first, in England, it was considered that the compulsory legalisation of education would provide for these children. When it became clear that some middle-class children were gaining more from their education than some brighter working-class children, an attempt was made to equalize opportunity with the development of the IQ test section of the eleven plus examination. The ideology of those concerned in its development was a clear attempt to provide *equality of educational opportunity* for bright working-class children. There was an assumption that within this competitive, rather than ascriptive, system every child had an equal chance to compete, and therefore all those children who were gifted would be recognized and given every opportunity to develop to their full potential, thus joining the rest of the elite. Kogan described this era in education as the *soft* concept of equality, which allowed for equality of opportunity, though not necessarily equality of provision (Kogan, 1975).

Disillusionment concerning IQ testing developed as a result of psychological and sociological research in the areas of IQ testing; the importance of home background for success at school (Peaker, 1967; Floud et al, 1957; Pidgeon, 1976; and Wiseman, 1967); plus the wastage from grammar schools of the working-class children (Jackson and Marsden, 1962). Kogan termed the era that followed as reflecting the *hard* concept of educational equality, where attempts were made to compensate for home deprivations. Plowden's Educational Priority Areas became half-hearted government policy (G.B.,DES, 1967), partly as a result of the vast regional (Taylor and Ayres, 1969) and local differences that existed in educational provision. In America specific programmes were developed for deprived children, an example being Head Start.

Compensatory education is, by definition, compensation for those who are deprived or less fortunate in some way by the provision of extra, scarce economic resources. To illustrate, one can imagine a see-saw with children sitting along the length of it. At one end are remedial, deprived and handicapped children. At the opposite end are gifted children. Every resource which is given to the children at either end will tip the see-saw one way or the other. Provision for the handicapped, whose needs are obvious, requires little justification. The belief that education can counter-balance social deprivation accompanies the natural desire to improve the educational provision of those children who are socially deprived. Any request for resources for the gifted, in times of scarcity, leaves a flavour of theft from the disadvantaged by the advantaged. This is further aggravated by the fact that children who are designated as being gifted, also tend to be middle-class (see Chapter 2).

In these circumstances there are several arguments which may be considered to justify helping the gifted. The first being that by fostering the gifted one can make them more able and qualified to help those who are less fortunate than themselves. Rawls suggested the *principle of difference*, which is that the better off shall have more, only provided that in having more, they benefit the worse off, and only if the worse off would have been even more worse off had the distribution been equal (Rawls, 1972). An example would be that of providing extra educational resources to enable a gifted child to become a doctor or teacher who might thereby benefit the children at the opposite end of the see-saw. However, any assessment of the amount of fostering of the gifted related to the extent of extra help to the less able by the gifted can only be subjective and speculative.

A further argument is that the gifted are a *national asset* and for the good of the country, and in order to prevent wastage, should be extended as far as possible. In America, at the time of Sputnik in 1957, considerable emphasis was placed on gifted children extensive resources being allocated to their identification and the development of programmes for their education (Newland, 1976). Renzulli suggested that there is some indication that society does turn towards and provide extra for its potentially gifted children in times of distress. Although the initial post-Sputnik interest in creative giftedness died down, it has again increased in America in line with economic hardship (Renzulli, 1981).

In England a similar pattern of greater interest in, and educational provision for, gifted children can be seen to accompany the progressive economic hardship of the late 1970s and early 1980s. This is reflected by the increase in booklets about gifted children published by Local Education Authorities (LEAs) around the country (West Sussex County Council, 1974; City of Birmingham, 1979; and Devon, 1977). Lawrence surveyed the LEAs of

Britain in December 1978 to determine if there had been any changes since Ogilvie's survey concerning giftedness in 1973. Although there had been some development in many LEAs in guidance and training for teachers and head-teachers about giftedness, the situation concerning policy, identification, and provision was almost identical to that found by Ogilvie. Yet individual areas such as Devon and Essex had made considerable provision for gifted children (Lawrence, 1980). According to a very recent survey, many LEAs are pub-lishing guidelines, establishing working parties and mounting conferences and courses for teachers. However, only 50 percent of the LEAs returned the survey questionnaire (Sherwood, 1983).

The commencement of the Assisted Places Scheme in the early 1980s may also be interpreted as a political move by the Conservative government to cater for gifted children by providing them with financial assistance to attend selected private schools. This implementation has been accompanied by considerable dissent. Those in opposition to the scheme posing arguments such as that the government should not distribute tax payers money into the private sector of education; that to remove gifted children from comprehensive schooling deprives such schools of their better pupils thereby lowering the standard and negating their comprehensiveness; that the policy implies that state education is inadequate to supply the needs of gifted children; and that it encourages elitism. A conflict exists between the needs of gifted children and the needs of other children. Stevens noted that whilst gifted children generally gained little from comprehensive schooling, their presence in the classroom invited a greater curiosity amongst the other children, and because of their inventive minds they made subjects more exciting (Stevens, 1980). So from this point of view their talents were greatly appreciated. There is also a possibility (which is developed in Chapter 4) that working-class children are not the children who necessarily benefit from policies such as the Assisted Places Scheme, although it was presumably the original intention that they should. However, recent newspaper articles have suggested that children who have won Assisted Places do come from low income homes (Albert, 1982; and Levi, 1982).

Painter saw the interest in giftedness in the context of industrial and technological societies,

> the fundamental reason for the high value placed upon intellectual ability by industrial countries is its essential nature in the maintenance of a technological society. Consequently, the full development of the abilities of gifted children is beneficial both for the children themselves and a source of enrichment to the community to which they belong (Painter, 1980, page 9).

Both of the arguments, that of the principle of difference and that of the gifted being a national asset, do not necessarily justify the provision of extra resources. Either argument may be countered if it can be shown that gifted children are adequately provided for in the normal educational system within which they may achieve their full potential. On the other hand if it can be shown that in being gifted there is a likelihood of the development of some disadvantage, then there would be a strong argument for preventitive action, and consequent resource allocation. In these circumstances, the gifted child is removed to the *disadvantaged* end of the see-saw, and is consequently entitled to special treatment, the need for justification is eliminated. There has been considerable research indicating the disadvantages of giftedness. The research outlined below reveals the academic under-achievement, bad class-room behaviour, delinquency and maladjustment of gifted children.

Vernon et al suggested that some gifted children do not achieve their full potential as a result of deliberate under-achievement and conformity to the norm in order to avoid the disapproval of their peers (Vernon et al, 1977). Bridges observed the work done by gifted children who were brought from surrounding primary schools in Essex into the Teachers Training College one afternoon weekly in order to work with students on an individual basis. It was noticed that the children appeared to conform to what was expected of them in quality and quantity of work, which Bridges termed the *stint* (Bridges, 1969 and 1975). Painter compared the IQs and achievement tests of seventy-three primary school gifted children with a bright control group. She assessed the performance scores of gifted children (the difference between the tested age and the mental age) as on average thirteen months lower in English and eight months lower in mathematics than that of the control group, who already had a minus performance score. These results may be partly explained by the tendency for children to do less well on achievement tests than IQ tests, thus giving an impression of under-achievement. It may also be a possibility that the tendency to teach to a chronological, rather than a mental, age, plus the inadequate time (their average age was 8.8 years) in which to acquire the mechanics of learning, might indicate reasons for the difference in the standard of work compared with mental age. IQ and achievement tests also measure two very different concepts which may not be expected to correlate in terms of age. Painter's explanation of her findings emphasized the low expectations of the gifted children by their teachers (Painter, 1977).

Mallett suggested that under-achievement in gifted children can lead to bad classroom behaviour (Mallett, 1970). This behaviour may eventually lead to the identification of giftedness if it becomes sufficiently bad for the educational psychologist to be consulted (Levi, 1975). Brooks described a school run specifically for bright delinquent boys. He found that an unexpectedly large number of the boys came from working-class homes, suggesting thereby that possible differences in intellect between parent and child could lead to delinquent behaviour (Brooks, 1972 and 1980). Pringle studied 103 children who had been referred for psychological assessment. The aim of the study was to investigate reasons for the failure and maladjustment of able children in school (Pringle, 1970).

The problems experienced by gifted children have become a prevalent theme generally, iterated in the newsletter produced by the National Association of Gifted Children (NAGC) and the press. Booklets have been produced which discuss aspects of the difficulties of the gifted (Lowenstein, 1981; and Painter, 1980). Many of the speakers at the 1982 Conference on Gifted Children in London concentrated in particular on this aspect of the education of gifted children (Chappell, 1982; Delisle, 1982; and Maker, 1982 and Maltby, 1983).

Recent research by the author indicated that teachers perceived many of their gifted children to be disturbed. It was suggested that this may be attributed to the greater likelihood of resource allocation to disturbed gifted children as opposed to gifted children (Maltby, 1979). This argument has recently been substantiated (Benn 1982a and 1982b).

The era of belief in compensatory education came to an end with such findings as those of Jencks. His interpretation of the statistics of the Coleman Report raised doubts concerning the feasibility of schools affecting areas such as educational attainment, occupational status, income, job satisfaction and so on. He suggested that it was the relative positions in social status that accounted for the differences (Jencks, 1972). Kogan proposed that present day education is in the third stage of a *psychological individual* approach (Kogan, 1979) which would seem to demand the need to provide for every child's requirements despite the scarcity of resources.

Kogan's contention may be supported with regard to gifted children in the recent concentration on the development of curriculum materials intended to be used for enrichment by gifted children individually or in small groups, and by an increase in studies which attempt to evaluate the gifted child as an individual. The studies concerned with the individualization of curriculum materials will be discussed first. Tempest selected fifteen children to form a class for the construction and testing of appropriate work cards for gifted children (Tempest, 1974). Funds were later provided by the NAGC for the follow up of these children in secondary schools (Waddington, 1979). Tempest's book contained curriculum suggestions, but the actual work cards were never published. The project is further described by the teacher who was involved in teaching the fifteen children (Callow, 1982).

After completion of the Schools Council Project (Ogilvie, 1973) Ogilvie was commissioned to prepare enrichment materials for use with primary school able children in the normal classroom. The result has been the Schools Council Curriculum Enrichment Packs (SCCEPs) the first of which were published in 1980 (Schools Council, 1980). The rationale and development of the materials have been described (Axon, 1982; and Ogilvie, 1980). Some counties, in particular Essex, have concentrated on the development of their own enrichment materials (Roberts and Wallace, 1980).

Hitchfield attempted to evaluate gifted children as individuals. She used the 1958 cohort of the longitudinal National Child Development Study when the children were aged eleven. Hitchfield's research investigated 238 able and gifted children, and gathered data from the children themselves, their teachers and their parents. It was frequently possible to make comparisons between the gifted children and the total cohort (Hitchfield, 1973). Freeman's Gulbenkian

Project was very similar to that of Hitchfield, except that each sample gifted child was compared to another child of comparable ability and a control child, all of whom were in the same class (Freeman, 1979).

It has been suggested that England has lagged behind the US in its interest in giftedness, for which there are several possible reasons. England never had quite such enormous economic advantages to allocate, even in the prosperous 1980s. It also had for many years an educational system which could have been considered adequate to cater for the special requirements of the gifted through its selective grammar schools and scholarships to public schools. It may be feasible to regard the change to the comprehensive system as being the time when some concern, especially parental, developed concerning the gifted (Benn 1982a and 1982b; and Maltby, 1979). This was shown by an increase in research, plus pressure group formation such as the NAGC. It is also suggested that the tendency of many primary schools to stop streaming accentuated the differences in ability among children, making teachers consider and be more aware of those at either end of the ability continuum.

Figure 1 represents many of the developments outlined in the present chapter in the form of a model. The broadening of the cone indicates the greater elasticity of criteria of giftedness and consequent inclusion of greater numbers of children. The conservative/liberal continuum flows from left to right, together with the expansion of the cone. The various types of educational opportunity are presented in combination with Kogan's definitions of them. The model should be viewed as a flowing process of general eras, but not specific dates. The format has been described in order to indicate a path through the literature concerned with gifted children and to aid its comprehension and clarification.

The Research Perspective

From the review of the literature concerning gifted children, it appears that there is a dearth of research in two connecting areas: that of children categorized as gifted by their teachers; and that of comprehensive studies of gifted children in their normal classrooms. Both these areas are considered to be particularly important for the following reasons. The majority of gifted children in schools who are perceived and treated as gifted will be those who have been categorized as such by their teachers. In recent times, with cut backs and increased pressure on the time of educational psychologists, the contingency of individual IQ testing for possible giftedness in children has decreased. Therefore, it is the minority of gifted children who will be revealed by individual IQ testing, except in those few geographical areas where particular interest has been shown in gifted children, or where a research project or individual researcher has screened for giftedness. This does not imply that gifted children will not be disclosed by group tests for indeed many schools do use such methods in order to screen for children of below and above average

Figure 1 An historical model of definitions of giftedness and educational opportunites

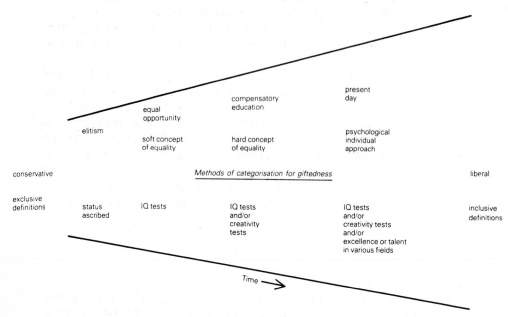

ability or intelligence. Secondly, it has been shown that the majority of LEAs do not make specific educational provision for gifted children (see Introduction). Thus in the UK, gifted children are predominantly present in normal classes. It would appear of paramount importance, therefore, to study gifted children who are most representative of their ability peers, those in the normal classroom.

Although the original intention was to study children categorized by their teachers as gifted, it became necessary early in the course of the research to change this intention. Access to the schools had to be negotiated through the headteachers rather than through the teachers. Therefore, in some cases, it would be more appropriate to define the children as ones categorized by the individuals in the school as gifted. This led to an interesting focus for study in itself, which will be explored in detail in Chapter 2. This book is a study of children categorized by their teachers and/or schools as gifted in the *normal* classroom. The methodology used in the study is described in detail in the Appendix.

Notes

1. In the relevant Local Education Authority (LEA) first schools are for children aged from five to nine, and in middle schools the children were nine to twelve years old. Eight years of schooling are examined altogether.
2. This may not always be apparent because of the differences in standard deviation between IQ tests. The Stanford-Binet Intelligence Scale has a standard deviation of 16, whereas the Wechsler Intelligence Scale for Children and the British Ability Scales have standard deviations of 15.
3. The broadening of Hitchfield's criteria for giftedness to include in her sample 42 per cent of the boys and 64 per cent of the girls with IQs lower than 130 might indicate that many of her sample of gifted children were not gifted. However, as pointed out in the Introduction, it may be that high IQ is not necessarily a definitive criterion for giftedness. Compensatory weighting was made on the Goodenough Draw-a-man test and school attainment to include more children from social classes IV and V.

2   The Categorization of Children as Gifted

This chapter is concerned with the manner in which children are categorized as gifted. It refers to the definitions of giftedness that are used by headteachers and teachers, and relates their definitions to the exclusive/inclusive continuum discussed in Chapter 1. An attempt is made to reveal that the concept of giftedness and classification of children as gifted is problematic. The nature of the problem is developed with illustrations from case-study material of children about whom there is discordance of opinion concerning their giftedness or non giftedness. Issues are raised in this chapter which are tentative and exploratory in nature. Many of these issues are pursued and expanded more rigorously in later chapters.

Before embarking on the main discussion, an examination will be made of the literature concerning gifted children with reference to the percentage of the total population who may be considered to be gifted. This will then be compared to the number of children categorized as gifted in the LEA studied.

When discussing gifted children it is normal to refer to the top one or two per cent of the population in a particular field. However, frequently there is disagreement concerning how many children would be involved. If more criteria than IQ alone are used for giftedness then Ogilvie found that general opinion among teachers focussed on the top two-six per cent as warranting consideration as gifted (Ogilvie, 1973). Even when IQ is the sole criterion used in the identification of giftedness, there is little consensus about what proportion of the population is involved.

The majority of recent studies in England take giftedness to be an attribute of those individuals with an IQ over 130, at which level Burt and Painter respectively suggested that 1.6 per cent or 2.28 per cent of the population would be included (Burt, 1962; and Painter, 1980). Burt further suggested that intelligence, rather than being distributed according to the normal curve of distribution, is in fact distributed according to Pearson's Type IV curve, which gives a higher percentage of cases at either end of the curve. Assuming a standard deviation of approximately 15 IQ, he estimated the number of gifted people to be expected at each level of IQ (Burt, 1963). According to Burt's figures, the proportion of the population with IQs of over 160 is more than ten times the number deduced from the normal curve of distribution. There is some support for this from the Devon County Council which found on screening their schools that there were more gifted children than would be expected if using the normal curve of distribution (Devon County Council, 1977). In any discussion of this area it needs to be remembered that there is a phenomenon of circularity. It is presumed that IQs are distributed along a normal curve of chance, therefore IQ tests are standardized according to this curve, and therefore IQs would tend to be distributed along the same curve.

The total population of children in the first and middle schools in the LEA studied was over 12,500. The number of children one would expect to be classified as gifted, according to the research already cited, would be in the region of 125 if only the top one per cent of children were categorized as gifted, and 250 if the top two per cent were categorized as such. In fact, only a total of sixty -five children were stated to be gifted by the headteachers, which is 0.52 per cent of the total first and middle school population. Clearly, far fewer children were designated to the category of gifted in the schools in the research area than would have been anticipated in the light of the research just discussed.

As already stated in Chapter 1, it was originally intended to study those children who were categorized as gifted by their teachers. However, because access to schools had to be negotiated through the headteachers, the initial intention was diverted. The headteachers varied in their approach of deciding which children were appropriate for the author to study. Generally the impression was given by the headteachers that they knew which children in the school were gifted, and were considered to be gifted by the teachers. In one school the headteacher was new, and he consulted the teachers about which children were gifted. Once in the schools it became apparent that there was not necessarily a consensus of opinion about the categorization as gifted of some of the children. For example, two teachers approached the author in the staff room to say that they had a gifted child in their class, and four teachers added children once the author was in their classroom. The headteachers appeared to be unaware that these children were considered to be gifted. There were also children whom the headteachers had recommended as gifted who were not considered to be gifted by their teachers. Consequently, this study is concerned with those children categorized as gifted by their 'schools'.

Within the main project a minor study developed of the perceptions of headteachers, teachers, previous teachers and educational psychologists, in their categorization of individual children as gifted. The total group of thirty-nine gifted children was divided into two sub groups. The first group included those who were perceived to be gifted by their present teacher. The second group were those gifted children who were not considered to be gifted by their present teacher, but were, or had been, categorized as gifted by past teachers or by the headteacher. The two groups of *gifted* and *non gifted* will be

Figure 2   Names of gifted children categorized as gifted and non-gifted by their present teachers[2]

Class	Gifted	Non-gifted
FIRST SCHOOL		
1	Arthur	
2	Ricky	Karl
	David	
	Don	
	Rita	
3	Robert	Mary
	Jim (two teachers)	Jim
4	Maggy	Keith
	Hugh	Liz
	Rosemarie	Vi
		Alexandra
	Benny (two teachers)	
MIDDLE SCHOOL		
1	Sandy	Benny
	Vicky	Hank
	Peter	Kathy
	Ann	
	Ken	
	Lilo	
3	Laurence	Nicholas
	Les	Mandy
	George	Tony
	Sylvia	Pat
	Jo	
	Christopher	
4	Angela	Dennis

Plus Geoff (Music) and Adrian (Football) – Total of 39 gifted children.

referred to throughout the thesis. The names of the children in each group are given in figure 2.[1]

Definitions of Giftedness by Headteachers and Teachers

During the initial screening of children for the study, the influence of the headteachers became apparent, consequently they were interviewed as well as the teachers. Eight out of the thirteen headteachers were asked about their definitions of giftedness. Six of these headteachers mentioned high IQ as a criterion for giftedness. The cut-off points mentioned by four of the headteachers were 140 plus, one suggested 145 plus, and one 150 plus. Four of the headteachers qualified their IQ definition with statements such as

It involves attitudes and ability, and the ability to follow an interest through.

. . . a facility for the remarkable.

High IQ, 150 plus, also some other qualification, which is undefinable, a special interest in something, such as music or art, something which needs special training. Could be high IQ only, or number work, or English.

When related to the historical model of attitudes to giftedness (Chapter 1) the definitions of four of the headteachers would be placed at the exclusive end of the continuum. Those of the other four headteachers would be placed at the opposite and inclusive end of the continuum, with definitions of giftedness such as

Young children capable of doing things at a higher level.

Giftedness is relative, one is gifted only in relation to what others can't do.

An analysis of the definitions of giftedness used by teachers showed that they were less test-score orientated than the headteachers, and reflected a concern with the practical relevance of ability, the predominating factor being school attainment. A simple explanation for this may be that headteachers are usually less involved with the more practical day to day classroom interaction, and may consequently place greater reliance on more test based assessments. Teachers, on the other hand, are in very close contact with the children and their work. Their concern is with the progression of educational attainment, its assessment being continuous and ongoing, though possibly in a subjective manner rather than by the use of test scores.

The teachers could be placed into three main groups according to the definition of giftedness that they gave. Nine teachers considered that the gifted should be 'all round' in their abilities. Nine teachers mentioned IQ in terms of the application of intelligence. Eight teachers referred to excellence in attainment by the gifted in comparison with their classroom peers. One teacher required a specific ability, such as in music. The three main groups will be discussed in turn.

Nine teachers felt that to be gifted, children should be all round in their abilities. The most extreme teacher in this group stated :

Teacher of Vi and Alexandra, first school, year 4

A striking outstanding quality, for example playing Chopin at six and an IQ over 165.

There is considerable dissension concerning all round or polymathic giftedness. Burt was of the opinion that the abilities of gifted children develop fairly evenly, and that they are normally gifted all round until the time of specialization. Therefore, if one chose a group of children who were gifted in one area, it would be highly probable that they would also be gifted in other areas (Burt, 1975). Conversely, Ogilvie considered that it was incorrect to expect giftedness to be all round, and ability to be equal in more than one area (Ogilvie, 1975). He also suggested that the greater the requirement for polymathic capacity, the greater the chance of ending up with no gifted children at all (Ogilvie, 1973). The demand for polymathicism would appear to be exclusive for categorizational purposes. In this study seven teachers who looked for polymathic giftedness categorized as non gifted nine children who were previously labelled as gifted, thus reflecting the exclusive nature of their own definition of giftedness.

One middle school teacher considered giftedness to be ability in a specific area such as music. Being specific may also be restrictive for the categorization of giftedness.

Nine teachers mentioned IQ in terms of the application of intelligence. It was interesting that intelligence alone was not a sufficient criterion of giftedness, and other factors were also mentioned. For example, five teachers required advancement in work beyond their classroom peers by the gifted children; one teacher wanted a high reading age; and two teachers mentioned creative thinking.

Eight teachers spoke in terms of excellence of attainment in relation to the children's peers, which was qualified in terms of conceptual ability and language. This comparative notion will be highlighted in many of the case-studies explored later in this chapter. It appeared to be the basis for many teachers for their categorization of children as gifted. Frequent references were made by teachers to their 'amazement' at the quality of performance as compared with other children. Disappointment in expectancy of attainment frequently resulted in decategorization.

All thirty-nine of the children had been called gifted by one or more individuals at some time (usually recently) in their careers. In seventeen cases the label of gifted was reinforced by an IQ score as a result of individual testing by an educational psychologist. Yet, of these thirty-nine children, fifteen children were not considered to be gifted by their present teacher (excluding Geoff and Adrian[2]). This decategorization phenomena became a major concern of the present research. An attempt will be made to analyze and explain the processes by which it happened. However, the data used in the discussion of this problem is mainly illustrative and not conclusive. Several questions will be raised concerning the decategorization, such as whether the children had changed over time and were thereby no longer applicable for classification as gifted; or whether the changes were caused by differing teacher perception; or variance between individuals and their application of categorizations of giftedness. In other words, which factor was the most relevant for categorization, the teacher or the child?

While questioning the importance of the teacher or the child, it is recognized that processes of categorization involve the interaction of both parties. It is also acknowledged that teachers are not theorists or philosophers, and they will not be fully comprehended by examination of their definitions. They are professional practitioners, whose perceptions may be more fully understood by the exploration of the world within their classrooms. The analysis of data gathered in different situations in this chapter, mainly teacher interview and classroom observation, overcomes what Hargreaves calls the *third party relation*, where typifications of gifted children are expressed outside the normal direct face-to-face environment of the classroom (Hargreaves, 1977). It is also understandable that concepts which appear clearly defined in an interview situation should be altered once the multi-faceted circumstances of the classroom come into play (Keddie, 1971). In this study it has been possible to ask the teachers questions, and then relate the answers to what occurred in the classrooms; and also to develop questions according to observations made.

The remainder of this chapter discusses many of the children who had been removed from the category of gifted by their present teacher. The first section will examine differences in the perceptions of individual gifted children by past and present teachers. The attention will then focus on test scores, and differences in perceptions of headteachers and teachers.

Teachers versus Teachers

The differentiation of classification that occurred between teachers concerning individual children will be examined with reference to Benny who was observed twice over a period of time, and to four children whose present teacher did not consider them to be gifted (in other words decategorized them) and where it was possible to interview a previous teacher who did consider the children to be gifted.

Benny, first school, year 4 and middle school, year 1

Benny was observed in the January of his fourth year, aged seven, in first school. The headteacher stated that the school drew from an upper working-class catchment area. Subsequently, an opportunity occurred for Benny to be re-observed at the end of his first year in the middle school, aged 8.6. According to the headteacher there, the school drew children from a primarily middle-class area. The definitions of giftedness employed by Benny's teachers would place them in the same definitional category, yet they did not agree in their categorization of Benny. The first school teacher considered him to be gifted in everything except art work, as shown in the following interview transcript.[3]

He doesn't have terrific co-ordination and doesn't like wasting time doing a picture unless it has a purpose, like a map or chart, ordinary painting no. He was noticed because of his speed of work, he kept coping with harder and harder work. He wanted books from the teacher's shelf and reads adult books. He is keen on history and literature. I had heard that he was bright, but no one said that he was gifted. (There was a letter in his records from a consultant psychologist dated the previous year, stating that he was of exceptional ability and qualified as a gifted child.) He is totally reliable in his work. It is a problem because he is so fluent. Communicating with him is like talking to an adult. Once, when I was hearing him read, he said "This is an awful waste of your time. It might be more useful to hear Dave". He always brings in some books from home. I always think that he regards them as his emergency supply in case I run out of things for him to do. (First school teacher)

The teacher also emphasized her assessment of him as a gifted child in the records that went on to the middle school, where the headteacher stated:

We have no doubts about his capabilities as a gifted child . . . we have no doubts about his intelligence. In class he works reasonably well. He wants to be first. (Middle school headteacher)

Conversely, the middle school teacher did not consider Benny to be gifted, although many of her perceptions of him were similar to those of his previous teacher:

Benny, because he's finished his work first, and gets it right, is anxious to go on to the next step. He does produce the goods, but he needs a lot of prodding to do it. He is obviously well read. He has good general knowledge and knows of things above the average of the class. But I find extraordinary lapses in common sense, and I think giftedness is a roundness of being good at everything. Perhaps that's why I don't think about Benny in that way. For example, I asked him to find the middle of the book, and he didn't know how. Less able children were able to do it and it annoyed him. (Middle school teacher)

Benny was seen by both teachers almost identically in terms of his ability as compared with other children. So the reasons for their variation in his categorization need to be explored in other areas, such as his classroom activity, as observed by the researcher. He immediately stood out as a child who was very demanding of attention. In the interactive analysis, he achieved thirty-seven interactions with the first school teacher out of a total of 217, and with the middle school teacher thirty out of 240 interactions, one of which was for five minutes.[4] Clearly he was getting far more teacher time than he was entitled to in comparison with the other children. He had various techniques for achieving this, such as when there was a queue at the teacher's desk Benny went to the opposite side of the desk to gain her attention; or when he observed that the teacher was not speaking to another individual he would impart a piece of information, or show his work to her. He was also very keen to answer questions and give information during discussion lessons. The following is an extract from a history lesson with the first school teacher. The section lasted approximately eighteen minutes (The asterisks refer to other children speaking).

The teacher reads a section from a book about Captain Cook.
Benny's hand goes up.
B-Mrs ... I know his middle name, it was Stuart.
T-Very good, how did you know that?
B-I've got it in my History book.
T-Good, you'll be able to help me then.
T-All right Brian, you can do the sum.
*

T-What's an errand boy? (Benny's hand goes up first) James?
*(wrong answer)
T-Benny?
B-A boy who runs messages.
T-What's a harbour? Paul?
*

T-Adrian?
*

T-How did they travel?
**

B-(Calls out) And the people in the middle used carts.
T-That's right.
T-They didn't know about the whole world, maps and so on. (Benny's hand goes up) What is it Benny?
B-Did they know about America then?
The teacher reads about Cook and the shilling he was supposed to have stolen.
B-(Calls out) They could have got hanged in those days for stealing a shilling.
The teacher is talking about how Cook learned to navigate.
T-Navigation. What is it? Jenny?
*(Wrong answer)
T-Paul?
*(incomplete answer)
T-All right Benny?
B-It tells you where you are and where you are going.
The teacher is talking about navigating by the stars, and
tries to get them to use the word sextant.
T-Malcolm, in your project you did stars.

B-(Interrupting) Mrs ... My grandfather was a sailor.
T-What did they use to hold up to the sun Wayne?
*

T-Try to think Benny, I'm sure you know this.
***
B-Binoculars.
Colin-Sun dial
Barry-Binoculars.
**

T-I have a job for you all. I want you to find out what a sextant is. I know you'll find out (pointing to Benny) but I want the others to find out too.
***

B-(Benny's hand goes up, and then he interrupts while another child is talking) Mrs ....
Benny and the teacher go over to the globe to show Benny where the North Sea is.
***

The teacher is describing press gangs. (Benny's hand is up)
T-What is it Benny?
B-My grandfather taught me about that because he was a sailor.
T-Yes, but he wasn't press-ganged was he? (Benny shakes his head)
*

B-(Calls out) My grandfather was about forty when he was a sailor.
*

Benny was obviously a keen participant in verbal lessons, and had information, relevant and irrelevant, to impart. During the above extract there were eleven interactions with the teacher, some quite extended in length. Five of these interactions were achieved by ignoring the conventions of classroom behaviour and calling out or interrupting other children, but always with his hand up.

In a lesson in the middle school Benny had fifteen interactions with the teacher. During the question and answer section he called out less, though he tended to stand with his hand up to gain attention. The class then drew pictures and Benny went up to the teacher three times at her desk to give her various pieces of information concerning the topic. There would appear to be strong similarities in his behaviour in class between schools. However, when his distraction was timed[5] it had deteriorated from 42 per cent in first school to 66 per cent in the middle school. This should indicate a lower level of output of work, but in fact he still tended to finish his work before the other children, and was ahead of the rest of the class in mathematics and English specifically. It is interesting to note that his middle school teacher was under the impression that he was not in advance of a particular child in School Mathematics Project (SMP Mathematics)[6]. He was in fact ahead by six cards. This is remarkable considering the way he worked during SMP as shown in the following extract.

The whole class are doing SMP mathematics. The trolley containing most of the equipment is at the front of the room, and Benny sits near the back. The children collect their cards and equipment as required. The extract lasts half an hour.

Partial plan of the classroom

				Richard
				Benny
		Camela	Tanja	
Jane	Ian	Alexander	Miles	
TROLLEY			TEACHERS	
			DESK	

Benny talks to Tanja and Camela on the way to the trolley, and then talks to Alexander. The teacher tells off three other children for talking. Benny returns to his desk and starts working. He drops his pencil and turns round to talk to Richard in the process of picking it up. He gets up and goes to the back of the room.

T-Now Benny, where have you gone now?

B-I'm getting the cubes.

Benny works quietly for a time. He goes to the trolley and chats to Alexander and Ian. He returns to his desk. He has finished his answer and jiggles the cubes round noisily. He takes the cubes back and chases Jonathon.

The teacher notices this and says to the author — All the time I have to chase him to get on, otherwise he gets into mischief. It's very hard work sometimes.

While Benny is chasing, he is watching the teacher to see if she notices. She ignores it, but tells him off when he starts talking to Richard.

Miles to B-Your're trying to trip me up aren't you?

B-No I'm not.

Benny goes to the teacher to get his card marked.

T-Class-I will now have five minutes silence.

Benny goes to the trolley to get another card. He pretends to Jane that a letter is a gun.

T-Jane-Are you talking?

Jane-No.

T-B-Come on.

Benny pretends to Ian that a letter is a beard. He carries on playing the fool to Jane and Ian at the trolley. When the bell goes he runs across the room pretending to be a clown with big boots on.

T-B-Could you try and walk across the room?

Benny had special activities in English that he did because he finished so far ahead of the class. When the other children finished they read a book. Benny appeared to be producing equally advanced work for both his teachers, and therefore the difference in classification between the two teachers cannot be attributed to the work produced. It is possible that Benny's middle school teacher required greater application of his abilities to his work and the expected conventionalities of classroom behaviour, which did appear to have deteriorated with the second teacher. This deterioration may be attributed to her perception of Benny as non gifted; on the other hand, his poorer behaviour may have acted as a contributory factor in her decategorization of him.

The differentiation of classification that occurred between teachers concerning individual children can be further examined in the cases of four children whose present teacher did not consider them to be gifted, and where it was possible to interview a previous teacher who did.

Karl, first school, year 2

It was Karl's previous teacher from class one who had initially considered Karl to be gifted. She approached the author on the subject once present in the school. Her definition of giftedness was

> Children who are probably seeming to be two years ahead of a child of that age, not only in school things, but in perception and general understanding. (Previous teacher)

She considered Karl to show his giftedness in

> his excellence in conversation and general knowledge. He seemed to have mixed largely with adults (he is an only child). He seemed not to have been talked to as a baby and seemed completely grown up in his language use. He was one of the youngest in the class ... He did everything two times as quickly as everyone else. He was blasé about things that caused problems to the others ... He was impatient with infantile things. He was probably so far ahead that it was not worth bothering about. He knew his sounds before he came (to school). He used to know all the details about his holidays, how he got there, how long it took, where it was, how long he was there for, etc. That is unusual at that age. He's a very pleasant child, clean and wholesome. (Previous teacher)

Karl's present teacher did not consider that he was gifted. Her definition of giftedness was,

> A child who from a very early age shone in all areas and could turn their ability in lots of different ways. A sign of it is needing further stimulation.

She perceived Karl in a less favourable light than his previous teacher, and accounted for his earlier classification as gifted in a variety of ways, as shown in the following extract,

> He is good at manipulating adults. I reckon that the reason he appeared special is because he can hold his own with adults. He has an uncharacteristic amount of attention at home. They had probably stimulated him, and he probably joins in the conversation at home like an adult. All the teachers talk about him because he goes to the teacher in the playground and introduces himself. He can get personal, which they find funny, but I find irritating.

She considered him to be poor in his social attitude, which for her appeared to be an overriding dimension, and felt that there were other children who were performing better than him at school work.

> Others of the same ability are more socially aware. He is selfish and uncaring about others, and self indulgent. He likes to write stories and make little books because I think they make him feel secure, because he does a lot of that at home. He then wants his story read to the other children. I don't do that because I feel that it is wrong to expect praise in that way all the time. All the children should have a chance. In number work there are two others who are better than him in the class. He is not the best reader. Others are more consistent with their number work. It's the conversation that makes him singled out. Not the vocabulary because M ... showed surprisingly the ideas of meanings. V ... will often understand words when Karl doesn't. I don't actively dislike him, but I feel that something has to be done about him now because his behaviour is disturbing ... He has to be made to get on better with others.

There could be several reasons for the differences in opinion between the two teachers. The obvious one is that a change had occurred within the boy over a period of time. The majority of the staff considered the school to be *rough*. From what Karl's second teacher said, the advantage of his encouraging home background had diminished with time, and he appeared less outstanding as the other children caught up with him. A second reason may be that the two teachers had different concepts of giftedness. The first teacher considered attainment as related to peers, whilst the second teacher required polymathic giftedness, in which she put a high premium on social awareness. Finally, on a personal basis the second teacher found Karl to be less likeable. A particular incident illustrates this. Karl came into the classroom and told her that he had kissed the previous teacher. She asked the teacher what had happened.

Apparently she had stopped him to do his shoe laces up and he had kissed her. You see, she lets him do things like that and likes it. (Conversation with the author).

The following two children reveal the tentativeness that can occur in classification. The first child, Pat, had been called gifted for many years. Six months after observation he won a musical scholarship to a prominent public school. The second child, Dennis, had never been considered gifted officially, but a previous first school teacher decided retrospectively that he was.

Pat, middle school, year 3

Pat's previous teacher defined giftedness as:

A child who stands out from other children in one or more respects. (Previous teacher)

She then described how Pat complied with this definition,

He stood out. He was unusual in the way he carried out tasks. It's not just that he always finished first and was brilliant, but he had an air of confidence all the time. I was the first person to label him as gifted. He always did outstanding work, mainly in English imaginative work. He was outstanding in his ideas. In Art he had more than other children, I put it down to maturity. He was attempting perspective at the age of seven. His maths was very good, but he wasn't outstanding there. Music of course. He wouldn't bother to tell you about the prizes that he won at music, you would get to hear of it some other way. He never boasted, though he must have realised he was gifted. He streaked ahead in the first year I had him. (Previous teacher)

His present teacher defined giftedness as follows:

Gifted children should stand out in comparison to the rest of the class in all respects. In all their work one should be impressed a lot of the time, amazed.

This teacher then presented a confused picture of how she saw Pat before she was his teacher, and now, as his class teacher, bearing in mind his musical ability.

When he was little it was obvious that he was odd and gifted. You only needed to look at him to see. He is definitely gifted musically. He was in a musical show, I was astounded. His teacher said that he was good at everything else too. I heard about him long before I had him. I expected more.

The teacher had had expectations of Pat before she became his teacher, which may not have been clearly defined. She then found that these expectations were not fulfilled.

> He is very very good, but I just don't know if it's good enough to be gifted. He had a label, so he's expected to be gifted. I looked at his work, his work is not fantastic.

This description of Pat's work does not appear to comply with that of the previous teacher. However, the next extract indicates that Pat had very high ability. The present teacher appeared to be reluctant to call Pat gifted, and there is an apparent mis-match between what she described and her conclusion which she reached that he was not gifted.

> It's good (his work) he picks up everything that one says, but is that gifted? Perhaps he just wants to learn. He listens to everything and gets it down. This year he does not stand out as much. He always finishes first, he rarely does not know the answer. He can work things out. He is very modest but knows that he is gifted, he must know. He almost doesn't like to tell you if you make a mistake. You can see he is uncomfortable and doesn't know what to do about it. He hasn't got a sum wrong in maths homework all year. He is gifted in music and his musical gifts make one think that he should be gifted at everything. If there's something he's not good at, for example games, he tries desperately hard. He is not artistic, his work always stands out because he's thought it out, but I don't think he's good at art. He just has good ideas and does it intelligently, coming prepared and having thought out what he wants to do. I am not impressed or amazed at his work. He seems slow putting his hand up (observation had shown that his hand was up almost continually). I still don't know if he is gifted. He doesn't stand out as much as when he was younger though he is top of the class. He makes a lot of mistakes. I have suggested that he enter for a scholarship to a public school.

There would seem to be several contradictions in this extract, such as never making mistakes in mathematics homework and he makes a lot of mistakes; the fact that he must know he is gifted, but not thinking he is gifted himself, (unless this referred to his music); and his work is not fantastic, but he is top of the class. Pat's academic record for the previous two years showed As for grade and effort in everything except physical education where he got a C grade with an A for effort. Interpretation of the teacher's meaning indicates that although she accepted his giftedness in music, and although he was easily at the top of the class, yet she was disappointed with his academic standard which did not achieve her criterion for labelling as gifted. The perceptions of two further teachers were available for the same year.

> He has got grade five in cello. They are usually thirteen or fourteen when they do that. One must have grade six before one does A level, which indicates what a high standard he has reached. The others who started the cello at the same time are on grade two. (Music teacher)

> You ask such obvious questions. He is the best of the class obviously.

He is excellent, he has been from the start. He is very matter of fact, and takes it all for granted that he finds it easy. Although he's clever he doesn't get bored, he's active all through the lessons. (French teacher)

In class Pat had his hand up almost continually, and in French the teacher frequently turned to him as a last resort when the other children were unable to answer a question. His concentration was excellent (see Chapter 5). He produced neat work, which was lengthier and of a higher standard than his peers. In tests he almost invariably received full marks.

Dennis, middle school, year 4

Dennis's fourth year teacher in first school mentioned Dennis as being gifted during an interview concerning Benny. She felt that she had been too inexperienced at the time to recognize his giftedness, but retrospectively considered him to be gifted. Dennis's present teacher in the fourth year of the middle school stated to the author on the telephone that he did not feel that Dennis was gifted and that there were other children who were as good as him. By the time the research was started in the school the teacher was very excited because Dennis had just come first for his year in the National Foundation of Educational Research (NFER) tests. The teacher had not previously put him at the top of the class because his presentation of work was not particularly good. The teacher emphasized the importance of presentation especially with maps and illustrations, which may be attributed to the teacher being a geography specialist. He reported that at the beginning of the year the class had done some work independently, which required thought and the ability to organize information. Dennis had done this particularly well, but the teacher had found it too hard for most of the class, and had concentrated more on presentation for the remainder of the year. Dennis was at the top of the class with his reading age which had been tested the previous year and was 14.8. The next nearest child to him was 14.2. His mathematics, science and French teachers considered that his work stood out from that of the other pupils.

At the end of the week the following conversation with Dennis's teacher occurred because of what appeared to be a slight change in his attitude.

> * R-If he had been defined as gifted in the first school rather than retrospectively, would he have been seen as gifted all the way through?
> T-Yes, I'm sure he would. It was only after talking to you on the phone that I started to think about it. Would you say that he is?

* Researcher

The part played by an enquiry on the subject of giftedness in alerting teachers and schools to consider the subject was noted by the survey conducted by HMIs, where a member of the team stated:

Several members of the staff commented upon the salutary nature of this HMI enquiry in that it had drawn the staff's attention to an area which had previously been overlooked (G.B., DES, 1977, page 10).

Nicholas, middle school, year 3

In this section, which has contrasted the perceptions of four gifted pupils by previous and present teachers, Nicholas is the only child who had been given an IQ score as a result of being tested by an educational psychologist (see figure 3). His IQ score was extremely high despite the fact that his mother tongue was not English.

Nicholas's previous teacher defined giftedness as,

The ability to tackle new concepts with achievement if they were explained in adult terms. (Previous teacher)

This teacher found him to be two to three years in advance of the rest of the class, especially in mathematics, where he was doing the Kent Mathematics Scheme on his own.[7] She considered that his knowledge of vocabulary was enormous, but he did not appear to use it when doing English, where his writing was unimaginative. She found him interesting, because he was immature with sudden bursts of brilliance, though she also found him frightening because he was cleverer than she, which she combatted with her own experience. During that year she was worried because there was no competition for him in the class. However, at the beginning of the year in which Nicholas was observed, Jo arrived in the class and provided the competition.

The present teacher considered Jo to be gifted, but did not think that Nicholas was gifted. She found Nicholas to be more *all round* in his abilities than Jo in that Jo was not as good at English as Nicholas, but she considered Jo to be gifted in mathematics and probably science (though they had not started this subject yet, so this was based on an assumption). When asked if Nicholas's mathematical ability had deteriorated since the previous year when he was considered to be so good, she stated,

Well it isn't now. Jo is much better and there are others in the class who are at a higher level.

This was queried with the headteacher, who organized the matrices in mathematics for the children. He stated,

Nicholas is scoring 96–100 per cent at level three. He is taking less than a month with each matrix. His rate of working may have dropped off, but there is no significant falling off in the quality of work. Jo scores in the eighties though he is probably working faster. He is consistently taking one month. Jo is on number eleven, Nicholas is number seven. They started the matrices at the same level. Jo missed out most of the fractions, did later tasks in number, and went all the way through on Geometry. Nicholas has started further back. There is not a great deal of difference. (Headteacher)

It appears that the fact that the teacher was not in control of what was happening in mathematics, and was not in close communication about it, had led to a misunderstanding of the situation, which had contributed to her decategorization of Nicholas.

So far the discussion has attempted to contrast the stated definitions by teachers of giftedness, and related these definitions to the perceptions by teachers of specific gifted children who had been decategorized by the present teacher. Four out of the five present teachers had different definitions of giftedness from the previous teachers, and in three of those cases the present teachers had a polymathic definition. This may have partially contributed to the decategorization of the children to the non gifted group, but does not totally account for it. From classroom observation and statements by the teachers there does not appear to be any firm evidence of deterioration in the ability or attainment of the children. The next section uses independent measures of a variety of test scores to compare the two groups of gifted and decategorized non gifted children.

Test Scores versus Teachers

Seventeen of the sample of gifted children had been tested by an educational psychologist. Schools vary in their policy of calling in the educational psychologist, and some restrict the testing to those children who have educational or emotional problems. The schools also vary in the importance that is placed on testing and scores generally. Figure 3 gives the test score results of the children, who are divided into the gifted and non gifted groups according to the perceptions of their present teacher. Eleven of the twenty-four children in the gifted group, and six of the fifteen children in the non gifted group had been tested by the educational psychologist.

The IQ scores are problematic in that the same test was not used for each child. Scores on one test do not necessarily mean similar scores on another, as shown by the differences between WISC and Peabody in the cases of Ann and Ken. Also one has to consider that the children were tested at very different ages. The tests are standardized for each age range, and comparison across ages is somewhat suspect. However, detailed knowledge of the intricacies of IQ testing is rarely available to teachers, and it may be more usual for them to attend to the final IQ number, probably the highest. Taking the Full Scale score for WISC and the Peabody and Stanford-Binet scores (where both were available the highest was used) the gifted group averaged 153.5 IQ and the non gifted group average 150.3+ IQ (the plus sign is because of Mary). There would seem to be little apparent difference between the gifted and non gifted groups.

Figure 3   The test scores of first and middle school children categorized as gifted or non-gifted

Year	Name	WISC(1)			S. or S	Binet(2) Peabody MA	Neal RA(3)			RA(4)	Other(5)
		V	P	FS			FL	Acc	Comp		
GIFTED											
(a) *First School*											
1	Arthur	None									
2	Ricky									4.1	
2	David									2.6	
2	Don	None									
2	Rita				140	SB				2.7	
3	Robert									5.6	
3	Jim (6)									3.10	Youngs NV IQ off scale
4	Benny (6)			160							
4	Maggy										NFER 135, Young NV IQ 127
4	Hugh									3.8	NFER 130, Young NV IQ 128
4	Rosemarie										NFER 139, Young NV IQ 125
(b) *Middle School*											
1	Sandy									3.7	NFER 116
1	Vicky	131	123	130						3.4	
1	Peter	155	136	151			4.4	4.8	3.1		
1	Ann	148	135	146	126	Peabody	1.6	2.10	1.10		
1	Ken	133	127	133	156	Peabody	3.1	3.7	3.5	4.7+	
1	Lilo	143	143	147						4.7	
3	Laurence	137	128	136						2.10	Spelling age 1.7
3	Les	137	143	143						2.7+	Spelling age 1.0
3	George									3.6	Spelling age 2.5
3	Sylvia									3.0	Spelling age 1.11
3	Jo	None									
3	Christopher	144	115	133			3.6+	3.7	1.7		
4	Angela	145	139	146						4.6	Cog Ab V 145+ Q 142+ NV 144+
NON GIFTED											
(a) *First School*											
2	Karl	None									
3	Mary				169 + (off scale)						Youngs NV IQ off scale
3	Jim (6)									3.10	Youngs NV IQ off scale
4	Keith										NFER 124 Young NVIQ off scale
4	Liz										NFER 139 Young NVIQ 130
4	Alexandra	138	135	140						3.4	
4	Vi				143	Peabody					
(b) *Middle School*											
1	Kathy	138	147	146						2.6	
1	Benny			160							
1	Hank									2.5	NFER 140
3	Mandy									4.0	NFER 130, Nelson V 141, Q 132, NV 135
3	Tony									4.1	NFER 127, Nelson V 136, Q 128, NV 130
3	Pat									4.2	NFER Math 139, Eng 137, VR 134
3	Nicholas	138	149	147	137	MA 15.5	4.8+	2.4	2.3	3.8	
4	Dennis									3.8	

(1) Wechsler Intelligence Score for Children, Verbal, Performance and Full Scale.
(2) Stanford Binet or Peabody IQ tests, Mental Age.
(3) Neal Reading Age, Fluency, Accuracy and Comprehension (The figure given is the number of years above the chronological age).
(4) Reading Age (The figure given is the difference between the chronological and the reading age. Where several reading age test scores were available the mean is given).
(5) Youngs Non Verbal IQ score
National Foundation for Educaional Research
Nelson-Verbal, Quantitative, and Non Verbal
Cognitive Abilities-Verbal, Quantitative, and Non Verbal
(6) Jim and Benny appear on both lists (see note 2).

Further examination of figure 3 reveals some interesting points. Schools differ in the IQ cut off point for their criterion of giftedness, for example Vicky had a Full Scale WISC score of 130 which would have excluded her from being categorized as gifted in Lilo's school. Also, schools vary in their policy of administering group tests. Where these were administered there tended to be several children in a class who were categorized as gifted by the school and/or teacher. This will be examined in more detail in the section concerned with differences in categorization between headteachers and teachers.

It is also normal practice for teachers to use Burt or Schonell reading tests[8], which give a reading age. Figures 3 and 4 give the difference between the chronological and the reading age, which allows comparison across age groups. Where test results were available for more than one year, the differences between the chronological and reading age were totalled, and then averaged. Figure 4 gives the reading ages of the gifted and the non gifted groups. Several teachers mentioned as their criterion for giftedness achievement which was two years above the norm.[9] It appears that in reading, as far as testing of this kind shows, these children did indeed perform two years above the norm. There is also some indication that in this area the non gifted group had an equivalent standard of attainment to the gifted group. This would provide strong indication to the effect that the differences were not necessarily in the children, but in the perceptions of the teachers.

Figure 4   Reading age scores for the teacher-classified gifted and non-gifted groups

Reading age*	Gifted	Percentage	Non-gifted	Percentage
Over 4 years	5	31%	3	33%
Over 3 years	7	44%	3	33%
Over 2 years	4	25%	3	33%
Total	16		9	

* Number of years average difference between chronological age and reading age.

The cases of four children in two classes will be explored in greater detail. They are particularly relevant, because each pair had similar IQ scores as assessed by an educational psychologist, yet in each pair the teacher considered one to be gifted and the other child to be non gifted. The differences between the children, and the perceptions of the teachers of the children will be traced.

Alexandra and Vi, first school, year 4 (Previous teacher interviewed was the teacher of David and Don. Don was Alexandra's younger brother)

Unfortunately the present teacher of Alexandra and Vi was unwilling to cooperate fully in the research. He did not give a complete interview, nor did he allow classroom observation. It was possible to include the two children in the present research because there was considerable data available about them. They had both been subjects in previous research (Maltby, 1979); a previous teacher gave a very detailed interview; the children themselves were interviewed; and their present teacher allowed access to the class to collect the sociometric and Guess Who data (see Appendix).

Vi had been tested by an educational psychologist when attending nursery school. She was one of the first of several children considered to be gifted who had stimulated among the staff of the nursery school an interest in the question of giftedness. Her nursery school teacher stated that

> At the time, in the group there was no one of her ability, she was alone intellectually. (Nursery school teacher)

Vi's school records had a card attached giving the information that she had a high IQ of 143. Her previous teacher stated that,

> I suppose my definition [of gifted] would be that they've got a talent in some field that is more than the average child would have, not necessarily all over, but in a certain area they seem to show a particular bias, or whatever you would call it, ability. (Previous teacher)

The teacher then went on to explain that despite her knowledge of Vi's very high IQ, she did not consider her to be gifted.

> I was told the facts about her [Vi's] IQ before she started school. When I had her I would not have called her gifted, nor would I have noticed her as such. She was causing a lot of problems and I felt that I ought to go along and find out as much as I could, so I went to some lectures on gifted children. It was very reassuring to hear from other teachers that a lot of the other [gifted] children had terrible problems in reading or writing and the physical presentation of things. Which is quite reassuring in a way, because you tend to feel that because a child is gifted they should be good at all things. (Previous teacher)

When Vi was compared with Alexandra, whose IQ was 140, her ability was not considered to be as high. The comparison was made from different perspectives by the mother and the teacher.

> There was always this competition from her mother about why she wasn't doing as much as Alexandra. But they're completely different sorts of children. Vi wasn't reading when she started school, Alexandra was on to book 4 Ladybird. (Previous teacher)

The teacher attributed the difference in achievement of the two children to differences in their home background, and problems in Vi's home,

> As far as I could see in class she was perfectly happy, that's to say she wouldn't come in screaming or anything, but mother had terrible problems actually getting her to school, which she said was the fault of

the school, it was what we were doing in school that Vi didn't like, but she could never find out what it was. Actually in school Vi was quite happy ... She always needed terrific reassurance, she was very reluctant to do anything new until she was certain that she could do it. But I think the main problem was that Mum was making all sorts of problems, coming up to see me and speaking in front of her about it. I felt there was more going on at home than we knew about, which we later found out was true. I think Alexandra and Don have got everything at home they could possibly wish for. When I went to Vi's home it was a spotlessly clean flat, it looked like something out of a magazine. It didn't look as though a child lived there, whereas [Alexandra and Don] have got a playroom and they do painting and all sorts of things, certainly a different sort of background. The strange part was, that made me sort of wonder, was this business of not wanting to come to school nearly always happened the week before a holiday from school ... as if it was the holiday coming up and she didn't want to be at home. (Previous teacher)

The teacher then went on to describe the ways in which she found Alexandra to be gifted,

Alexandra struck me as something different, I suppose because she was so good at her reading, general knowledge, vocabulary and her whole attitude. She had problems with writing, and I felt she became frustrated because she'd got all the ideas, but whenever she wrote it always looked such a filthy mess. (Previous teacher)

Their present teacher felt that Vi was outstanding in her reading, and well above average in English. His definition of gifted was,

a striking outstanding quality, for example playing Chopin at 6 or IQ of over 165. Neither Vi or Alexandra would be that gifted. Both are well above average with very keen intelligence.

The headteacher also did not consider Vi to be gifted, but did think that Alexandra was. She attributed this to differences in home background, Vi's home was emotionally problematic and intellectually lacking, she came from a working-class home; Alexandra's home was middle-class and intellectually and emotionally supportive. (The effect of social class and perceptions of home background will be examined in the next chapter).

Clearly neither child would or could comply with the extremely restrictive definition of giftedness of their present teacher. The reason for the difference of opinion between the school and the educational psychologist concerning Vi may be that a high IQ score was not sufficient as a criterion for giftedness, especially when the testing had been instigated by a previous school. The present school required more concrete evidence in the form of high attainment, though Vi's present teacher seemed to find her standard of work very high in some areas. It may be that Vi's home background was sufficiently difficult to prevent her from producing work of a higher standard. Also there is the possibility that the contrast of achievement and/or attitude was exacerbated by the presence of Alexandra who showed qualities which complied with the school's expectations of giftedness.

Kathy and Lilo, middle school, year 1

There was one point difference in the Full Scale WISC scores of Kathy and Lilo, Lilo's IQ being 147, and Kathy's being 146. However, Kathy's reading age score was lower than that of Lilo. The educational psychologist and the headteacher considered both the children to be gifted, but the present teacher did not agree with reference to Kathy. Her definition of giftedness was,

> In advance of their chronological age in all subjects, and IQ of 140 plus. They could be gifted in one particular sphere if one takes what the word means.

She then went on to describe how Lilo was gifted.

> Lilo is fantastic at English vocabulary. There is no cockiness there, she is perfectly natural. She is gifted and would survive in a third year class. She will always read, she is never at a loose end. She is keener than Kathy once she has got something that gets her. The reading lab is new, and she is more advanced than the others, and she wants to get on. She is very strong on the English side, has a good sense of humour and plenty of originality. They both understand new things very quickly.

The reasons for the two girls being tested by the educational psychologist were different. Lilo was tested because of her obvious ability, while Kathy was tested because her brother had been gifted and had won a scholarship to a public school. Kathy 's reputation from her previous school appeared to influence the teacher's impression of the child, and the teacher felt that her ability in class was not in advance of the other children.

> Kathy had the attitude that if her brother goes to one of these schools why can't I. I have heard that she can be a madam, I have not had trouble with her myself. Kathy is thought by the educational psychologist and Head to be gifted, the potential is there, but she is not gifted. Orally she shows that she is bright rather than gifted. She is good verbally, but she doesn't show up in class. Her maths is not particularly good and her work seems no better than M ... 's. She won't fall over for work, but her brother was the same. Not lazy, but she does what is required.

The teacher had not sat Kathy on the top ability table. Perhaps this contributed to the child's poorer output of work.

I chose where they sat, the middle table at the front is the brightest, where Lilo sits. I missed Kathy out by accident. It does Kathy good to keep her on her toes, not letting her think that she's best. I'm only going by what I heard from last year. They are both very nice, Lilo is more so that Kathy because she is so natural. Kathy is very pleasant but has an air that she wouldn't demean herself too much.

Ten extracts have been chosen from classroom transcripts of interactions between the teacher and the two girls. The extracts illustrate an apparently more favourable attitude towards Lilo on the part of the teacher, reiterating the impression given by the interview. The first seven are between the teacher and Kathy and show a mixture of negative and positive remarks made by the teacher to or about Kathy.

Extract 1

The class are doing the answers to a mental arithmetic test. The teacher is asking specific children to give what they have written.
Kathy giggles.
T-What's the joke?
K-I put twenty-two.
T-Oh, that wasn't very good.
The teacher asks the class to get out their bingo cards for multiplication tables. Each child has their own folder for this.
K-You said I could choose.
T-Yes, which do you choose?
K-Two times table.
T-Lazy, very lazy.

Extract 2

The class are lining up for television.
T-Oh yes, you're sensible Kathy, you can go to the back.

Extract 3

Children who have copied a word wrongly in a particular exercise that morning are called for by the teacher.
T-Hands up those who have to write out a word ten times.
So few, I thought there were more.
Kathy puts her hand up.
T-Ah yes, Kathy, quite a common event with you. Careless.

Extract 4

Reading around the class. Kathy reads a section.
T-You read that pretty nicely. The only thing is, did anyone notice any changes she made?
Children-She added an 'and'.
Kathy mutters an indignant 'well' under her breath.

Extract 5

The class are doing patterns on paper. Kathy shows hers to the teacher.
K-It went wrong a bit.
T-Good idea. It was a good idea you tried.

Extract 6

The class are doing some writing and the teacher is going round looking at their work.
T (in a raised voice)-Kathy that is absolutely disgraceful. How do you spell John?
K-J-O-H-N.
T-Then why do you spell it J-H-O-N? You will stay in at play and do it again. Do you want to do it in the library?
K-No
T-No, because last time the Head saw you.

Extract 7

The children are giving the results of their test.
K-Fourteen out of twenty (looking very shamefaced).
T-At least Kathy you didn't cheat. That's important to remember and that's the most important of the lot.

When a comparison is made between these extracts between the teacher and Kathy and those given below between the teacher and Lilo, it will be seen that there appear to be differences. Lilo received bantering and favourable remarks from the teacher, whereas a considerable number of the interactions between the teacher and Kathy may be considered to be negative.

Extract 8

The teacher interrupts the verbal work that the class are doing with tables.
T-I have noticed that Lilo has taken note of something written above the blackboard. I put the notice up because I was fed up saying it [Are you wearing SPECS?]
L-What about you?
T-I only wear them when I'm reading.
L-I only wear them when I'm concentrating.
T-Aren't you concentrating now? You should be.

Extract 9

Some new Geometry books are given out. Most of the children flick through looking at the pictures. Lilo looks at the index first.
T-(to the class) You can see there are all sorts of things in this book.
T-You think it looks interesting Lilo? (Lilo nods) Good.

Later

L-Would you say that a circle has one side?

T-Ah! This is a very good question. How many sides has a circle got?

Later Lilo has her hand up.

T-Yes Lilo.

L-My book keeps bouncing up. (It is a new one)

T-Well we'll have to see what we can do about that in a minute. It is annoying when a book does that. That's a good way of describing it.

Extract 10

The class are doing their SRA Workbook.[10] Lilo is flicking through the book.

T (To the class)-By now you should be old enough to listen without looking at a picture. You should be able to listen and resist the temptation of turning over pages. Shouldn't you Lilo? (Lilo grins and nods her head.)

The interview with Kathy showed that to some extent she was aware of the differences in attitude by the teacher towards Lilo and herself.

K-I'd like to be Lilo because she always gets nice jobs and always being picked to do things. I don't normally get picked to do things. I'd love to do library duty in the playtimes.

R-How do you get chosen to do that?

K-Well um Lilo got chosen because when she hurt her eye she couldn't go out to play. She was sitting in the library and she got library duty, and other people in the classroom got it in their dinner times. I suppose it's just because I go home to dinners, but I could have done the one for people who do go home to dinners at playtimes ... the teacher just chose people, she didn't say do you want to do it or don't you, she just chose people, in her spare time asked people.

However, these extracts may give a distorted picture of the situation. It would be impossible for a teacher to be aware of and comply with every desire of every pupil. There are some grounds for the teacher to perceive differences between the two children, such as their reading age scores. Lilo was exceptionally keen to participate in any classroom activity, and performed at a higher level than Kathy in class tests and SRA.[10] Kathy presented a somewhat sullen aspect, and reciprocated the teacher's attitude as demonstrated by the following extract from the interview with Kathy,

(Kathy had just passed an examination to attend a selective girls public school)

R-Is there any reason that you'd want to go to your new school?

K-Um. It sometimes gets a bit boring here when there's not enough to do, and you have to wait for people and everything is explained six times to everybody and it gets a bit boring then. Quite a few people find that ... that was partly why I took the exam.

It would be difficult to assess which came first, Kathy's or the teacher's attitude. Very possibly they escalated in combination, but there did seem to be a personality clash between the teacher and the child. Once Kathy was at the new school her work improved, and she gained an Assisted Place two years later.[11] The interpersonal evaluation by teachers of gifted children in the handling of their talents will be examined in more detail in the following chapter.

Consideration of the three pairs of children in the same classroom has been valuable, and leads to some tentative conclusions. In each case one of the children had been decategorized, despite a high IQ. Therefore there would appear to be fair indication that test scores provided by educational psychologists are not necessarily conclusive in a teacher's categorization or continuance of pre-classification of a child as gifted. Similarly, (as discussed in the next section) school administered tests may not be definitive either. The teachers in this study seemed to base their judgments on the children's classroom activity. This is supported by research in America by Salmon-Cox where it was found that a child's classroom performance was given more weight by teachers than a standardized test score (Salmon-Cox, 1981).[12] The teachers demanded excellence as compared to the expectations of the norm for the age of the children, the lack of fulfillment resulted in declassification. The presence of another child in the class who performed better or was perceived by the teacher to perform better, such as Jo, Alexandra and Lilo, would also seem to contribute towards decategorization. This may be attributed to an exaltation of standards and expectation.

Headteachers versus Teachers

This section examines the differences in perception between headteachers and teachers concerning the giftedness of children. Out of the total of thirty-nine children, there were eighteen children about whom there were differences of opinion. In twelve cases the headteacher perceived the child as gifted and the teacher did not, and in six cases the position was reversed. Some of these children have already been discussed in the previous sections. The children are listed in figure 5.

Karl, Sandy and Vicky's headteacher had newly arrived from a more middle-class school, and was of the opinion that, seen in the context of such a school, these three children would not have stood out. The two teachers involved in the categorization of the children had worked in the school for a considerable time, and the headteacher felt that their standards had altered accordingly.

The remainder of this section will examine one particular first school involving eight children and five teachers. Particularly interesting is the fact that one of the children, Jim, was taught by two of the teachers (morning and

Figure 5   *Perceptions of giftedness by headteachers and teachers concerning individual children*

Year	Headteacher positive Teacher negative	Headteacher negative Teacher positive
FIRST SCHOOLS		
2		
3	Mary Jim	Karl (previous teacher)
4	Keith Liz Alexandra	Maggy Hugh Rosemarie
MIDDLE SCHOOLS		
5	Kathy Benny Hank	Sandy Vicky
7	Nicholas Pat Mandy Tony	

afternoon) and they differed in their classification of him. Figure 6 shows the children who were involved together with their categorization as gifted or non-gifted and their test scores. The school appeared to use tests more frequently than may be considered usual for a first school. The headteacher stated that this was partly to screen individual children, especially those at either extreme of the ability range. She said that she had taken advice from an educational psychologist concerning which tests to use, in order to alleviate the need for an educational psychologist except in extreme cases. This was because of the increased pressure on the educational psychologist service, resulting in their time becoming less available to schools.

The headteacher's definition of giftedness was,

> I think there are two different categories ... in some cases it's an outstanding talent in a particular field where that child's ability is way above the other children. And then ... there's an all round sort of ... where children have been thought to be able to be educated with the older children, perhaps because they have been thought to be parti- cularly bright and adult, or generally if they seem to be far in advance of the other children ... it's a sort of general ability which is well above the average, and I think it's a particular talent. (Headteacher)

This would put the headteacher into the inclusive definitional category. In many ways the children discussed in this school repeat some of the observa-

Figure 6   Differences in categorization between headteacher and teachers in one school

Class	Name	Teacher Definition	Teacher Category	Headteacher Category	Educational Psychologist	Reading Age	Youngs N/V	NFER
2	Rita	IQ + other	Gifted	Gifted	St. Bin. 140	2.7		
3	Mary	Attainment	Non gifted	Gifted	St. Bin. 169+ off scale		off scale	
	Jim (morning)	Attainment	Gifted	Gifted		3.10	off scale	
	(afternoon)	All round	Non gifted					
4	Maggy	IQ + other	Gifted	Non gifted			127	135
	Rosemarie	"	Gifted	Non gifted			125	139
	Keith	"	Non gifted	Gifted			off scale	124
	Hugh	"	Gifted	Non gifted		3.8	128	130
	Liz	"	Non gifted	Gifted			130	139

tions made previously, and they also highlight the differing perceptual positions of the teachers and the headteacher, who was interviewed in some detail with reference to each child.

Mary, first school, year 3

As can be seen from figure 6 Mary was recorded as having an exceptionally high IQ at nursery school. This was repeated after the period of observation with Youngs Non Verbal IQ where she was off the scale. There are similarities with Nicholas, Vi and Kathy in that there was another slightly older child in the class, Rachel, who was performing in reading considerably better than Mary. The teacher considered Rachel to be brighter than Mary, though not gifted. The two children worked closely together. For example they were on the same mathematics page, which was two books in advance of the rest of the class. Rachel was several reading books ahead of Mary. The teacher stated that apart from Rachel there were two other children who were ahead of Mary on the reading scheme, which was not apparent during observation. The teacher also said that Mary wanted to read the same books that Rachel had already read, and did not wish to miss any out, furthermore Mary did not become bored. The reading system used by the teacher was that the children read a specific number of pages to themselves, then read them to the teacher, before they went on to the next pages. The teacher said that Mary did not need to look over her reading, she was able to pick it up and read it, therefore she tended to hear her earlier. The teacher felt that Mary should be able to read on, but that Rachel was more able to do this. When Mary read to the author she appeared to be extremely fluent, and there were no words in the remainder of the book that she did not know. In the Where Are You game (see Appendix) she had indicated a degree of dislike for school work. She was questioned about this during her interview, and revealed that many of the perceptions of the teacher were not quite correct.

Interview with Mary

I don't like looking at reading very much because it's boring 'cos I know it a lot you see 'cos when I look over it the teacher calls other people out before me 'cos they need more practice and I get a bit bored just sitting there looking over it again and again. We have reading cards and she says how many pages you've got to do. You start at the beginning and you've got to go right to the end of the book, you do it gradually page by page ... the ones that I'm on at the moment are quite easy. I don't like going over the reading book because it's not that I've done it before, it's because it's quite easy and it's a bit boring.

The teacher's definition of giftedness indicated a demand for high performance,

> A child who obviously was far and above the capabilities of the norm
> in a certain area, it could be in music or drawing ... they are quite
> often found beyond the teacher's capabilities.

It is clear that Mary was not fulfilling this demand for high performance in her
teacher's estimation, and therefore would not comply with the teacher's
definition of giftedness. On the other hand, there is some indication that this
may be a result of the system of progression used in the class, and Mary would
have been able to progress in her reading at a faster rate. When her very high
IQ was mentioned the teacher attributed it to the fact that Mary got a lot of
support from home. The headteacher considered that the teacher was wrong,

> ... because I think she's operating at a good level for her age she's at
> and I think perhaps that that is what they're looking at, but I'm
> inclined to think whoever tested her was right. I think she'd cope with
> it, [harder work] I really do. I thought that last year she did stand out,
> and again, perhaps not in the work that she actually presented but in
> very many ways ... Her understanding seems to be so much more
> advanced than the others, and her approach. She has got a maturity
> that the rest of the children have not got. It's a bit nebulous, it's
> difficult to just put your finger on it, but for instance when you've got
> a new teacher she helps her settle in, showing where everything is,
> etc. (Headteacher)

The Youngs Non Verbal IQ test results the following month showed that
Rachel's IQ was high, but not nearly as high as Mary's which was off the scale.
The position was reversed with regard to reading ages. It would seem that the
teacher's assessment of Mary's reading performance was correct, though it
may be reasonable to expect some correlation between reading age and level of
material read. It would also seem that in this case IQ results were considered to
be more important by the headteacher than by the teacher.

Jim, first school, year 3

Jim had been identified by a previous teacher because of his language and
reading ability which she had particularly noticed when he had read fluently a
meteorological report from one of the higher level newspapers, and had
understood it. He was able to read on his arrival at school, although he had
never been taught. Jim was taught by a teacher in the morning who had an
attainment definition of giftedness, and in the afternoon by a teacher with a
polymathic one. His reading age was 3.10 years above his chronological age.
When he was IQ tested by the headteacher after the observation period he was
off the scale and even higher than Mary.

Jim's morning teacher described him as being gifted in language, especially reading, where he was able to read ahead so far that he was able to put on
different voices. However, she found that his creative writing did not reflect

his language ability. She thought his ability in language, English and reading was sufficient for him to be accelerated by two years, but did not consider that it would benefit him socially. In mathematics he worked on a more advanced book from the rest of the class. She did not find that he learnt new mathematical concepts particularly easily, which surprised her. She considered Jim to be a leader, and found him extremely helpful when she first arrived in the school.

Jim's afternoon teacher did not believe that Jim was gifted. She was particularly concerned by his lack of application, where he was satisfied with less than he was capable of. His handwriting was poor and slapdash, and he lacked concentration. This was brought out during observation where he was distracted 38 per cent of the time, mainly chatting with the other children at his table. The teacher attributed a lot of his problems to his home environment. The parents were divorced, both parents had remarried and had recently had new babies. The teacher found Jim to be a bright child, with a ready sense of humour and wit. He contributed well at discussion time, revealing keen observational abilities. She was under the mistaken impression that Jim was not in advance of the rest of the class in mathematics. She found him to be stimulating, and with plenty of potential, which she thought would not be realized, especially in comparison to some other children, unless his concentration improved, which was why she did not consider him to be gifted. This is an interesting qualification to the concept of giftedness. It appears that there were two criteria that were important for this teacher. The production of work at the time, and some indication that he would be able to fulfil his potential in the future. She did not perceive that Jim satisfied either of these criteria.

There were similarities in perception between Jim's afternoon teacher and Benny's middle school teacher, as there were in some of the behavioural characteristics of the two boys. This teacher also described an incident rather like Benny not finding 'the middle of the book', which reflected the same concern for 'common sense' or 'recognition of the obvious',

> Jim wanted to do his own picture to go round the maypole, and we had talked at some length about holding up the ribbon. He always comes to school very smartly dressed, and he did take great trouble in depicting his suit, but that's what he produced, someone with their arms firmly at their sides, and there were two others that afternoon who did much the same thing, in other words they didn't have their arms raised. So I cut out those that were suitable and when they were all sitting down quietly I produced these and I said "I can't put these people on the maypole, can you tell me why?" and one or two of the children in the class had a bit of a giggle. "Now come on, don't giggle, what is wrong?" I held Jim's up, and he said "Well, I look like that." I said, "Yes this is a very good painting, but why can't I put it round the maypole?" It took him quite a long time to realise that he hadn't got the arm up. (Afternoon teacher)

The headteacher was in agreement with the morning teacher and also considered Jim to be gifted,

> Jim stood out from the others more or less from the word go, and again I know he doesn't in the actual presentation of his work, in some of the work anyway. And again the teacher doesn't think he's gifted, but I don't think I'd agree with her. We've watched Jim for a long time and his powers of observation, and his powers of reasoning and logic are exceptional for his age. His previous teacher thought he was, and that was where the original idea of his giftedness started, and I'm inclined to agree with her. In some ways we could have pushed him, reading wise especially. We knew his reading was far in advance of the rest of the class, but I don't think we were quite prepared for the incident with the newspaper. It wasn't just that he read it, but he understood it, and it was the same with his reading in school, he wasn't just reading and not understanding. With Jim you could ask him all kinds of questions about comprehension and you could get him to interpret and predict without any difficulty at all. And again I'll be interested to see what the IQ turns out to be. (Headteacher)

As both teachers taught Jim at the same time, the discordance in classification can be taken as differences between the perceptions of the teachers rather than differences in the boy. The two teachers did have different definitions of giftedness, which would contribute to the dichotomy. The afternoon teacher seemed to demand more than ability, she required that Jim achieve to his fullest potential. The headteacher had the opportunity to observe specific children over a longer period of time, and make comparisons with larger numbers of children.

Maggy, Rosemarie, Keith, Hugh and Liz, first school, year 4

There were five children involved in the final class, and there was complete dissimilarity between the headteacher and the teacher. In discussion they appeared to be using different concepts. Each child will be discussed in turn. Keith was off the scale in the Youngs Non Verbal IQ test, but the teacher did not find his class work exceptional, though very able, and she did not consider him to be gifted. The headteacher did think that Keith was gifted, presumably because of his IQ score.

Rosemarie had a lower IQ which contributed to the headteacher's classification of her as non gifted, but her teacher was amazed at her story telling ability, and allowed her to perform to the rest of the class. She would start a story, with no apparent idea of the ending, making it up as she went along. It would be colourful, imaginative, and complicated enough to keep the class spellbound for a period of ten minutes (as observed). Presumably, as this happened during classtime, it was not an aspect about the child of which the headteacher was aware.

The headteacher used Hugh's test scores in deciding her nongifted classification of Hugh. His teacher felt that he had a lot of imagination and an original approach to answering problems. She found Hugh handicapped in writing, but was impressed by his ability to pick up a piece of writing after an interval of two days and regain the threads immediately.

Liz was noticed by the headteacher for her high test scores as well as her unusual artistic talent. This had been revealed the previous year. She drew a very large card depicting all the children in the class. Each individual child was recognizable, she had drawn the hair correctly and had caught their facial expressions. Her teacher recognized her artistic talent, considered her to be highly intelligent, but found her to be easily confused, especially in topic work, and did not find her gifted.

Maggy had been accelerated by a previous headteacher (acceleration is discussed in more detail in the next chapter). There was some doubt amongst the staff as to whether this was because Maggy was considered to be gifted, or because of class numbers, and there is no mention of the acceleration in her records. The present headteacher considered the situation impossible because it would have meant her spending two years in the top class where she would have lost all her friends. Maggy therefore repeated the third year with a different teacher, allowing her to make friends in her year group, with whom she would go to middle school, while her previous class was still in the school. The headteacher had discussed it with the staff, who had agreed that Maggy was bright but not gifted, which was reflected in her test scores. She was also thought to be rather immature. Her present teacher did think that Maggy was gifted, especially in mathematical and logical thinking. Maggy read fluently and had covered all the reading schemes in the school. The teacher encouraged her to read other books around the school, but found that she picked out rather simple books. This contrasted with what she did at home, where apparently she read Shakespeare for fun, and quoted bits of Macbeth to her parents. The teacher described her as lacking in confidence in class discussion and considered her work to be slapdash. The teacher felt that she may have some hidden ability that was not totally reflected in her work or in her verbal approach to things.

This particular headteacher based much of her opinion on test scores, but her staff did not necessarily do so, which was queried during the interview with the headteacher,

R-Do you think that IQ is necessarily the same as ability in children?
H-Yes I think it is the same as ability. It definitely doesn't always show at some stage in their education, in fact it often doesn't. In some cases it does because they can do everything without you being there to help them and that would be the sort of child that I would consider to be a very high IQ and generally gifted. Rita fits into that category . . . It is a personal thing [categorization] isn't it? Unless they have an IQ over 140. I suppose that's really a thing that you can go by . . . I don't think that their IQ is always reflected in the work at school for various

reasons. I mean I don't think that it's always the teacher's fault, but sometimes their view of a child is coloured by what they expect. A child with not so high an IQ . . . on these NFER tests can come up with a very high score, alternatively somebody with a very high IQ may not be able to read, but that doesn't mean to say that the IQ is wrong, there is something wrong with the way they've been learning to read, I'd suggest, rather than the other way round . . . I think it depends on how people look at what is gifted. (Headteacher)

The differences in perception between headteachers and teachers concerning the categorization of individual children as gifted may be attributed to differences in the criteria for giftedness that they used. This was illustrated at the beginning of the chapter, where definitions were analyzed, and also in the case-study of the school. The headteachers used a *universal or relative* definition and application of criteria for giftedness to individual children. On the other hand, the teachers appeared to be more *specific or absolute* in their theoretical and practical applications of their concepts of giftedness. The teachers were liable to ignore test scores if they did not comply with their own class-based estimate of the child's ability. There appears to be some indication that headteachers would agree with test scores. Steadman and Goldstein, in a study which included eighty headteachers, found that 60 per cent of headteachers regarded test scores as correct when the score was higher than expected (Steadman and Goldstein, 1982). To some extent the differences in criteria used may be attributed to the different roles of headteachers and teachers, where headteachers have more opportunity to acquire an overview of larger numbers of children. Primary school teachers are more limited in the numbers of children with whom they come into contact, and the comparisons that they make between children tend therefore to be within class comparisons. This may account for the decategorization of some of the children when more than one gifted child was present in the class.

This chapter has illustrated differences in perceptions of teachers and headteachers with regard to giftedness and individual gifted children. The two groups of gifted and non gifted children will be returned to in the following chapters. For the purposes of this research the non gifted group are included in the sample of gifted children because they were considered to be gifted by their schools or their previous teacher. In the next chapter an examination will be made of the actions by children which led to their categorization as gifted; perceptions by the teachers of the children's home backgrounds; and an attempt will be made to explain the decategorization of some of the non gifted group.

Notes

1. In the interests of anonymity, and at the request of many of the headteachers, the names of the children have been changed. Throughout the book teachers

will be referred to according to the names of the gifted children that they taught.

2. Two children frequently appear in the figures twice. Benny was studied twice, once in his final year in first school, and once with a different teacher when he was in the same class as another child, at the end of his first year in middle school. Jim had two teachers, one in the morning and one in the afternoon. Two children are frequently excluded in discussions concerned with academic ability because they were not considered to be academically gifted. Geoff was a gifted musician, and Adrian was a gifted footballer.

3. Unless otherwise stated quotations are taken from the interview transcripts of the present teacher.

4. The area of how much teacher time as a scarce resource gifted children are allocated, or allocate for themselves, will be explored in detail in Chapter 5.

5. See the Appendix for the methodological difficulties of timing concentration and distraction.

6. The School Mathematics Project (1964–) is designed to develop mathematical concepts for children using practical methods. The mathematics is built up in a progressive way, and is suitable for a broad range of ability. The children work on their own or in small groups on workcards, and progress at their own pace.

7. The Kent Mathematics Project (1978–) is a series of graded workcards in mathematics. The aim of the design is to provide a course in mathematics for each individual child suitable for all abilities of children between nine and sixteen years; a scheme which is flexible within which teachers can introduce their own interests and skills; a system in which children will accept responsibility for most of their own learning, and so on.

8. The Schonell Graded Word Reading Test (Schonell et al, 1972) is one of the most widely used reading tests in the UK. The Burt Reading Tests 1–5 were some of the earliest reading tests devized and are still used in some schools (Burt, 1921).

9. In fact being two years ahead in ability does not necessarily coincide with an IQ of 140, especially as children become older. For example a child with a chronological age of eight and an ability age of ten would achieve an IQ of 125 ($\frac{10}{8}$ = 125) and a child with a chronological age of ten and an ability age of twelve would achieve an IQ of 120.

10. The Science Research Associates Reading Laboratory (1961–) covers an age range of twelve years. The series is constructed on a multilevel principle and presents reading materials at different levels of ability and skill development, accomodating individual differences. The material is presented in the form of work cards coloured according to the level of difficulty. The children start at a point commensurate with their ability, and progress at their own speed.

11. The Assisted Places Scheme will be discussed more fully in Chapter 4.

12. The self fulfilling prophecy will be discussed in Chapter 6.

3   Labelling and Giftedness

In the Introduction it was explained that initially this research was based on a dissatisfaction with two assumptions emphasized in previous research on giftedness. The first was that there was a specific group of children who were gifted, which group could be identified provided that the *correct* screening procedure was used, usually that of tests of IQ and/or creativity. The second assumption was that frequently teachers were not considered to be efficient or effective in their screening of gifted children, which was related to the teachers' ability to identify the same children as the tests.

If one reverses the priority of judgments vis-a-vis tests and suggests good classroom performance as being an indicator of academic success, then it may be that tests are only partially adequate for identification, whereas teachers, who are able to observe the classroom performance of children may be more efficient than they were previously considered to be. There was some indication in the previous chapter that ability on tests was not considered to be reflected in the classroom performance of some children. Jackson reported a general distrust by teachers of tests. The teachers considered children to behave atypically on tests, and the tests frequently did not confirm the teachers' judgment derived from classroom performance (Jackson, 1968).

In Chapter 1 changes that have occurred in definitions and methods of identification for giftedness over the last sixty years or so were discussed. It was pointed out at the beginning of Chapter 2 that the proportion of the population considered to be gifted varies according to the criteria of giftedness in use. This statement was expanded in the consideration of previous research, and in the examination of the categorization and decategorization of children as gifted by teachers and headteachers in the present research. It was shown that there was dissent between teachers and headteachers in their perceptions and interpretations of the behaviour of individual children, which was partially attributed to the dichotomy between people's use of universal, as opposed to specific criteria of giftedness as applied theoretically and practically.

It appears that the composition of the *group* of children identified as gifted is unstable. It fluctuates in historical terms, and also at any one time according to the perceptions of the individuals concerned. Therefore, there is some indication that a deterministic model of giftedness is inadequate. In other words, children referred to as gifted are not objectively given, but subjectively problematic. The historical indecisiveness concerning giftedness, together with the diversity of perceptions between individuals when judgments of giftedness are shifted to the practitioners' level, lead to the suggestion that a social theory would be appropriate when studying the re-structuring of the concept of giftedness.

The *interactive labelling theory*, as an approach, may fulfil this requirement for a social theory. Previously it has been used in the study of deviances, such as prostitution, homosexuality and so on. The orientation is that individuals do not necessarily belong to a particular deviance group because of some inherited characteristic, or because society has forced them into it. They belong because they have been labelled as deviant by others. This is what appeared to occur with the children in this study.

Warren and Johnson suggested that labelling theorists only partially advanced to a phenomenological view of man as an actor, in that they perceived the individual as able to make decisions and have a will of his own, but still within the restrictions of society (Warren and Johnson, 1972). As with the majority of theories, labelling theory cannot be judged separately from previous sociological and social-psychological contexts, for it is through comprehension of these that new conceptualizations evolve. Schur stated that the labelling approach complements elements of previous sociological theories of deviance, such as functionalism, and that rather than being a formal theory is an orientation or broad interpretive framework (Schur, 1979).

The labelling orientation emphasizes the importance of the perceptions of social groups in the categorization of candidates to a deviant group. Becker explained the process of deviance labelling as,

> *social groups create deviance by making the rules whose infraction constitutes deviance*, and by applying those rules to particular people and labelling them as outsiders. From this point of view deviance is *not* a quality of the act the person commits, but rather a consequence of the application by others of rules and sanctions to an 'offender'. The deviant is one to whom that label has successfully been applied; deviant behaviour is behaviour that people so label (Becker, 1963, page 9).

Previously, labelling theorists have tended to study groups that were considered to be stigmatized, groups which deviated from the norm. As stated by Goode, the word deviance implies a negative concept (Goode, 1978). This would appear to deny the application of labelling theory to the gifted. However, to be gifted is to be deviant, to be well outside the norm in terms of ability in one or more fields. Also, although being considered gifted does not inevitably mean consideration in an unfavourable light, it can be, as indicated by some of the research mentioned in Chapter 1. The literature has logically been concerned with those children who have been classified as gifted, in other words the label has already been applied. The group labelled as gifted have been so labelled by another group, whose definition of giftedness is socially constrained, as is the methodology used for their recognition.

The discussion so far may be clarified using an illustrative model which shows the labelling of children as gifted, figure 7. The term negotiative arena is used to reflect the dynamic process of discussion and decision — making concerning the label of gifted. It is probable that the process is restimulated when changes of teacher and/or school occur. The model refers to the dominant adult participants. The centre represents children about whom there is total consensus concerning the label of gifted. Partial agreement is when there is dissent between one or more of the participants concerning a particular child. For example, in the case of Mary (Chapter 2) the headteacher agreed with the educational psychologist about the label of gifted, but the present teacher did not consider her to be gifted. The past teachers are represented in the model by the dotted line.

The application of labelling theory to the study of gifted children involves four areas of research. Many studies concentrate on only one or two areas, thereby presenting a one-sided picture. The present research is committed to presenting a comprehensive perspective and will therefore attempt to cover all four areas, which are the process of labelling; the study of the labelled; the reactions of the labellers to the labelled; and the setting in which the above three areas occur. These will be discussed in turn.

Figure 7   The negotiative arena

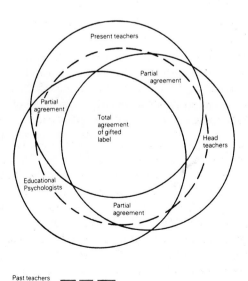

Past teachers   ___ ___ ___

There are two important aspects to the study of the process of labelling. The first is that the labelled must behave in a manner which leads to the instigation of the process. The examination of this behaviour is important to understand why and how that person was labelled. Secondly, the perceptions of the labeller need to be understood in order to comprehend the labelling of the labelled. Hargreaves emphasized that care must be taken not to impose the researcher's definition of the situation which may not be salient for the teachers and pupils (Hargreaves, 1977).

Gibbs was puzzled by labelling theorists' focus on the labelled when the theory appeared to be about reactions to the labelled (Gibbs, 1966). However, without observation of the labelled, the reactions to deviation would not be fully understood.

There are several aspects to the reactions of the labellers to the labelled which will be explored in this research, especially in terms of how the teachers deal with the gifted children. Hawkins and Tiedman suggested that within the study of reaction there are several possible studies, such as why behaviours are selected out for some official intervention by society; the origination of social policy; and the application of existing legal definitions (Hawkins and Tiedman, 1975). To some extent these have already been explored in Chapter 1, but they will be referred to again in Chapter 4.

Understanding about the setting in which the above processes occur would appear to be essential for comprehension of the processes themselves. Yet this is an area which is frequently excluded in research, reliance being placed on statements and perceptions of the participants. Chapters 5 and 6 of this research would comply with the suggestion of Manning that the mode of analysis be interactional, considering to some degree simultaneously both the labeller and the labellee within a transactional setting (Manning, 1975).

In the remainder of this chapter the concentration will be on the first perspective of the process of labelling. Initially, consideration will be given to the activities of the children who inaugurated the labelling process. The focus will then change to the teachers as individuals, looking at the sources from which they get their knowledge about giftedness; and speculations will be made about pressures from outside the classroom which may affect the teachers, such as parents, colleagues and so on. An examination will be made of the teachers' perceptions of the home backgrounds of the children, and the methods that the teachers use in the assessment of the relative academic positions of the children. Both these areas will be related to social class.

The process of labelling may be considered to be a slow and gradual one, proceeding through various stages, including observation by the teacher followed by internal questioning, external questioning of colleagues including the headteacher, sometimes culminating in official designation by, for example, an educational psychologist. Although the concentration here is on the teacher it has already been shown in the previous chapter that headteachers may instigate the labelling process, usually on the basis of a child's performance on standardized tests.

Concurrently with consideration of the process of labelling, an attempt will be made to unveil some elements of the decategorization (or delabelling) of some children by their present teachers. This was discussed in the previous chapter, but the following notes will refresh the reader's memory. The total sample consisted of thirty-nine children, who were considered to be gifted by the *schools*. Out of these thirty-nine children, one was considered to be gifted solely in music, and one other in football. Consequently when academic giftedness is discussed, these two children are excluded. Turning to the remaining thirty-seven, twenty-four children were perceived to be gifted by the teacher they had at the time of observation; fifteen children were not considered to be gifted, and are termed decategorized or delabelled (two children, Jim and Benny occur in both groups because they were with two teachers who differed in their perceptions).

The Child

Labelling theory would suggest that in order for the process of labelling as gifted to commence the child has to act in a manner which indicates to the observer (in this part of the study the teacher) that there might be a possibility of that child being gifted. To reverse the quotation from Becker given above, the child has to break the rules which consititute being not gifted. According to Hargreaves, the labelling theory perspective suggests that any act is potentially deviant. The act becomes deviant when it is perceived to be so by another person or group (Hargreaves, 1976). Labelling theory is always in operation, in that the majority of children are labelled normal. The initiation of a process leading to the allocation of a different label comes when the criteria of *normal* are abused. It has already been shown in the previous chapter that within classroom comparisons are important for some teachers. Because of the research emphasis in the past on those children categorized as gifted by the researcher or identified by criteria chosen by the researcher, there is very little knowledge available about how teachers decide that the label of gifted is appropriate for a child. Nor do we know about the complexities involved in labelling. As Jordan suggested, some teachers may be more inclined to label than others, some teachers may be more inclined to use specific labels; and some teachers may be particularly rigid in maintaining a label once it has been applied (Jordan, 1974). This has already been indicated in the examination of the teachers' definitions of giftedness, and will be explored in more detail here.

The behaviour/s or activity/ies of the child are taken here as initial trigger mechanisms or indicators for the teacher of possible giftedness. The data for these indicators gathered in the study has been retrospective, being the verbal reports of teachers, headteachers, plus school records (where available). While acknowledging that retrospective data can be criticized because of possible distortion over time, of memory and varying methods of school record keeping, they may still be considered to represent some of the factors which are perceived as important by the participants. The examination here is limited to the child in the school situation. This should not be considered to eliminate the possibility of a pre-school child being identified as gifted by parents or health visitors. Indeed, there has been a recent increase of interest in giftedness by health visitors. However, in this study no child had been identified (as far as is known) as gifted, prior to entry to school or nursery school. The types of activities on the part of the children which initiated the labelling process will now be discussed.

Classroom performance is an important factor. The arrival at school of a child who can already read is frequently considered by teachers to be sufficiently unusual, compared with other children, to activate consideration as to possible giftedness. In some cases a specific occasion was pin-pointed as an initiator, as in the case of David,

David, first school, year 2

I first noticed David when I was writing out a notice for the wall and he was reading it out to me *upside down* (author's emphasis). The notice said "The handsome prince heard the witch say 'Rapunzel, Rapunzel, let your hair down'. He saw the beautiful girl at the top of the high tower. She let down her long golden hair, and the old witch climbed up. The prince rescued Rapunzel and married her. We don't know what happened to the witch. Do you?" The only word he couldn't read was married, and that was probably because of the way I wrote it. I then gave him a reading age test on Burt and it was eight, he was 5.6.

The occasion when Jim astounded his teacher by being able to read the newspaper meterological report (Chapter 2) was another example, as was Ken who amazed the headteacher,

Ken, middle school, year 1

When he came to the school aged less than five he could read, he had taught himself. He read to me a copy of a letter which I was sending out to the parents and understood it, apart from the word co-operation which he thought was to do with the co-op shop. This was a remarkable feat, because there were some very long words in it. (Headteacher)

These three precise instances were obviously very clearly implanted on the memories of the teachers and the headteachers, and were brought out as unusual examples of outstanding reading ability. Alexandra's previous teacher put pre-school reading into the context of her school, which drew from a low social class catchment area,

Alexandra, first school, year 4

Alexandra, because she was just so different from everybody else in the class, the way she read, her whole attitude, her general knowledge, that may be what made her so different, the fact she started school reading which is most unusual for round here. (Previous teacher)

Lilo's teacher showed herself throughout the interview to be influenced by reputations built up in the previous school. Interestingly, Lilo is the only child to have her pre-school reading ability actually written into her school records. Her teacher said,

Lilo, middle school, year 1

It was brought to notice with Lilo in the first school She could read when she came to the school.

Ricky's teacher was unaware that a previous teacher had already identified him as being gifted, nor had she known that he could read before he came to school. These facts were only brought out during a staff room conversation with the author, and were not stated in the records,

Ricky, first school, year 2

Previous teacher – Have you seen Ricky. He's gifted. His mind is so bright and with it. When he came to school at three and a half he could read and was writing stories.
Top class teacher – He came into my class once (seven to eight year olds) and they were watching a reading programme for remedial readers. They flashed words on the screen and he could read every one. He probably had a photographic memory.
Present teacher – He came to me fluently reading, with inflection, and really understanding what he was reading. (Staff room conversation)

The next group, including Karl, Rosemarie and Arthur, learnt to read particularly fast. This was used as a partial indicator of giftedness together with language, mathematical and other abilities. The quotation from Arthur's teacher is a fair example of the group.

Arthur, first school, year 1

He is a very good reader. He is on the highest reading book that anyone has ever had with me. He started at school without being able to read, and this is only his second term. His writing and picture drawing are good. In Maths he is [doing work], which is very good for his age. He grasps concepts very quickly. You only have to explain something to him once and he has got it.

The interviews with teachers showed that reading ability related to a part of the school curriculum which was important for them in considering a child as gifted. In order to be able to assess whether this had been the case for all the children, the available thirty-one school records were examined (excluding those of Geoff and Adrian). This made it possible to follow, to some extent, the school careers of the older children with reference to reading. Twenty-seven children had comments about reading in their first two school years, such as 'excellent reader', 'reading fluent', 'excellent progress reading'. Thirteen of the thirty-one children had reading noted under special interests and activities for the same years.

Twelve children were noticed by their teachers because of the excellence of aspects of their classroom performance and/or the fact of being able to do work in advance of the other children,

Hugh, Maggy and Rosemarie, first school, year 4

I think that with Hugh, Maggy and with Rosemarie I felt that they were well ahead of the rest of the class at least in certain aspects, and that their general way of approaching certain problems, discussion, aspects of topic work, general discussion, little bits of information that they added or questions that they asked, showing their own way of looking, of thinking about things, alerted me to the possibility that they might be gifted.

This also reflects the concern with originality of thoughts and opinions as reiterated by Don's teacher,

Don, first school, year 2

Don is different in the way he'll answer from the rest of the group. He thinks about things before he says the answer. He seems to please himself. He's quite independent compared with all the others. For example, the reason I saw him as being potentially gifted was when we were doing *Meg and Mog* stories and they all liked them, but he didn't because they weren't interesting. I feel that a child who is prepared to stand against public opinion like that must be gifted. He stands out.

Standing out in comparison to the other children was an obvious trigger mechanism which instigated the consideration of the label gifted. At the same time, presentation and tidiness of work were criteria that appeared important for some teachers. It has been suggested (Gallagher, 1964; Ogilvie, 1973; and Tempest, 1974) that if those children who are tidy in their work are most highly regarded by their teachers, then inaccuracy in the assessment of children may result. Acklaw and Wallace stated that 'Many gifted pupils are untidy, careless, and reluctant to write with their speed of thinking' (Acklaw and Wallace, 1982, page 2). Therefore, manipulative difficulties, revealed in poor or untidy writing, may contribute to lack of initial labelling of a child as gifted, or the delabelling of a child from the category of gifted. Eight children were mentioned by their teachers as having difficulties with their writing and/or presentation of work, five of whom had been delabelled by their present teachers. These were Hank, Kathy, Jim (afternoon teacher), Dennis and Alexandra.

There are a variety of ways in which delabelling may occur. In Hank's case the teacher appeared reliant on presented written work for her assessment of his abilities,

Hank, middle school, year 1

Hank's writing is almost negligible. This is why we're waiting for the NFER scores. His writing is untidy, imaginative I suppose, though I don't always see it. One week I sent him to the headmaster to get a 'good' because it was neat, but it was the only time. At one point the output was so negligible there was nothing to judge him by.

Although Dennis did not have manipulative or co-ordination difficulties, his presentation of work was not sufficiently good to satisfy his teacher's standards.

Dennis, middle school, year 4

I've done one or two simple tests, and he's come out near the top but not the top. On presentation as well, which is something I have to assess as well as their actual ability, how well they can present the work, especially at the beginning of the year, that's when it's the time to set the standards, and so I really hang on presentation. It's got to be beautifully set out, all the maps have got to be drawn just so, and the diagrams and illustrations. At the beginning you've got to set the standards. On those, that drops him down to just about half way I'd say, just roughly speaking. His presentation is not as good as some of the others who perhaps take longer, don't dash it off so fast ... That would have lowered his marks. So that means that in the first instance my placing of him would be lower, because this is a criteria which I include.

The lack of perfection of Dennis's work was clearly a contributing factor to his teacher not recognizing Dennis as gifted, yet, when work was set that required thought, he was able to do what the other children in the class were unable to do,

> I do remember that his first piece of Geography um mark, I really did leave them on their own a little bit, I'd given them a talk about South East England being the gateway to Britain, invaders coming ... and there was a page from a book which we'd read, and then I elaborated on it, and they had to do a couple of maps and some writing on what I'd spoken about, and Dennis did it particularly well, the writing he'd noted all the points and he'd done very well ... maps were OK. Again presentation let him down a little bit. It was very good. And then I found that some of the others in the class, even though it's our top class ... that it was beyond ... some of them. They couldn't cope with being left on their own ... Then I started hammering the presentation and easing up on the brain work, I thought we could do that later ...

The example of Dennis illustrates a competing objective in the teacher's overall aims between presentation, rather than quality of content.

For some teachers, therefore, presentation of written work may be an important factor in the labelling as well as the delabelling process. Writing difficulties will be referred to in the next chapter in the context of educational provision for gifted children.

The next criterion to be considered is test results. Four children entered first school already designated by the educational psychologist as gifted (when in nursery school). The nursery school had had these and other children tested because the staff felt that they were particularly bright and wanted their impressions confirmed. There were four areas of ability which encouraged the nursery school teacher to instigate assessment procedures. They were,

> ... excellence in language, concepts of ideas, memory and sometimes they had behaviour problems which made us believe that something else was needed. (Nursery school teacher)

The children concerned were Vi and Mary (already discussed in Chapter 2) Rita and Peter.

The children may also be identified by tests used by the schools themselves. Thus Keith's headteacher said,

Keith, first school, year 4

> Now Keith was a great surprise. Keith's always been good, but it was really the IQ test that brought his name up. (Headteacher)

However, change of school may affect the labelling of the child.

Hank, middle school, year 1

I have to go on the scores from the form before. We picked out children with the highest IQ scores. [The idea of Hank being gifted] came from the teacher in the second year at first school plus NFER 140. (Present teacher)

He is utterly utterly brilliant. People have been telling us that he was very interesting. He is not producing the goods so we have had the educational psychologist come to see him. He gives the impression of an absent minded professor at the age of eight. He forgets to bring his materials on a Monday three times in succession. One feels frustrated when people say that a child is gifted and that child persists in behaving like a remedial child. (Headteacher)

In Hank's case the headteacher considered him to be gifted, but the present teacher did not. Christopher was identified by IQ testing after his younger brother had entered the school eighteen months younger than normal. Christopher had been pointed out as being gifted by the headteacher and previous teachers to his present teacher, who felt that he would have considered him to be gifted anyway.

Christopher, middle school, year 3

I think his behaviour stands out, his being such a loner, he's very socially immature, and emotionally immature. I think those things would have brought my attention in any case to his academic capabilities.

Children can be identified because of a talent which may combine with academic ability, as with Liz, Mary and Pat.

Liz, first school, year 4

Liz had come up before, in different ways ... She had always been good in her performance ability. It was last year in her artistic ability that really made us sit up and take notice, and then it was really born out in the IQ test and the NFER. She has a particular gift as far as her artistic work is concerned. It was at the beginning of last year that she began to stand out and we noticed her particularly, I mean you never notice Liz by what she says, because she doesn't say anything. (Headteacher)

Mary played the cello exceptionally well. Pat was the boy who won the music scholarship to a public school.

Children may also have a talent and not be particularly able academically.

Geoff and Adrian came into this category, and have therefore not been included in the discussions which refer to academic ability and test scores.

Geoff (Interview with headteacher when Geoff was aged eight)

> He has grade four piano. He composes very adequately. He learnt the violin very quickly, and after three months was in the school orchestra, which is quite a feat. He has private lessons, which are a struggle for the family to pay for, the mother has to go out to work. He comes from an ordinary home, and is encouraged. There will always be someone better, but he has outstanding ability in relation to the rest, or considering that without the opportunity at school he might not have had a chance to show it. He plays the piano so brilliantly that it is obvious that he is gifted. (Headteacher)

Adrian's class teacher was unaware of his talent as a footballer, but the PE teacher, who was keen on developing the football team, considered Adrian to be gifted in sport.

Adrian, middle school, year 3

> He is gifted in sport. He is a brilliant footballer and rugby player. He belongs to the town football club. He played for the school team when he was eight, and was the best one there. In two years the League Clubs will probably look for him. If he maintains the same progression in the next five years he could be in the English team in the future, but a lot depends on personality and determination because it is so competitive. In seven years of teaching I have never seen anything like it. One only has to show him something once and he can do it. He is extremely talented. He is regarded as a sort of God by the other boys. He is confident in his ability and it came as a bit of a shock when he couldn't do craft. When the secondary schools came to see the football they were all asking what school he was going to because he stood out so much, and they all wanted him for their school team. (PE teacher)

It is interesting that so few children were mentioned for a talent alone, especially in the light of the recent literature on giftedness (Chapter 1) which has emphasized talents at the inclusive end of the continuum of definitions of giftedness. An American study by Munday and Davis found that there was correlation between accomplishments in comparable extra-curricular activities at school with adult accomplishments of academically talented persons, whereas test scores, high school grades and college grades were uncorrelated with adult accomplishments (Munday and Davis, 1974). A possible prescription from these findings would be that schools should encourage extra-curricular talents. This was also emphasized in the HMI report, where it was stated that :

for some activities for example sport and music, time lost before identification is claimed to be time that can never be regained. It is no use for a child to be identified as a gifted gymnast in the last year of school (G.B., DES, 1977, page 18).

It may be that at primary school level lack of talent labelling is a consequence of limited expertise on the part of the teachers. In particular, music and some sports are solely extra-curricular or out of school activities, and class teachers are usually concerned only with the academic curriculum in the classroom. It may be that schools assume the talents to be provided for outside the school. German in a study of one LEA suggested that provision for physically gifted children was made not according to who or where the talent was, but haphazardly according to parental pressure and fashion. He found that very often it was difficult to assess if particular children involved were talented or just interested and there were no clear identification and selection procedures yet established (German, 1979). Furthermore, identification of specific talents does presume provision, for example it would be hard to identify a child as gifted at squash if there were no squash courts and he had therefore never had the opportunity to play the game. There are enormous variations between schools in what they can make available to their children. Factors such as the size of the school; number, keenness and expertise of the staff in providing school clubs; geographical viability; availability of facilities; and economic constraints, all play a part in what is offered by individual schools.

To summarize, the main types of child activity that are likely to instigate the labelling process are pre-school reading; learning to read on entry to school particularly rapidly; working in advance of peers; achieving high test results; having a gifted sibling; or showing a talent. Inevitably, it is the child's uniqueness in specific areas to which the teacher may react. The effect on the teacher of any of the instigating activities by the child will depend upon the context in which they occur. For example, as already pointed out in Chapter 2, an excellent reader may be more noticeable in a school that draws from a working-class catchment area; whereas the presence in the class of another child, whose classroom performance is relatively better, may reduce the impressiveness of a child's actions. Also, for a child to work obviously in advance of the others, he has to be in an environment in which getting ahead is permissible, and not one where all the children are required to work at the same pace.

The attention now turns to the teachers, and factors which may affect the teachers' reactions to the children's activities.

The Teacher

As already shown in Chapter 2 teachers vary in their conceptions and perceptions of giftedness. It was suggested that teachers varied in their labelling of a child, despite similar actions of that child. There was evidence of reluctance on the part of some teachers to accept children, or a particular child, as gifted. The assumption may be made that what teachers read and hear concerning giftedness will affect their position towards it, and it was considered that their sources of knowledge were important. Teachers were therefore asked what they had read or heard about gifted children which had influenced them. The outcomes were notable in the sense that despite having a gifted child in their class, out of a total of twenty-four teachers, thirteen had done no reading on the subject. However, the teachers' time is limited and there are the pressures of the rest of the class to consider. Of the rest of the teachers, one mentioned the influence of the press.

> Well, there's been quite a lot in the paper about gifted children, how they fare in a class of varied abilities, the fact that perhaps they don't always find their own level, that they do get held back by other children.

Another teacher stated,

> It doesn't seem worth reading around the area when nothing is done about them. I've only read articles.

A further teacher had seen several programmes on television. Three teachers had done some reading, one of whom had read the West Sussex pamphlet (West Sussex County Council, 1974). One art specialist had been influenced early in his career by an American's work with children. One teacher had read the Hoyle and Wilks booklet published by the DES and supplied by the NAGC (Hoyle and Wilks, DES, 1974),

> I did send for some booklets from the gifted children society two years ago because I had a child who had a very high verbal IQ but was handicapped with handwriting and in other ways. I wasn't sure in my mind then if he was gifted or not, I wasn't sure what kind of work to give him to do in school, therefore I read their booklet, and they do have some materials that they produce, but I haven't sent for them.

Two teachers mentioned that the subject of gifted children had been a small part of their teacher training course. One of these teachers had been trained fifteen years previously. The other teacher had had a lecturer who has recently edited a book about gifted children (Povey, 1980) and had given his students his own booklet on the subject (though this teacher had been more interested in remedial education at the time). Vi's teacher had attended two LEA lectures about giftedness, because she had been concerned about Vi.

In contrast, several other teachers mentioned the lack of training while they were students concerning gifted children. It appears that this lack was not generally counter-balanced by courses or reading once the teachers had such a child in their class. It would also seem that much, if not most, of the research literature concerning giftedness is unlikely to affect the teachers attitudes, perceptions and actions towards their gifted children. The findings here are supported by the recent Schools Council 'Impact and Take Up Study' (Steadman *et al* 1981). The study found that primary school teachers had little knowledge of the existence of reports, working papers, research studies and so on from bodies like the Schools Council, though specifically there was some awareness of Ogilvie's book *Gifted Children in the Primary School* among primary headteachers, 23 per cent of whom had read all or parts of the book.

The teachers in the present study are the ones that would be most expected to be interested in information about gifted children, because of the presence of such a child in their class. The fact that what information they did gain was through the media of television and newspaper or magazine articles might indicate the benefit of in-service courses run by the LEA and/or advice from an Adviser specializing in gifted children. The latter policy has been followed in other counties such as Devon and Essex.

Berlak and Berlak referred to influences in schooling which they term as *dilemmas* (Berlak and Berlak, 1981). These are factors which conflict in their influence on teachers in the classroom, thereby creating conscious or unconscious dilemmas with which the teacher has to cope. Berlak and Berlak referred to knowledge, in the form just discussed, as part of the teachers' social history. A teacher's social history may include beliefs about teaching methodology, and politics, insofar as they affect pedagogy, such as attitudes about discrimination in education. Beliefs such as these may influence the teacher's attitudes towards the concept of giftedness.

Turning to the question of external influences on teachers, pressures from outside the classroom may not be specific to giftedness, but may be considered relevant to the process of labelling as gifted. One of the most critical influences would be expected to be that of colleagues, according to Lacey (1977), in that it would be assumed that some considerable importance would be placed on the opinions of the child's previous teachers through personal consultation, or reading the child's school records. Hargreaves referred to *idiosyncratic deviants* as children about whom teachers disagree concerning a label; and *consensual deviants* as children about whom there was a consensus of opinions among the staff of a school. He suggested that consensual deviants were more common because the discussion in staffrooms facilitated the labelling process (Hargreaves, 1976). Fifteen of the gifted children in this study were delabelled, and they were taught by ten of the twenty five teachers. These children would be *idiosyncratic gifted*.

Parents can be affective in pressurizing the teachers. This is frequently related to social class, in that middle-class parents may be more able to challenge teachers' opinions (Morrison and McIntyre, 1971); interfere on behalf of their children (Ball, 1981; Hitchfield, 1973; and Lacey, 1970); and involve themselves in the educational process (Halsey et al, 1956). As parents, they tend to be more knowledgeable about their rights of access to educational agencies. For example, the following extract shows that Les's parents approached the educational psychologist directly,

Les, middle school, year 3

> Les was referred for assessment and advice by his parents initially. I
> agreed to see him only if they first discussed the matter with the
> headmaster. They did this. It was generally agreed that Les should be
> seen at home during the lunch hour as this was the parents' special
> request. (Educational psychologist)

The parents' desire to make decisions about future schooling can encourage a
school to call in the educational psychologist, which may finalize the school's
labelling of a child in terms of an IQ score, which is entered into the school
records.

This process occurred in the cases of Benny, Laurence, Robert and Les.
Robert's teacher illustrated both the influence that colleagues can have, as well
as that of parents' intervention,

Robert, first school, year 3

> Well it's very difficult because you get the idea from other teachers that
> the child is gifted. Before you get the child you've got this, you've
> absorbed other people's ideas and opinions. I suppose somebody like
> Robert who is obviously ... you know when you talk to him he talks
> like an adult, doesn't he really? And you can almost converse with him
> on adult terms, and I suppose this in a way is gifted. Yes, and then of
> course his parents did say, they did go and see the Head and said
> "Look all parents think their children are brilliant so we realise that it's
> one of those things that all parents think, but we would really like to
> have them [brother and sister] tested", and he was. Obviously I'd
> heard about it. I'd had his sister and found obviously that she was very
> bright, and it was talked about in the staff room, so I was aware that I
> was going to get somebody who was very bright.

There is some expectancy for a teacher to conform to the policies of those
in higher authority at various levels, such as the headteacher or LEA, although
the teachers' consciousness of the policies may vary. For example, a teacher
will be aware that a school is streamed, and of LEA demands concerning
testing or screening, because of the administrative demands on the teacher.
The level of awareness concerning policy, such as of within class ability
grouping, will be dependent on the effectiveness of the headteacher's dissemi-
nation of such policy.

Erikson pointed out that it is necessary in a definition of deviance that
there is conduct about which something is done (Erikson, 1973). In the
particular LEA in which the study was conducted there had been recent
interest about gifted children. This took the form of a letter from the local chief
educational psychologist encouraging headteachers to formulate lists of chil-

dren labelled as gifted, plus an elusive promise of some educational provision for gifted children. These events may have activated some interest for the headteachers in the classification of their gifted children, in order that their school and children may benefit from the resources becoming available. There is a possibility, therefore, that the LEA may act as an influence on the teachers through the medium of the headteachers.

Rubington and Winberg stated that social definitions are more likely to be accepted when a high-ranking, rather than a low-ranking, person does the categorization (Rubington and Winberg, 1973). Schur suggested that there is an inherently political issue to the assessment and categorization of behaviour (Schur, 1980). This is reflected by children who had not been considered gifted for several years by their teachers or headteachers in classroom terms, yet were still referred to as gifted in administrative terms, such as on their school records, or when the school was asked for lists of gifted children, and so on. This appeared to be because of an IQ number which had been allocated by an educational psychologist. There were also children who were not included in the study who were *discarded* from the possibility of being labelled as gifted when the educational psychologist allocated an IQ which came below the required level. Children were also referred to in Chapter 2 who were not put forward as gifted by their headteacher, but were considered gifted by their teacher.

It can be seen from the discussion so far that there are several influences acting upon the teacher at a variety of levels. These may be considered to create dilemmas for the teacher, and thus to have an effect on the labelling process.

The Teacher in Relation to Social Class

The next area to be considered is the effect that the social class of the child has on the perceptions of the teacher. There are two methodological problems in this study which adversely affected the exploration of this particular area. The limitations are a result of the initial intentions of the research which did not encompass a large scale survey of gifted children and social class. Consequently, the sample is too small to make any definitive statements about the relationship between the social class of children and teachers' identification of them as gifted. Secondly, the focus of the interviews with the teachers was not on this area. However, figures 8 and 9 show two points which do need clarification. The first is that there is a tendency for children from middle-class homes to be over represented among those labelled as gifted, despite the smaller population numbers.[1] This repeats the pattern found in previous research (Bridges, 1969; Freeman, 1980; and Terman, 1925). The second point is even less well supported by the data because of the smallness of the group. It appears that once labelled as gifted there is some tendency for children from working-class homes to be decategorized. Possible interpretations of this tendency would be that the childrens' home backgrounds were such that they were no longer able to perform to as high a standard as previously; they were performing in the same manner as before, but their teachers did not perceive them to be; they were performing less well because they were affected by their teachers' perceptions of lower ability; or because they were being treated differently by their teachers. The social class of the children together with their categorization as gifted or non-gifted is given in figure 10.

There are three directions in the analysis which were used in an attempt to give some explanation concerning the under-representation of working-class children labelled as gifted, and the over-representation of the working-class children among those who were decategorized. The first direction is previous research about social class and educational achievement. An assumption is made that the majority of teachers are aware of the main findings of this research, and are consequently influenced by it. Secondly, as the research progressed, an awareness developed to comments made by teachers, especially those concerned with the teachers' perceptions of pupils' home backgrounds. The third direction is concerned with the teachers' assessment of relative academic positions in the class, in other words the methods that teachers used to assess the ability or performance of each child in comparison with the other children.

Changes in the emphasis of research in the social sciences from a predominance of macro towards a tendency for micro research has expanded the explanations for the relationship between social class and educational success or failure. Large scale survey research has repeatedly demonstrated the poorer performance overall of working-class children in the school situation. Among others, Floud et al, and the Newsom and Plowden Reports found that working-class children were under-represented among those who succeeded in schools (Floud et al, 1957; G.B. DES, 1963 and G.B. DES, 1967). A body of research concentrated on the differential social class home influences, especially parental encouragement (Douglas, 1964; Douglas et al, 1968; Frazer, 1959; Mays, 1965; and Wiseman, 1964). Differential language use between social classes was also posed as a difficulty for the working-class child on entering the predominantly middle-class environment of the school, (Bernstein, 1971; and Lawton, 1968). The generalized impression was that the working-class children came from disadvantaged homes which contributed fundamentally to their failure in passing through the educational system.

Further research, usually micro, concentrated on individual schools and individuals within schools, particularly on perceptions and actions of individuals. There was more criticism levelled at teachers themselves as unconscious reinforcers of social class structure by selection within the educational system in terms of grouping, streaming, and curriculum restriction which resulted in consequent social reduction to the same or similar occupational level as the parents (Ball, 1981; Hargreaves, 1967; Jackson, 1964; Jackson and Marsden, 1962; Keddie, 1971; Lacey, 1970; Nash, 1973; and Sharp and Green, 1975). The implication of these studies is that it is the teachers who define the parameters within which children can achieve. On the other hand, Willis

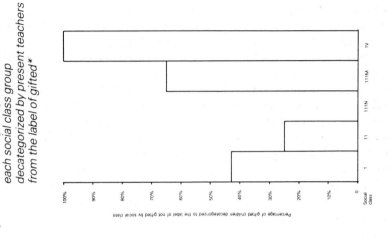

Figure 9   *Percentage of gifted children from each social class group decategorized by present teachers from the label of gifted**

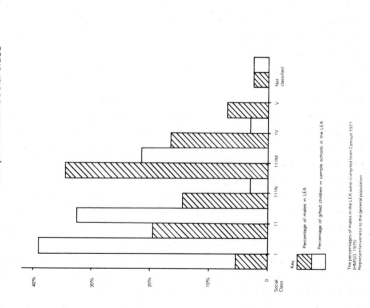

Figure 8   *The percentage of males in each social class residing in the Local Education Authority compared with the percentage of gifted children in the sample in each social class*

Figure 10   Social class of the gifted children

Gifted Name	Social class	Non Gifted Name	Social class
Angela	1	Alexandra	1
Ann	1	Benny*	11
Arthur	111N	Dennis	111M
Benny*	11	Hank	1
Christopher	1	Jim*	111M
David	111M	Karl	111M
Don	1	Kathy	11
George	11	Keith	1V
Hugh	11	Liz	11
Jim*	111M	Mandy	1
Jo	11	Mary	1
Ken	111M	Nicholas	1
Laurence	11	Pat	1
Les	1	Tony	111M
Lilo	11	Vi	111M
Maggy	11		
Peter	1		
Ricky	unknown		
Rita	11		
Robert	11		
Rosemarie	1		
Sandy	111M		
Sylvia	1		
Vicky	11		

Plus Geoff (Music) and Adrian (Football) — total of 39 children

* (two teachers)

suggested that there is a point at which working-class children 'choose' to opt out, and thereby refuse to fulfil their potential for educational success (Willis, 1977). Croll pointed out that differences in teacher expectations of working-class pupils does not mean that the teachers cause lack of progress, but that they may make accurate predictive assessments of those pupils. He felt that differential treatment for pupils from different class backgrounds provides stronger evidence of teachers affecting differential social class achievement but 'leaves open the question of whether the treatment causes the progress or whether it has been accurately matched to levels of attainment' (Croll, 1981, page 115).

Possible explanations for the under-representation of working-class children in the total gifted sample are to be found in the literature about social class and educational achievement. The evidence indicates that the frequency of contact with possible gifted children is likely to be higher for teachers in middle-class schools than it is for those in schools with a predominantly working-class intake, and therefore the concept of giftedness will probably be more familiar to them. This is illustrated by Robert's teacher, whose awareness of gifted children was increased by having had one before in her class.

Robert, first school, year 3

> Having had this child right at the beginning of teaching and wanting to do my best as you always do in your first year, I did pay particular attention to him and I used to go to the library and get books out for him, and he used to do little projects on his own ... Yes I did make a big effort with him, and having had him I am aware of gifted children.

On the other hand, gifted children who attend a school which is predominantly working-class may well appear more exceptional to the teacher in comparison with their peers. This was pointed out in the previous chapter by reference to several children, including Nicholas, who lacked competition, and Alexandra with her pre-school reading ability which was exceptional for that school. During the initial approaches to schools to gain access for the research, headteachers were asked if they had any gifted pupils in their schools. The headteachers of schools in working-class catchment areas frequently commented in the following manner,

> Oh no, we don't have any gifted children at this school, if anything they come from the opposite end of the spectrum here. (Headteacher of non-sample school)

The theme of social class backgrounds affecting academic success has been researched since the 1940s and may therefore be considered to be *common knowledge* among teachers. However, it would seem unlikely that generally teachers are aware of the possible effect they can have as individuals on the achievement of children as revealed by some of the micro research. Sharp and Green referred to a *social pathology* view by teachers of working-class home environments lacking in the type of stimulation and encouragement conducive to educational success (Sharp and Green, 1975). This is clearly reflected by Ken's headteacher.

Ken, middle school, year 1, social class IIIM

> He is and will be intellectually outstripping his parents. His mother said that before he came to school he was asking questions that she did not know the answers to. The father is more intelligent, and spends time with him. His problem is his home background. He is disturbed, and was before he came to the school. He would not stay to dinner for a long time, and his parents brought him right to the door of the school

until he was quite old. In twenty years of teaching he is the oddest child I have met. He is very attached to his home. Normally, he dashes home and his door is ajar and he scuttles through. If it isn't, he panics. I asked him what he wanted to be when he grew up, and he said a bricklayer. What a waste of a fantastic mind. He needs more stimulation. (Headteacher)

Teachers in first and middle schools are well aware of the home background of their pupils, there being many indicators such as speech, dress, and what the children write or say about their homes, as well as parental visits. Much of the information appeared to be used by teachers to assess the home as an *educational resource*. However, many of the teachers' judgments may be considered to be based on extremely flimsy evidence and hearsay. It is possible that teachers select facts to fit their preconceived notions. Both Goodacre and Nash have found there to be a low correlation between actual and teacher perceived social class of children (Goodacre, 1968; and Nash, 1973). The extracts that follow will highlight the factors that appeared to be important to the teachers.[2] Interviews with teachers indicated that they considered home encouragement to be an important factor in the educational success of many gifted children. This is fully reflected in how the teachers answered the question 'What are the parents like?' where they concentrated mainly on what the parents were like as educational *scene setters*.

Twelve (out of thirty-seven) of the children were described by teachers as coming from supporting and/or stimulating homes. This seemed to refer to several areas, such as support within the school (which is usually more relevant in some first schools where parental help is encouraged); stimulation within the home environment; and direct encouragement for the child. The following extracts are typical:

Kathy, middle school, year 1, social class II

Kathy's mother is willing to come on school outings and help if asked. She likes to see children working. There is no pressure workwise, though there may be behaviour wise.

Dennis, middle school, year 4, social class IIIM

I've only met mother. Very helpful, very friendly. I think father's a carpenter ... obviously he's got support there at home, dad will help him out. You tend to find the ones in the top streamed classes are the ones with the supportive parents, buy them books and help them to get on, pretty typical.

Jim, first school, year 3, social class IIIM

He's obviously got plenty going on at home. He's taken out, if you name somewhere he's visited it, he's got a very stimulating home background. I think he's from an enabling home.

Les, middle school, year 3, social class I

Stable and sensible support from the parents. They don't expect too much but they are pleased to support when they can.

The teachers showed concern for those gifted children who were perceived to come from homes which were lacking in stimulation, which tended to be working-class ones. Vi's home (father – skilled manual) was compared with the home of Alexandra (father - professional) by the teacher (Chapter 2). The limited cultural support of the home was considered to be a contributing factor for the lower school performance than would be expected with Vi's high IQ. The headteacher stated in an interview two years previously.

Vi and Alexandra, first school, year 4

The mother complains to the school that they are not doing their job properly, because she knows the child's IQ and doesn't understand why she is not playing chess like Alexandra, but the backgrounds are different. (Headteacher)

Ken (father – skilled manual) was mentioned above. The following child, Keith, who is the only one in the sample whose father was an unskilled manual worker, was felt to come from a happy environment, but lacking in the home resources needed for full educational development.

Keith, first school, year 4, social class IV

Keith's parents seem very pleasant people who are proud of this boy of theirs who they say has got on so well now, because I think in the records in the school he was very nervous when he first came to school ... but this year he has not been reluctant to come to school and they feel very pleased about that. I think they were moderately surprised how much he is capable of, as his sister was not very bright.

The teacher then went on to elaborate the ways in which she considered the home to be supporting, such as in its demand for discipline and provision of security,

> I should think their standards of discipline are quite high, but
> pleasantly so. He's a very orderly well mannered nice child, a very
> well brought up child, and from a loving home, very secure. He has a
> home background that does not provide enough stimulation.

There is then a distinction in the mind of the teacher between the happy secure
home, and the home that is lacking culturally, which makes the task of the
school more difficult. In other words, there are too few books, and too much
television.

> I don't think there are many books. He wrote a list of TV programmes
> that he's watched, he obviously enjoyed the stories but he seems to
> spend quite a lot of time watching TV. When they have a chance to use
> the school library he said to me "I don't want a book", and I managed
> to speak to his mother who works in the school [skilled manual
> worker] and said that I thought it would be nice for him to have a
> book, and can she tell me why he didn't want a book, and she said that
> "He might be a bit nervous about forgetting to bring it back at the right
> time." "I don't make a great to do about that but tell him not to
> worry." I think he ought to have some books. He's still a bit reluctant,
> and I think he likes factual books, but not story books very much, but
> he needs an awful lot of encouragement to read for the sake of
> reading, and I've tried to say to her that he ought to belong to a library,
> even if he wants to read factual books, not to worry about that, but to
> encourage him to read a bit to himself. I think perhaps the father is
> quite clever at his work, or using his mathematical ability. They
> weren't all that surprised that he was good at maths, but I think the
> other aspects of his learning, of finding out about the world would be
> more *encouraged in a different type of home*. (Author's emphasis)

In these extracts there is clearly a strong belief that a working-class home is less
beneficial for a gifted child than a middle-class home. This belief is reiterated in
the discussion about Sandy.

Sandy aroused amazement and admiration among the teachers and the
headteacher because of her ability to deal with her (in the teachers' view)
detrimental family environment, support her mother emotionally, and still do
exceptionally well at school. The parents were divorced (father – skilled
manual) and the teacher went into great detail about the kind of situations with
which the child had to cope,

> *Sandy, middle school, year 1, social class IIIM*
>
> The parents are divorced, and there is another man. Sandy takes on a
> lot. She seems to be Mum's emotional support, and takes it on. I
> haven't met Mum. I don't think she and the Dad are very intelligent,

going by the sort of jobs that they do. *She doesn't have books or a cultural background.* (Author's emphasis) The urge is from Sandy rather than from home. She organises everything at home. The mother is wet and unable to cope with the new baby. They live in a small council flat. She has a boyfriend and they fight a lot. One day the mother phoned the school to say that a next door neighbour had been taken into hospital and could Sandy go home to look after the baby next door. She was sent home, and rushed off with an anxious look. The staff thought it was wrong to put those sorts of responsibilities onto a child, and thought she coped very well. The father came to collect Sandy and her sister after school, and was very upset when they were not there because that would mean that he would not see them for the next two weeks. He was cross that she had been asked to do such a thing, and said that it was not the place of a child.

The responsible attitude of the child was admired by the staff of the school, and was used by them. She was placed in charge of helping the other children in the class to find equipment for practical mathematics when the class was left in charge of a temporary teacher. She was asked by her younger sister's teacher to help her sister with her reading. This she did so efficiently that it was almost immediately apparent in her sister's work. Despite her many good personality characteristics, her teacher perceived a change in facets of her character which she attributed to her home background.

Sandy is sharp, kind in a way, but there is a certain hardness creeping in, probably as a shell. She protects her little sister. She can use some bad language and her fists. She is a hard nut. I get the impression that she's used to street play and standing up for herself. The boys don't often tangle with her.

This type of character and home connection may be one of the reasons why her headteacher assumed that she would become a school drop out, despite her current good school performance. She was very highly motivated, which was revealed in her interview, where she stated that she took mathematics work cards home nearly every night of her own accord.

Six of the children were considered to come from 'pushing' homes. In only one case, that of Vi, was the background working-class. As already mentioned above, and in Chapter 2, Vi's mother could not understand why her daughter was unable to do the same things as Alexandra. The differences between the two children were mainly attributed, by the headteacher and the teacher, to the different cultural resources of the two homes. The pressure from the mother was also considered to contribute to the need for the child to attend a family consultation unit twice weekly. The detrimental relationship between pressure from the parent(s) and the emotional stability of the child was reiterated in the following two extracts concerning Sylvia and George, both by the same teacher.

Sylvia, middle school, year 3 social class I

Sylvia is a bit insecure. I get the impression that she is pushed at home in directions she doesn't want to go. I think it might be the mother who is very intelligent and dominating. Women teachers have to be careful with her [Sylvia] because of this. One can get at her [Sylvia] through humour and she appreciates when one makes an effort. Sometimes when she [Sylvia] is in a bad humour I can shivvy her out of it. She is able to concentrate, but she turns anti school if I push her in a way she doesn't want to go, which is because of home.

George, middle school, year 3, social class II

There is a lot of tension in that family. His family is well off, and he is the only child which is why he is spoilt. I suspect that the father is intelligent and very anxious for the boy to do well, but the mother wants something different for the boy. I don't know whether it's maternal attachment or what, but there seems to be a sort of tug going on.

Maggy's parents gave the teacher an impression of putting pressure on the child to succeed at school. This knowledge appeared to have been gained from information concerning the child's father being in politics, rather than anything else. In Christopher's case the mother's pressure was in the form of anxiety that he (and his brother Peter) should fulfil his or their potential. Both children spent considerable time doing school work at home.

Christopher, middle school, year 3, social class I

His mother does take an interest in him, and does set him specific sort of project work and things like that. She does a lot of good things for him, I'm not saying she doesn't, she shows a definite interest in him educationally, takes him to Museums, Art Galleries, things like that. His mother is very anxious that Christopher should fulfil his potential. She's overanxious really.

Finally, Benny's mother revealed her anxiety through her frequent visits to the school. The visits were concerned with his behaviour and future choice of schooling.

Six children were mentioned as coming from 'happy' homes, typified by that of Robert.

Robert, first school, year 3, social class II

The parents are very nice, and very balanced and know they've got two very bright children, but don't ... you know ... they're quite happy if the children ... so long as they're happy in school and doing well and doing the work that everybody else is doing, so long as they feel that they're working to the best of their ability. I think basically as long as they're happy, I think they realise that having bright children they're going to go on fairly well.

In two cases the teacher concentrated on the home environment in terms of a one parent family and mother's qualifications.

Jo, middle school, year 3, social class II

Jo is living with his mother. They have moved around a lot. It has been mostly mother and son, and friend, they lived in a commune for a while. She has some qualifications. She is very bright and is something in computers. Jo is particularly good at maths.

In two instances the parents were described as 'nice and ordinary'.

Lacey in *Hightown Grammar* developed the composite notion of *Psycho-socio-cultural resources* in examining the relationship between academic achievement, social class and parental encouragement. He described these resources as:

1. Psychological. In addition to the pupil's IQ, this variable includes the emotional resources of the family unit.
2. Social. Includes all the resources which stem from the social position of the family unit. Indicative of this variable are occupation and income.
3. Cultural. Includes the parents ability to understand and manipulate an 'academic' or 'school' culture. An important indicator of this is their educational background (Lacey, 1970, page 125).

Sharp and Greens' *social pathology* and Lacey's *psycho-socio-cultural resources* would seem to complement each other and in combination fit the conceptualizations of the childrens' home backgrounds, as revealed by the teachers' descriptions of them. There would seem to be a clear distinction between the teachers' impression of the working-class home, which is deprived in psycho-socio-cultural resources, and the middle-class home with its supportive parents, provision of books, stimulation provided by excursions and activities. The former typology of home background was considered by the teachers to be detrimental to the intellectual and educational advancement of the children. There would also appear to be a fine distinction between the culturally advantaged happy home and that which puts such pressure on a child as to become emotionally disadvantageous. The concepts used by the teachers appear to be based upon assessments of the parents in terms of the support that they give at home which aids the teacher in her work. As already stated, how far the parents were accurately classified by social class would be difficult to ascertain. There were definitely occasions when the teachers were vague about the fathers' specific occupations, although this is not the sole indicator of social class.

The methods used by teachers to ascertain a child's relative academic position within the class will now be analyzed. The working hypothesis here is that the more objective the teacher was in assessing academic position, the less likely it would be that non-academic factors, such as social class and personal feelings, would affect the situation. The methods used by the teachers to position the children academically relative to the other children in the class were placed on a subjective/objective dimension. The subjective end of the dimension involved no testing of any kind, and assessment decisions were based entirely on the judgment of the teacher. In the middle were teachers who used their own within class testing or assessment as a method of differentiating children. The objective end was where standardized tests were used which did not rely on the total within class ability and performance. Data are available for sixteen out of the total of twenty-four teachers.[3]

Complete subjectivity would be represented by the following teacher who applied no actual criterion to her assessment.

Ricky, first school, year 2, social class not known

I don't know how [you estimate relative academic positions]. You just know, don't you, you know how they're getting on and where they all are.

The following two teachers mentioned instinct, although the first one relied extensively on the previous teacher's assessment for dividing her children into mathematics and reading groups, which preconditioned the level of their work.

Ann and Ken, middle school, year 1, social class I and IIIM respectively

I don't bother at the beginning of the year. It is done by instinct, apart from silent readers.

Nicholas and Jo, middle school, year 3, social class I and II respectively

Sheer years of teaching. What they do in their work. How they relate to each other, instinct. One knows with experience. Their attitude to work.

One teacher stated that he used a mental overall standard. A first school teacher gave an impression of not wishing to assess the children relative to each other, but found that she was doing so.

David and Don, first school, year 2, social class IIIM and I respectively

I suppose you do subconsciously yes. It wouldn't be fair for me to say no I don't. I suppose I do it basically judging it on their reading ability at this stage.

Another first school teacher had been unaware that she had been assessing the children academically, and that she was using relative positioning to group the class by tables. It became apparent to her when she chose for the author those children who were capable of filling in the sociometry and Guess Who (see the Appendix) as a group on their own, and those children who needed to do it individually with the author. She clearly differentiated between intellectual and performance ability.

Jim, first school, year 3, social class IIIM

I thought I wasn't doing it, and it wasn't until they filled in the forms that I realised I was. At this age it's probably the ability to answer questions, like questions I pose, where only Jim could answer one or two of them. If you asked me to put them into intellectual ability order, it wouldn't be how they are sitting now, because there's Russell over there [seated on a table which was not the high ability table] who's low in number, writing and reading, but he's a very able little boy. So they are more by ability rather than intellectual.

Within class comparison has an implicit variation which is a reflection of the age differences of the children, in that pencil and paper tests are more appropriate for older children. The following teacher was in a first school,

Robert, first school, year 3, social class II

I ask the previous teacher roughly what she thinks, and usually she gives me about four groups, and usually to begin with I let them sit anywhere, and we do quite a bit of work on paper and for usually two weeks I let them work in books. I just watch them and see what they're reading and I give them a variety of different sums and writing and this sort of thing and from that I usually group them, sometimes the groupings work out a little bit wrong, you can't group them exactly.

Two teachers are represented by the following extract,

Christopher, middle school, year 3, social class I

Whatever we do in the classroom is tested and retested after revision, which gives one an idea of where the childrens' abilities lie. Even without those, the amount of oral work that we do is a very good indicator as well.

The next two teachers border the within class assessment and standardized testing. It is mainly because of their lack of reliance on the latter, that they are placed in the middle of the objective/subjective scale.

Peter, middle school, year 1, social class I

Well I gave them a maths test and then I set them some English work which was nouns, I think it was, and I just sort of from looking at their work saw how they got on, and I tried to sort of mix it really, a maths test plus an impression of their English work and they are now more or less in ability groups.
R-Do you do any reading or spelling ages and so on?
T-Well we don't do very much because reading is more in the infants school.
R-Do you do any achievement tests?
T-Yes we do at the beginning and end of the year. They're not very important,

Les and Sylvia, social class 1 ⎫
Laurence and George, social class II ⎬ *middle school, year 3*

I would do so mostly by what they achieve in the tasks that I give them to do, so you can only relate them comparatively with others or on tests I think are far less reliable. For instance the tests that we use in school would give very little indication of a child's real quality, the Richmond, they are all of the same type, multiple choice questions, that kind of thing I think are ... unless you get a great deal of other evidence, they give a very false impression. I'd be interested to know how a skilled psychologist would tackle it.

The above examples do not necessarily mean that the teachers did not use standardized tests, but in answer to the question 'How do you ascertain the relative academic positions of the children?' the majority of the teachers did not consider the tests as relevant as other information.

Before discussing the group of teachers who used objective criteria for their assessment, an examination of figure 11 is appropriate. It gives a breakdown of teachers' subjective/objective methodology for academic posi-

Figure 11   Figure showing teachers' methods of academic positioning, children grouped according to label of giftedness, and social class of the children.

	Gifted No. of teachers	MC	WC	DK	**Both** No. of teachers	MC	WC	**Non Gifted** No. of teachers	MC	WC
Subjective	(5)	3	3	1	(1)	2	0	(0)	0	0
Within class testing	(5)	8	1	0	(0)	0	0	(0)	0	0
Objective	(1)	1	0	0	(0)	0	0	(4)	4	1

Total 16 teachers, 24 children

tioning; labelling of children as gifted or non gifted; and both (the presence of two or more children of both perceived categorizations); together with the social class of the relevant children. It can be seen that the teachers who found objective methods important, also tended to decategorize their gifted children. The resultant assumption would therefore be that the delabelling of gifted children was done using objective methods. The teachers who used objective methods will be examined in more detail.

Karl's teacher was placed at the objective end of the dimension because she did not use within classroom criteria. However, the guidelines and schemes she mentioned in the extract that follows were presumably not standardized on a total population, which makes her incorporation as objective debatable in this context.

Karl, first school, year 3, social class IIIM

There are guidelines and schemes which were made by working parties. I use these to estimate the ability to cope with items in all subjects.

Karl was the working-class child who was decategorized, or labelled as non gifted, and appears in the objective section in figure 11.

The remainder of the children who were decategorized by teachers who used objective methods to assess the academic positioning of their children, came from middle-class backgrounds. Pat, Mary, Hank and Benny were included in this group. Figure 3 (Chapter 2) shows that both Mary and Benny had very high IQ scores, and Hank had a very high NFER score. There would therefore appear to be some contradiction in what the teachers stated to be the criteria that they used, and what actually happened.

When Mary's extremely high IQ (which was off the scale) was mentioned to the teacher, she attributed it to a favourable home background, and also said,

Mary, first school, year 3

> She gets a lot of support from home. I think there is some confusion
> between verbal ability because of home and IQ.

Pat's teacher stated that she used reading tests in her assessment.

Pat, middle school, year 3

> They have tests every so often. By the work that they do. The spelling
> group they belong to which goes with their English work. Their
> *Schonell test reading age.* (Author's emphasis)

This teacher had decategorized Pat, despite the fact that he normally got full
marks in any test, and as shown in figure 3 (Chapter 2) he had one of the
highest differences between reading age and chronological age of the total
sample, namely 4.2 years.

Initial examination of figure 11 might indicate that decategorization of
gifted children was done by the teachers as a result of the use of objective
evidence. However, close analysis revealed that the use of objective tests by a
teacher did not necessarily result in that teacher's acceptance of the results.
Therefore, the criteria used by some teachers for delabelling gifted children
did not apparently lie completely in the direction of teachers' reliance upon
some objective measures.

In this chapter the usefulness of labelling theory in the study of teachers
and gifted children was proposed. The processes by which children became
labelled as gifted and by which they became delabelled to the non-gifted
category were examined. A variety of factors which may be considered to
influence the processes of labelling and delabelling were outlined, such as
sources of knowledge for teachers, pressures on teachers, teachers' impressions of the home backgrounds of the children, and the assessment of
childrens' relative academic position within the class. The appropriateness of
labelling theory as an approach to giftedness cannot be objectively assessed,
but allows a critical framework within which an analysis can be made.

Notes

1. The social class of the children was ascertained by relating father's occupation to
   the classification of occupations coding index, (G.B., HMSO, 1980). The groups
   were divided as follows:
   I   Professional etc. occupations
   II Intermediate occupations
   III Skilled occupations
       N Non-manual
       M Manual
   IV Partly skilled occupations
   V   Unskilled occupations

The limitations are that the information entered by the parent on the school records can be insufficient, for example engineer; and the use of father's occupation alone is crude, though powerful in Weberian terms as an assessment of socioeconomic status of a family (Weber, 1948). It is usually considered more effective to use a combination of factors to assess social class, including length of education of one or both parents, occupation of mother, reading matter in the home, and so on. This information was not, and could not be available to the author.

References to middle-class include the first three categories, I, II, IIIN; working-class includes the bottom three, IIIM, IV,V.

2. The reasons why the parents were not included in the research are explained in detail in the Appendix.

3. The number of teachers for most discussions is twenty-four (twenty-five when Geoff is included). Vi and Alexandra's present teacher refused to be interviewed or observed. However, these two children were discussed extensively by their previous teacher, and were subjects in previous research (Maltby, 1979).

4   Educational Provision for Gifted Children

The previous chapter explored the process of labelling, and to some extent the delabelling of children as gifted. This chapter examines the transactional setting of the classroom in which the interactions took place between gifted children and their teachers, and gifted children and their classroom peers. The investigation will be in terms of the educational provision that was made for the children within their own classroom and within the school. This will act as a background to the following two chapters where the interactions themselves are discussed.

The analysis of the interactional setting of the gifted child was stated, in the previous chapter, to be important because it leads to a comprehensive perspective and deeper understanding of the process of labelling, the study of the deviant, and the reactions of the labellers to the deviants. With reference to the gifted children, some of them may be seen to be provided for in an unusual manner within their educational environment. Without some knowledge of their treatment in class it would be difficult to obtain a complete understanding of the perceptions held of them by their peers and teachers. As stated previously observation within the classroom overcomes some of the problems of Hargreaves' third party talk (Hargreaves, 1977).

The first section of the chapter will define the various forms of educational provision that may be made for gifted children. These methods of provision will then be discussed with reference to the socio-political arguments outlined in Chapter 1. The successive sections will describe what happened to the sample of gifted children in their own schools.

Definitions of Methods of Educational Provision for Gifted Children

The terms used for describing educational provision specific to gifted children can be categorized into three main areas consisting of differential grouping or segregation, acceleration, and enrichment.

There are three levels of *differential grouping*. The first is special schools which in England tend to be for music, with schools such as the Yehudi Menuhin, the Chetham School of Music in Manchester, and the Wells Catherdral school, plus ballet schools such as the Royal Ballet School. At LEA level, Ogilvie's survey and Lawrence's follow up survey both indicated that approximately 50 per cent of the LEAs awarded full-time scholarships and exhibitions, especially to the above type of school (Ogilvie, 1973; and Lawrence, 1980). However, there are only a few schools in England that specialize in intellectually gifted children such as the Dolphin School in Berkshire which provides a stimulating educational environment on an individual basis. Havighurst suggested that special schools for gifted children were more likely to work in large communities where they were more anonymous and therefore created less jealousy (Havighurst et al, 1965). The tripartite system of education in England provided for higher ability children in the sense that it selected approximately the top 20 per cent of children for grammar schools, some of which in turn had express streams, which catered for the most able and intellectually gifted children. Some LEAs went further by providing scholarships to Direct Grant schools for approximately the top 1 per cent of children. When the grants to these schools were stopped by the Labour Government, a small percentage of LEAs carried on catering for their gifted children in the private sector. This practice was eventually discouraged by the Secretary of State. With the change to a Conservative Government the Assisted Places Scheme was implemented, commencing in 1981. It was intended to go some way towards reinstating the policy of providing scholarships aimed at gifted children whose parents were unable to afford private education. Public schools frequently bestow scholarships, normally aimed at the most intellectually able children selected from the private and maintained sector. So, although special schools for the intellectually gifted are extremely rare, it may be considered that some sections of the private sector cater for gifted children. The question of private schooling and scholarships was mentioned spontaneously in early interviews with teachers, and was therefore included in the interview schedule. For the discussion that follows, private or public schools will be considered under the section of special schooling.

Special classes are ones which are comprised of intellectually gifted children. On the whole, the formation of special classes is not a policy which is used extensively in England, especially at primary school level. There have been exceptions, such as Tempest's group, which was formed in order to develop curriculum materials for gifted children suitable for use in the normal school (Tempest, 1974).

Partial segregation entails gifted children being brought together as a group but working with their normal class for the majority of the time, as described in the Brentwood experiment (Bridges, 1969). This type of provision has been used in many parts of England. There are published accounts from areas such as Devon, Essex, and in the past, West Sussex. Chappell also described her experiences with a group of maladjusted gifted children (Chappell, 1982; and Maltby, 1983).

Acceleration is the process by which a child is put with a class of children of a higher age group. This can be done in several ways, by allowing a child to enter first school early, and progress with the same age group right through the educational system; to skip a class; or to enter secondary school early. The Plowden Report advised, that within a range of six months of the normal age, children should be allowed to transfer to primary and secondary school early, provided that overall development was taken into account, as well as friendships. Their survey showed that only forty-four out of 20,000 children were transferred early, which was considered to be an under-estimate of the number of children who might have benefited (G.B. DES, 1967). In 1978 ten children entered secondary school a year early in the county of the LEA studied in this research. Hitchfield found that the gifted had more nursery education and an earlier start at infant school than the population at large. Half of her 238 children were accelerated at some time in the primary school (Hitchfield, 1973). Robb suggested that it was advantageous for gifted children to be placed with children two years, and exceptionally two and a half years, older than themselves (Robb, 1974).

Enrichment basically refers to study, experience or activity which is above and beyond the normal curriculum followed by the other children of the same age. There is enrichment by depth, where a topic is covered more fully; and there is enrichment by breadth, where broader and more varied topics are explored. A point about enrichment which is frequently made (Renzulli, 1977; and Wood, 1973), is that children who finish their work quickly should not be given more of the same work to complete. Not only is that not a form of enrichment, but it is precisely those children who least need to do more of the same work as they have already grasped the principles involved. With enrichment the gifted children remain with their own class.

The socio-political arguments for and against educational provision for gifted children were discussed in Chapter 1. The same arguments will be applied in this section to the various forms of educational provision in the order in which they were defined.

The arguments used against special schools or classes are that they promote elitism; prevent gifted children from learning to interact with their normal peers; and stop other children from benefiting from their presence. Whereas partial segregation allows the gifted children to interact with others of their own ability, thus achieving better comparative understanding of their personal intellect, as well as meeting mental challenge and stimulation. Ogilvie recorded extreme disapproval for special classes for gifted children from his sample of headteachers and teachers (Ogilvie, 1973).

As far as acceleration is concerned there are several problems associated with this practice which relate to differential social or physical, as compared with mental, development. As a method of provision, it is generally only considered suitable if a child is polymathically (all-round) gifted, at least in terms of academic subjects (see Chapter 2). Also, to be successful, the following stage of schooling has to accept the early entrance of the child, otherwise that child has to repeat a year at the top of the previous school. Ogilvie reported that 56 per cent of the LEAs in his survey provided for early admission to secondary schools, which figure was reduced to 46 per cent at a later date according to Lawrence (*op cit*).

The more extreme the action that is taken on behalf of the gifted child, as opposed to other children, the greater the need for justification in terms of the needs of the child as compared with others, and benefit to the child itself. Also, the more extreme the method of provision, the more visible it is to public view. Therefore, justification for the criteria used in selection for segregative and accelerative methods of provision is required, as is a strong indication of objective impartiality in application of the criteria to specific children. This may be a forceful theme underlying historical dependence on test results of the IQ type, which tend to be acceptable evidence for most parents as to whether a child is gifted, as opposed to what could be considered to be subjective methods, such as teacher labelling. From the point of view of a headteacher, the likelihood of the demand for the justification of action is lessened with the choice of enrichment, in that the policy will be less obvious to parents and outsiders.

Segregation, partial segregation, and to some extent acceleration frequently involve collaboration with the LEA. In areas where the first two methods exist, they have usually been organized and financed by the LEA. For a child to enter secondary school early, the permission of the LEA has to be obtained as well as that of the headteacher of the more senior school.

The use of enrichment as a method of provision is perhaps less controversial, from a political and economic point of view, for several reasons. It is possible for it to exist in a school without parental knowledge because it is less overt, and therefore the justification of selection for it may be less demanding. The extent of parental lack of knowledge concerning what occurs in the classroom itself, especially with regard to the curriculum, was found by the *Accountability in the middle years of schooling project* (Becher et al, 1981). Enrichment does not normally require permission or collaboration with headteachers of other schools, or the LEA, and therefore allows individual headteachers greater autonomy. The identification and designation of the children as gifted can be less official or final.

Segregation and acceleration would appear to be almost totally dependent on the approval and/or instigation of the headteacher. Enrichment, on the other hand, may occur within a class without the headteacher's knowledge. Therefore, the autonomy of the teacher need not be challenged. The headteacher's influence on enrichment, the occurence of enrichment, and the form in which it will occur, is more dependent on the headteacher's relationship with the individual teacher concerned. That a headteacher may make suggestions was shown in Sandy and Vicky's class, where there were a lot of children on the slow learners table, three or four of whom wer extremely remedial. Their teacher had specialized as a remedial teacher for many years. The headteacher encouraged her not to concentrate on the remedial children to the detriment of the rest of the class, but to give them 'busy' activities. The autarchical nature of the classroom is mirrored in the description by Sharp and Green of 'Mrs. Lyons' who was able to perform in her classroom in a manner which opposed the ethos of the school, but provided a 'correct' impression to colleagues by the use of appropriate verbalizations (Sharp and Green, 1975). Teachers can normally be assumed to be sufficiently self-governing in their own classrooms to make organizational decisions affecting their classes as a whole, and gifted children in particular.

From the viewpoint of the social development of the child, the provision of an enriched curriculum would appear to be theoretically the most satisfactory of the three methods. The gifted child is not withdrawn from his peers in any way, and is not made to appear different from them, thus allowing ease of social interaction. The child is mentally stimulated, the educational horizons are extended, and the child may therefore be satisfied intellectually. The only disadvantage would appear to be that when there is only one gifted child in a school, that child may be isolated from the possibility of meeting others of the same ability, who would presumably create intellectual challenge. However, the assumption that is made in this argument is that the peers of the gifted children are age equals, rather than intellectual equals. Certainly in adulthood the tendency would be to choose to interact with those who are similar to oneself intellectually or in social class background rather than those who are necessarily identical in age (Ball, 1981; and Lacey, 1970). On the other hand, during teenagehood the chronological age peer group is an important reference group for many children. It would appear difficult to generalize about this point, because very little research has been done in this area with gifted children in England.

Ogilvie's survey indicated very strong approval by teachers, headteachers and LEAs for enrichment. This approval was particularly emphasized for first school children (Ogilvie, op cit). It is possible that enrichment may have been favoured for many of the reasons given above, as well as out of consideration for the benefits to the children.

The main problem with enrichment is that the burden of the work involved in providing it rests on the individual teacher, for example, with the preparation of materials, and management of classroom activities. Teachers are rarely in a position to create their own syllabus for one individual within a large class, because of lack of time, equipment, books, and in some cases expertise. Research concerning gifted children has been sparse in England, but in the area of the development of enrichment materials for the use of gifted children in the normal classroom, there has been considerable effort, as described in Chapter 1. The greater emphasis on materials for primary rather than secondary schools would presumably arise because of the subject expertise deficiency at the primary level, secondary schools normally having specialists who may be considered more able to develop their own materials.

The particular LEA in which this research was carried out had no policy for gifted children. The primary advisor reported that a working party had been set up to consider a policy regarding gifted children. However, the individuals involved had been unable to reach an agreement. Without such a policy, the types of provision made for gifted children in the area were relatively haphazard, as will be shown.

Before examining the provision made for the gifted children in the schools, there are two terms which should be defined, as they are used extensively in the description. These terms are *specific provision* and *circumstantial provision*. These expressions have been devized as a result of the analysis of the provision in schools, because they appear to be useful and relevant.

Specific provision involves some sort of action or decision being made as a result of the presence of gifted children, presumably for those gifted children. There are also several policy arrangements which occur normally within schools and which are made irrespective of the presence of gifted children. However, they may be considered advantageous for gifted children. These methods of provision may be termed circumstantial, in that they are accidental to the presence of gifted children and would occur regardless of their presence.

With respect to enrichment, specific enrichment is defined as occurring when the teacher provided, or tried to provide an activity which was specific to the interests, needs or ability of a particular child. Circumstantial enrichment is when a child is catered for separately from the other children as a result of having advanced beyond the syllabus on which the others are working. In other words, the child is on a higher reading book, work card, or mathematics book, but the other children would be doing the same later. Perhaps the most relevant differential for the teacher between specific and circumstantial enrichment would be that the former seems to demand more effort, flexibility, and imagination on the part of the teacher. The latter would be more limited to an earlier completion of the work that the rest of the class would be doing subsequently.

The next sections will examine the types of provision made for the gifted children in the present study. They will be covered in the same order as they have already been discussed, namely, segregation, acceleration, and enrichment. As already mentioned, private schooling will be taken as a form of segregation.

Segregation

There were no special schools or classes available for the primary age gifted children in the LEA studied. The partial segregation which occurred in the form of withdrawal groups will therefore be examined, before looking at the place of private schooling.

In the county a temporary arrangement existed, which lasted for approximately six weeks. Student teachers in their third year withdrew a small group of gifted (or gifted and very able) children one afternoon weekly, in order to learn more about gifted children. This arrangement affected Benny and Hank in one class, and Jo and Nicholas in another.

Of those schools, the headteachers already had a form of partial segregation taking place, though the first example might be considered to be borderline. In Benny and Hank's class a group of more able readers went to a special teacher once a week, in order to read some interesting books in a group. The teacher did point out that this was a policy aimed at able readers, and not gifted children. Hank was not included in this group, despite the fact that his Schonell reading age (note 8 in Chapter 2) was 2.5 years above his chronological age; he had been reported as an excellent and fluent reader in the first school; and he was off all the reading schemes in the final year of first school. He also stated in his interview that he enjoyed reading, particularly about animals.

Jo and Nicholas's headteacher had quite an extensive partial segregation programme for his gifted and more able children, consisting of a group of five children. The following extract indicates the rationale behind his provision for them,

Jo and Nicholas, middle school, year 3

> I feel that we have devoted too much to the lesser able child and ignored the more able. It's only in the last two years that I have realised the extent of the problem and the more able need help. I think one should extend their study skills so that they can stimulate themselves. My philosophy is that the needs of children of this age are very physical so they do a lot of swimming, and games, and camping, and walking, thus when they are asked to work they may be more willing. I wish to provide stimulating surroundings. I'm sure they are not extended in the normal class, especially in the verbal way. (Headteacher)

At the same time as recognizing a lack of extension and consequent need in the children, the headteacher was aware of the intrinsic disadvantage of segregation, namely that the children can be made to appear different from their peers, and they can also miss what is happening in the normal classroom.

> I resist the temptation of making a special class because I feel that they gain a lot from other children and give a lot to them in showing what work they are capable of. The withdrawal class have to be aware that they are being made to work. The others accept their going out to special groups without complaints. It has shown up problems in that when they are withdrawn they miss what other children are doing which can be valuable, for example science. This is where Saturday morning classes might be useful, because in that they could do extra science. I found that some of the work produced was excellent, but other children foundered. Perhaps I demanded too much, but no one

> knows what to expect. So little is known and I need to get together
> with people who know more. (Headteacher)

This headteacher felt an obvious need for contact and advice concerning giftedness. It is interesting how situations change with time. When Nicholas was originally studied during the previous year (Maltby, 1979), as a relative newcomer to the school, he was felt to be unique within that school, which had a predominantly working-class catchment area. Jo had joined the school since then. The other children who made up the special class would possibly not have had the opportunity of participating in such a group but for the arrival of the two boys in the school. The headteacher's desire for a Saturday morning club was reiterated by Jim's teacher, though for different reasons,

Jim, first school, year 3

> I'm sure the curriculum material is available. I think the shortage is in
> me more than in what I can get. I think if I had more time for Jim I
> would stimulate him by setting up more scientific things, but to do it
> for one is very difficult. That's why if he really is gifted I would like
> something like a Saturday morning centre where those children can be
> sent and somebody can spend a morning doing things to stimulate
> them. (Morning teacher)

Only one school out of the thirteen schools in the study had a within school withdrawal group for the purpose of curriculum extension. The implementation of such a policy may be considered to be dependent on the presence of sufficient number of children who would benefit. This is partly dependent on the size of the school; the social class of its catchment area, in so far as in schools that draw from a working-class area the teachers and headteachers appear to have fewer, or perceive themselves as having fewer, gifted children in the school; and the perceptions and definitions concerning giftedness of the headteachers and teachers (which were discussed extensively in the previous chapters). At the same time, there are economic constraints in the provision of space, materials, and teachers. Even when all these factors are favourable, a withdrawal group will not be considered unless the children are perceived to need such a provision. The one headteacher who had made a conscious effort in this direction noted that there were problems involved, such as the children in the group missing other classroom activities.

The question of private schooling will now be discussed. In Chapter 2 it was shown that the number of gifted children in the state schools in the LEA examined here was low in comparison to that which might be expected according to the literature about gifted children. This might be attributed to the perceptions of the headteachers and teachers and their labelling of children as gifted. On the other hand, it is a possibility that many gifted children had already entered the private system of education. There are two points which substantiate this suggestion. There was a decrease in the number of children in the sample who were in the fourth year of middle school (Chapter 3). This may be because a choice was made by parents in favour of private schooling as the time for entrance to the comprehensive school approached, or because schools had failed to support the giftedness of the child. This point is not supported by the data, because interviews with parents were not conducted. The second point is substantiated by the data that follow, which show that sixteen (41 per cent) of the gifted children in the sample were considered for private schooling by headteachers, teachers or parents.

In the area relevant to this research, it was normal practice for all maintained schools to be circulated by the local public schools asking for submission of candidates for the scholarship and Assisted Places examinations for day places. This usually took place when the children were in their third year of middle school. The extent of encouragement by headteachers for parents to submit their children's names would presumably vary according to the headteachers' political feelings concerning private education, as well as the headteachers' opinions of the academic standard of the children concerned. Before examining the gifted children who were, or had been, considered for private education, the working-class children, for whom the Assisted Places Scheme was supposedly designed, will be looked at briefly.

Only two of the sixteen children who had been considered for private education, by their headteacher, teacher or parents, were working-class, but in neither case, those of Geoff or Ken, was the possibility mentioned to their parents. For Geoff this may have been because his academic work was not considered adequate for him to get a music scholarship. Geoff was a gifted musician, and his orchestra teacher said of him,

Geoff, middle school, year 3, social class IIIM

If he was mine, I would think about sending him on a scholarship to a private school, but his academic work isn't good enough. It could be. He's got the brain, but he doesn't make use of it. He is gifted. He has the potential to be a professional but there's a certain spark that's missing. He doesn't seem to realise that he's going to need more than just music to get on professionally. (Music and Orchestra teacher)

In fact Geoff spontaneously brought the question of his academic ability up in his interview, and indicated that he was aware of his limitations in this area.

Interview with Geoff

G-I'd like to have a better mind for work, you know, school work.
R-Do you feel that you haven't?

G-Well, I've got a good mind for music, but not for school work. I don't know why.

R-Do you work at it?

G-Yeah, I work at it, you know. I do what I'm told at home, you know, I help mum and dad.

R-So why do you think that you haven't got a good mind?

G-Just not for school work, you know.

In the case of Ken, it did not appear from what the headteacher said, that the boy would be entered as a suitable candidate for a scholarship day place, although the reason was not clear, unless it was because the parents would not think of it.

Ken, middle school, year 1, social class IIIM

There might be a place in society for schools for gifted children. There ought to be a school for them, even if it had to be a boarding school from Monday to Friday. They need to be dealt with on a one to one basis. This would not be suitable for Ken because he is so attached to his home. Neither should he be entered for a scholarship because of his attachment to home. Probably in Sixth Form College things would change for that. It wouldn't strike the parents to think of any other form of education. (Headteacher)

There were three working-class boys who were old enough to have taken the relevant examinations. Adrian was the gifted footballer, and was not considered to be academically gifted, therefore there was no question of entering him. Dennis had not been considered gifted at the time (Chapters 2 and 3), and it is not known why Tony had not been entered.

The previous chapter described how some teachers and headteachers considered the homes of some of their working class pupils to be lacking in psycho-socio-cultural resources. The children that were referred to in this context, Vi, Sandy, Ken and Keith had not reached the appropriate age for scholarship examinations. During the interview with Sandy's headteacher he was asked a direct question about what would happen to Sandy if she went to private school,

Sandy, first school, year 1, social class IIIM

H-I don't know how she has come through so well because of her background. I feel that without something extra, like an interested person, or extra help, she will get lost in the system, leave early and get married, like the old grammar school early leaver.

R-What would happen if she got a scholarship to a public school?

H-She would probably go to University. (Headteacher)

It would be interesting to know if the working-class gifted children will be entered for the private sector when the time comes, as this form of education may be considered to overcome some of the supposed home disadvantages. Discussions concerning private education often do occur well in advance of the appropriate examination age. For example, in first school it had been suggested to the parents of Alexandra (social class 1) that the child would be an appropriate scholarship candidate, though Vi (social class IIIM), who was in the same class and had the same IQ, had not been considered. However, as shown in Chapter 2, Vi was not perceived to be as good as Alexandra academically. It may also be felt by teachers and headteachers that the working-class child would find it more difficult to 'fit in' to the private system, but such feelings were not voiced during the interviews.

There were fourteen middle-class children for whom private schooling was considered (twenty-seven of the sample were categorized as middle-class). The year following the field-work the author was informed that Mandy was going to attend a Public girls school. She has not been included with the fourteen children. It will be seen that the decision-making involved in each case was extremely complex. Factors which appeared to be relevant were numerous, and besides the attitudes of the teachers, headteachers and parents to private schooling, included considerations of the resources of the parents; the potential of the child; how far the school was able to cope with that potential; and the adjustment of the child.

The question of scholarships was not always appropriate as some of the parents did not qualify because of their financial position. Two of the headteachers and their staff had made considerable effort to ensure that four of the children went to public school. This is illustrated by the following extracts concerning Angela and Pat, who were at the same school; and the brothers Peter and Christopher.

Angela, middle school, year 4, social class 1

> The parents did not want her to go to Public school, because the older sister is at the local comprehensive. I went to her home twice about it. They were saying that there was no difference between Angela and her sister, I had to explain that she was in a different league. She wants to go to Cambridge, and I had to explain that she would. There are financial constraints. I explained that I would expect her to get an Open Scholarship to Cambridge. She ought to be at the private school. No reflection on the comprehensives but they can't cope with children like that. (Headmaster)

When Pat got his music scholarship the parents were unable to decide whether to take advantage of it. They were telephoned several times by the same headteacher before they decided to accept the place. This encouragement by the headteacher for the parents to enrol the child for the examination, and to take up the place, may be considered to be a form of sponsorship by the headteacher.

Peter and Christopher (brothers) took the pre-scholarship entrance examination to a preparatory school attached to a public school. This was done free of charge as they were from a one parent family, and it would have been impossible to pay the examination fees. Both boys sailed through, but there was no money available to send them to the school at the time. Later in the year in which Christopher was observed, he took the examination for and was granted an Assisted Place to the same school. The middle school had encouraged the mother to send the boys to one of about three Roman Catholic boarding schools, where they would have had their fees paid. The mother opposed the idea completely. The school felt that the boys should get away from the matriarchic over-protected environment. As Peter's headteacher said of him,

Peter, middle, school, year 1, social class 1

> He is a natural boy who joins in the hurly burly. By the time he is eight or nine he needs to leave the school and go to a boarding school where justice is done to his intelligence, although we can give him work at this school up to second year comprehensive level. It is criminal that his brains are not taken advantage of. (Headteacher)

Jo and Nicholas had taken the examination and failed to get a scholarship. Their teacher emphasized to the author that this did not mean that they had failed the examination, only that they had not qualified for the scholarship. The year before Nicholas took the examination his headteacher said of him,

Nicholas, middle school, year 3, social class 1

> He is highly gifted, and we need to do something for him in the way of a specialist education. The normal state system cannot accomodate him, he needs a private school. A special class is not on, he wants immersing in an academic and intellectual atmosphere. (Headteacher – the previous year)

The political beliefs of the parents of three of the children, Alexandra, Benny and Lilo, would not allow them to consider private education, although it had been suggested by the schools,

Alexandra, first school, year 4, social class 1

> But they've got very set ideas about things like private education and don't want her to be different in any way. I think they were told that

she could be a scholarship girl to ... school, or somewhere like that, but they don't want that, they want her to go to the local comprehensive, which quite staggered us, particularly as it is ... school, being the sort of child that she is. But they are very strong in their beliefs, you know, going to the local state school is being part of the community, that sort of thing.

The headteacher of Benny's first school had suggested private schooling, but at the time his mother had refused the suggestion for identical reasons as those given in the previous extract. However, by the time Benny was observed for the second time at his middle school, the mother was approaching the school regarding a scholarship.

Conversely, Robert's headteacher discouraged the parents from private schooling as reported by the teacher,

Robert, first school, year 3, social class II

He [the head] actually did talk to them, and they said "We think our children are a bit exceptional but we don't want to sound as if we're big-headed about them, but what do you think? Would it be a good idea to put them into private schools now?" And he said, "Quite honestly the way things are going you may have to pay for them partly to go to University eventually, so it might be better to save now, and let them go through the state system and then when it comes to another ten years things might have changed in that perhaps grants aren't so easy to come by, it might be then that you need to finance them in some way for further education." This was his advice anyway. He advised them to stay here, because they were happy and seemed to be gitting on well.

One child, Laurence, had briefly attended a preparatory school. He was an adopted Asian boy, and for the first time in his life was made to feel ethnically different while at that school. He returned to the middle school which was attached to the first school that he had previously attended. As can be seen from the following extract, this experience had had a long lasting effect.

Laurence, middle school, year 3, social class II

He went to another school for one year and he misses some of the things that he did there, for example science. On the other hand he appreciates being with the children here who are favourable to him. He does spend some time trying to belong to the group which is probably because he needs the security. When he's tested he shows up as being a very very intelligent boy compared with other children but it doesn't show in his attitude to teachers or his attitude to other children, because it's masked by emotional factors very often with him. He's very very emotional and sensitive to other children's opinions of him because he's had such bad experiences, and so he doesn't reveal himself. I gather before [he went to private school] he was very happy and it was really a shock to him, a tremendous shock when he found that he wasn't accepted by other children. Isn't that tragic?

During Laurence's interview he stated that he had left the private school for the following reason:

Interview with Laurence

L-1 didn't like the boys much, they weren't very nice to me.
R-Was the work harder than here?
L-Yes.

The children's feelings about private school varied. Nicholas's account of the experience of taking the examination seems ambiguous,

Interview with Nicholas, middle school, year 3

N-We did a test for ... school, that was a seven hour test, two hours for one day and on Saturday we had to do five hours. Jo didn't want to come the next day 'cos it was too much for him. He did come after all 'cos his mum told him to go. We didn't pass though.
R-Would you have liked to have gone to ... school?
N-Well, well I'd like to go to a normal school not a really high one, I'd just like to go to a normal average ... so well I wouldn't have really minded, but I wouldn't really have minded now that I haven't gone so it didn't really make any difference.

George had refused to take the examination for social reasons. His account of his ability to pass the examination is interesting, especially as in the Ability Placement (see the Appendix) he put himself between twelfth and seventeenth from the top of the class.

Interview with George, middle school, year 3, social class II

G-We had the ... school exams come up I think it was a month ago and my mum wanted me to take it, but I didn't want to go.
R-Why?
G-I wanted to stay at this school. I know I'd make new friends there. I

know a boy there called David and I still didn't want to go.

R-But you'll only be here for another year anyway.

G-Yeah well Paul and all my well my best friends, most of them'll go to ... school and I'll be able to go down the hill on my bike.

R-Would you have got into ... school do you think?

G-I don't know. My mum thinks I would 'cos I always ... well last year I came high in my Richmond tests and my reading and spelling tests, like my reading and even my spelling age I think I was top. Spelling I think I was equal top with Sue, and reading I was top fourteen years three months.

R-And that tells you where you are in the class?

G-Yes. I'm the top reader in the class.

Both Kathy and Angela were preparing to go to public school the term following the interview. Kathy's boredom with her present school was mentioned in [Chapter 2]. Her favourable anticipation of the public school was shown by what she said during her interview,

Interview with Kathy, middle school, year 1, social class II

Well, when we went for the test it seemed an awful lot harder the things that they had around the room, the things that they were doing with animals, it seemed much more interesting and also a bit harder, so you wouldn't have any time to get bored.

Angela, however, had ambiguous feelings at the prospect of moving to the public school. She wanted to go, but at the same time she wanted to attend the local comprehensive school because her sister was there.

Private education was considered seriously for many of the gifted children by both parents and schools. It frequently was regarded as a better alternative to the comprehensive system especially in those cases where the local secondary school had a poor reputation. It was also thought of as a method of immersing children in an educational environment that would stimulate them, and encouage them to reach their ultimate potential. Some headteachers and teachers felt that the state system of education was unable to provide the correct type of education for the gifted children. Also, when children were considered to be at risk because of their home environment, then boarding school was thought to be a beneficial substitute. It did tend to be the middle-class children for whom private schooling was considered. This may be because the middle-class parents were more aware of it as a possibility, and therefore able to make enquiries. The greater ability of middle-class parents to manipulate and intervene on their children's behalf has been discussed by Ball, Lacey, and Sharp and Green (Ball, 1981; Lacey, 1970; and Sharp and Green, 1975). However, the scholarship and Assisted Places Schemes are intended to provide educational opportunity for the children of less well-off parents. It is suggested that schools should, in the interests of equal opportunity, inform working-class parents of gifted children about their children's potential, and the educational opportunities available. This view would appear to be particularly appropriate in view of the teachers' perceptions concerning the lack of home stimulation in working class homes (described in Chapter 3).

Acceleration

The previous section examined partial segregation as a form of educational provision for the gifted child. Where it occurred it was generally specific provision made for the gifted child. In the present section another form of specific provision, that of acceleration, will be locked at. Reference will then be made to circumstantial provision of both partial segregation and acceleration in the section that follows.

In the present sample, Maggy had been accelerated in the past, but was no longer in a class ahead of her peers (Chapter 2). The reasoning was that she was not perceived as gifted by her headteacher, and would not be accepted into the middle school early, which would have resulted in her being separated from her peers, and repeating the final year with no friends in the school. So she repeated the third year with a different teacher. Peter combined the two methods of acceleration, by entering the first school early, and by skipping a class, which made him two years ahead of his chronological age group. As the only child in the sample who was accelerated, Peter's experience will be looked at in some detail.

Peter, middle school, year 1

Peter was initially designated as gifted in nursery school where his Full Scale WISC score was 151 and his average reading age differential was 3.6. The headteacher described how Peter was accepted into the school at an earlier age than was normal.

> The head of the nursery school phoned that she had an unusual child, who had a brother already in the school. We pressed the LEA to allow entrance to the school twelve months early. The educational psychologist sent a report to the Area Education Officer. He was started in the second year with children two years older than himself and held his own with the greatest of ease. By the age of eight, if he carries on, he will be capable of doing work of the top class of the middle school. His reading age is five years ahead of his chronological age. (Headteacher)

At the time of observation Peter was in the first year of the middle school (of a first/middle school) instead of the third year of the first school, aged seven years exactly. Peter had in the past found difficulty in writing the quantity that was expected, because he got tired due to his age. This problem had disappeared as he grew older. Despite the difference in age compared with the rest of the children in the class, Peter was on the top ability table. He was on one of the highest reading books in the class. He was observed to be among the fastest in the class to finish the work, though his teacher felt that he was slower at times.

> Then you have Peter, but in fact he doesn't cause me any problems as yet. I suppose it's because he's with older children. When he doesn't finish his work he takes it home.
> R-Does that happen a lot?
> Well, being younger he's a bit slower and chatters a lot. You can really see the difference in age when they're getting ready for PE because he's so much slower getting ready [observation indicated that six boys were faster and six boys slower than Peter]. I haven't let the rest take work home because they forget books. Peter's mother is very good because she makes sure that he has his book. He's used to taking work home as well. He's just started joined up writing. He's adamant to start it. His mother said, "He's having a bit of trouble with it" and he said "No I'm not, no I'm not". So his writing is very large and he's practising at home.

Observation of Peter in the classroom situation showed that despite working at middle school level, he was still very much in need of teacher contact and support. This is illustrated by the following extract from a lesson:

> The class are copying work from the blackboard with only slight murmuring. The teacher is making a list of the children who are unable to swim. Mary goes up to the teacher because she's finished the work. Peter goes to stand behind her.
> P-I can swim.
> T-I know you can swim Peter.
> Peter returns to his desk and carries on copying. He plays with Herbert and his ruler. Books are collected and books are given out. Peter sits dreaming. He has no books and goes to the teacher.
> T-Class, when you get your book, underline it, and put today's date. She gives out 'Beta 2'.
> P-Can I go and get my book?
> T-Yes, go and get it.
> Peter goes outside. He comes back two minutes later with his books. He returns to his desk and picks up the Beta book from the desk.
> P-I've already got one.
> T-Leave it where it is. When you've all written the date turn to page eight. Anna, will you read the title in a big loud voice?
> *(1)
> Peter gets help from Mary. They are doing the use of a ready reckoner

for adding. As the teacher goes past-
P-Does it mean the seventh row down? (ignored)
T*

P-Miss, we haven't done (and indicates two pages that they haven't done).
T-I know we haven't done that. It doesn't matter Peter.
T?(2)**

T-Using the ready reckoner see what the answer is.
Peter puts his hand up immediately without looking at the ready reckoner and mutters "I know this".
T-Next one.
Peter goes up to the teacher.
P-Six plus six is twelve.
Teacher indicates that she wants him to use the ready reckoner.
T?*

Teacher tells them to do the questions. They can use the ready reckoner but if they don't need to they don't have to use it.
The children swap books to mark section B. The teacher is going round the class looking at what they have done.
Katherine HU (3) What do I do when I've done D?
Peter goes up to the teacher.
P-Shall I do D? The class have already been told, and all the children around him have done that section.
T? Peter
Peter mutters "I've finished" and puts his hand up. The teacher comes and collects books and he asks if he should put his things away. Everyone else has an empty desk top.
(1) A child other than the gifted child speaks.
(2) The teacher asks a question.
(3) Hand up.

Judging by the questions Peter asked of the teacher concerning organization, he appeared to be dependent on the teacher. Intellectually he showed himself to be extremely capable. It would be hard to ascertain whether his questions and statements were a ruse to get teacher attention; a limitation of his age; or such deep intellectual concentration that he was unaware of instructions being given. This reliance on the teacher was mentioned to her, and she said,

> Yeah, but there are other children in the class who are the same. It's not the majority, but there are others. But I think it's because they're not used to having to do something and then go onto the next thing. Every time they finish something they bring it out. Well, I'm trying not to do that because otherwise I just have a big long queue.

The teacher's claim that other children reacted in a similar fashion had not been apparent during classroom observation, so the interactions were analyzed for a further three hours and forty five minutes (see the Appendix). In a total of 363 interactions between the teacher and the children, Peter interacted twenty-seven times with the teacher. The mean of the total class interactions was 11.7 (see figure 13 in Chapter 5). He was therefore getting more interactions than he was *entitled* to considering that there were over thirty children in the class. This would appear to have been achieved by going to the teacher to get her attention and occasionally being told off.

Problems related to the child's social development are frequently put forward as an argument against acceleration. In the present example, Peter had one main friend, Herbert, who sat at another table. When lining up to leave the classroom they invariably cuddled, or had some physical contact. They often played in the playground, together and with other children, and again there was considerable tactile contact. The sociometric data placed Peter just below the mean of the class in general popularity (see Chapter 6). He received positive choices from Herbert for sitting next to and playing with, which he reciprocated; and negative choices for working with and playing with from his opposite classroom neighour. His interview revealed that he never had children home to play, which was reiterated by his brother Christopher. They explained this as being because they lived in a small flat. They did not play out. This may have made it more difficult for Peter to extend his friendships. He saw himself as being in the middle for being liked. When his teacher was asked how the other children saw him she said,

> I haven't really noticed them being difficult to him. I mean this morning Matthew (middle ability table) said when he was reading to me from Blue book 6, I think it was ... "Gosh, he must be good at reading", but I think that they just accept him 'cos he's been in this class for quite a long time.

In the Guess Who (see the Appendix and Chapter 6) three children put Peter's name for being 'hard to get on with'. Two of these were girls who sat at his table, which was the top ability table. He perceived himself as being happy.

There was a steady competition at Peter's table concerning which questions individuals had completed, how many lines had been written and so on. His concentration was good. In twenty-six minutes he was distracted 9.6 per cent of the time, during some of which time he was listening to what the teacher was saying to other children. He saw himself as being eleventh or twelfth in the class in ability, though he also thought he was very clever. On the Guess Who one child thought Peter 'didn't have any trouble with his work and finished quickly' and three children perceived him as being 'good at everything he did without making an effort'. However, no one on the two top ability tables mentioned Peter in the context of academic competence. He liked school, though he did say that he did not like mathematics because he found it boring and hard. He thought he was obedient, which he seemed to consider important, judging from an extract from his interview,

Interview with Peter

The class were having art next door to the place of interview, and they were getting a bit noisy.

P-She keeps shouting at them. They should have a nicer time.

R-Why do you think they should have a nice time?

P-I said nicer time. because if they were more obedient than that, they could have lovely time.

R-So when you're obedient then you have a better time, do you?

P-Mm.

A further argument against acceleration that is frequently used is differential physical development between the gifted child and the older children. Usually the concern is about when the children reach puberty. Physically Peter was considerably shorter than the rest of the class but in PE he managed to keep up most of the time in running, skipping and similar races, though he had some difficulty in following the instructions.

The work of the class was well within Peter's capabilities and he was able to keep up physically. He had a friend, and was not perceived negatively by many of the other children. He enjoyed school, and was happy. There may be problems later, and he might have been happier still, for competitive or social reasons, with his own chronological age group, but there would seem to be little basis for making these assumptions. His brother Christopher, who was at the same school, was not accelerated. The headteacher said that this was because no one had realized that he was gifted until his younger brother Peter had entered the school.

Dennis, middle school, year 4

One other school operated a policy of acceleration. In Dennis's case this was used by his teacher to confirm that Dennis was not gifted in that he had not been accelerated,

> In the past there have been children who have been put up a year, and they have had to do two years in the top year because they were so bright. Partly also they were also normally a handful. They were straining so much that they had to be put up a year, and then you have to keep them in the top year for two years, which is again a problem, so other children have stood out more than Dennis has, that might give you some indication of whether he's gifted.

In some schools where the policy of acceleration did not exist, the question of its suitability for some of the children was brought up by their teachers. Lilo's teacher considered that she was able enough to be accelerated by two years. In her example it was mentioned as an indication of how gifted she was. Nicholas and Christopher were considered to be able to do the work of a higher class, but were not thought to be sufficiently mature socially. Similar statements were made about Mandy by her previous teacher, who thought her capable of doing English 'O' level when she was in the third year of the middle school, but unable to cope emotionally. Her present teacher said,

Mandy and Tony, middle school, year 3

It's a pity Tony isn't up with the fourth years. Mandy as well. There are several children where this should happen. In the fourth year the classes are smaller and they could get more individual attention and spend two years in the fourth year. With Mandy it would be good though it would involve her missing a whole year because she is younger and was in a different class. I have suggested this policy but the head wouldn't agree.

Pat's teacher mentioned that he would not be better with an older class, in fact he was one month too young to be in the next year, and thus almost qualified anyway.

Acceleration, as a method of educational provision, was not used extensively in the schools studied. It was only possible to observe one child, Peter, who was accelerated. In his case it did not appear to be detrimental to his social development, and he was able to work with the most able children in a class where the other children were chronologically two years older than he.

There are arrangements that are made in schools which are not specific to the gifted, but are already present in the organizational system of the school. These are defined as circumstantial provision, in that although they may benefit the gifted child, they are not primarily designed for that purpose.

Streaming, which is only possible in larger schools, occurred in two schools which affected three of the classrooms observed. The effect for gifted children may be expected to be an increased pace and/or higher level of class work. The following quotation is fairly typical of the reaction from the three teachers involved, of responsibility for, almost possession of, a precious object.

Kathy and Lilo, middle school, year 1

It keeps me on my toes having an A-stream, but I find it tiring. I am very conscious of the responsibility of having them, and stretching them. I find it very strenuous having an A-class because I'm aware of what they are capable of and I am conscious that I should stretch them to their limit.

On the other hand, streaming can create problems for the top stream, especially if it is done for the benefit of the lower streams, as would seem to be indicated by the following example:

Sylvia, Les, Laurence, and George, middle school, year 3

> I don't like having a streamed class because really only half of the class
> are A-stream calibre. The rest are not, and one or two are rather
> weak, but I have to have them because the B-streams need to have
> smaller classes. This makes me rather crowded because although I
> have a large room, half is for Art equipment, so we are very squashed.

Setting, which is also only possible in a large school, was done in two of the
schools for French and mathematics.

Streaming and setting are particularly relevant for gifted children in classes
where the normal method of teaching is to the whole class, and particularly
where the standard of work is aimed at the levels of those in the middle or
lower ability groups. It may be considered that in classes which have been
streamed or set, the level of work would be higher, and therefore the gifted
child would be better catered for. However, in classes where the children are
taught on an individual basis, the academic standard of the total class may
generally be considered to be less relevant.

Vertical grouping is when there is more than one age group in the class. It
is a system which has been considered to create a beneficial environment for
younger children, because it allows a child to develop a relationship with one
specific adult over more than one school year, which aids security. It also
develops responsibility among the older children who are encouraged to act as
monitors and general helpers to the younger children. The system was used for
the first two years at one first school, and involved Rita. It was also used
in Nicholas and Jo's class, where although they were third year middle
school children, they were with some fourth year children. Vertical grouping
is similar to acceleration for one year, but then deceleration for the following
year when a younger age group comes into the class, as observed by one
teacher.

Nicholas and Jo, middle school, year 3

> It is worrying me next year about competition for Jo. This year the
> fourth years are bright, but when they go.

Recent falling rolls have created difficulties at the classroom level, and
many of the smaller schools are having to *juggle* the children in order to create
complete classes. Occasionally this involves putting brighter children up a
year, usually temporarily. Again, there is a similarity to acceleration, but this
system does not involve such radical deceleration, in that at the end of the year
the children rejoin their own age group. This happened at two schools, but did
not affect any of the sample children. In Sandy and Vicky's case it had been
deliberate policy to exclude them,

Sandy and Vicky, middle school, year 1

At the end of last year six children were advanced into the higher class because there were too many children in that year. These two weren't. Sandy because it was felt that she had enough to cope with at home, and Vicky because she was so shy, and the mother didn't want pressure. (Previous teacher)

Six of the schools had no specific or circumstantial organizational policies which affected any of the gifted children.

Enrichment

Enrichment may be of advantage to gifted children in a social sense when it can be incorporated with ease into the classroom organization and teaching. If a class is seated in rows and taught as a whole class, a child who is doing separate work may be noticed and commented on by the classroom peers, and the child may then become excluded and be treated differently. If the class move freely, working on individual work and topics, it will not normally be so apparent to the other children that one particular child is working in a different way, or on harder topics or books, unless it is a scheme where the books are numbered. From the teacher's viewpoint, the incorporation of enrichment is organizationally facilitated when individual learning already occurs within the classroom. A teacher who is used to that method of teaching is likely to have materials ready to hand, or know where to obtain them. She will also be conceptually more able to organize for an individual, in that she will be used to thinking about thirty different pieces of work, rather than one piece of work done thirty times.

Pedagogically, enrichment reiterates values of individual learning to which many primary teachers supposedly adhere in varying degrees, as indicated by Kirby (1981). There are two forms of individual learning and teaching. The first is individualized, where the child has work which is particular to that child. For example, a child who is writing his *news* or an essay is working on his own as an individual, at his own pace and standard, and the content is original and unique to that child. Other children in the class may, or may not be doing the same activity. The second form of individual learning is individuated, where a child interacts with the teacher on an individual basis, such as reading to the teacher. Again, other children may be doing identical or similar work. As pointed out by Boydell when individualized work is in progress then individuated interaction is almost inevitable (Boydell, 1978). Perhaps the more normal use of the concepts in educational circles, is when children are set work, the level or standard of which is particular to an individual child or group of children. In other words, where the learning is at the child's personal ability level. For example, a child may go through a reading scheme at his own speed; or learn through discovery or interest, where a child would work on a personal or group topic.

Individual learning is sometimes associated with *progressive* methods of pedagogy. It has been suggested that the presence of such methods in primary schools is a myth (Boydell, 1981; and Simon, 1981), and Berlak and Berlak found very few classes or schools where such methods existed (Berlak and Berlak, 1981). Boydell, in her observational study of primary classes, indicated that teachers used a mixture of methods in their teaching, for example class teaching, group teaching, individual attention, and variations in setting of work. The present study confirms these findings, though it should be emphasized that no attempt was made to measure or assess the *style* of teaching in the classrooms as per Bennett (1976). However, as an observer, some assessment of pedagogic methods in classrooms was made.

The discussion of the provision of enrichment will deal with first and middle schools separately. This division is made because to some extent the nature of enrichment provision was found to differ in first and middle schools as a result of the differences in teaching style, the types of curriculum covered, and different problems associated with the variation in the ages of the children. The terms specific and circumstantial enrichment will be used. The former to describe activities which are specific to a gifted child and the latter work which is given to all the children, but which allows gifted children to work at a faster pace, placing little or no restriction on the speed of work. It will be seen that some children experienced both specific and circumstantial enrichment.

Alexandra and Vi will not be included in the survey of enrichment, as it was not possible to observe them in their class. Twelve out of the remaining fifteen first school children had some sort of enrichment provision made for them. Ken is also mentioned in the first school context because Robert's teacher, who had previously taught Ken, discussed him.

Enrichment in First Schools

Generally the work in first schools tends to be extremely individualized and individuated. A considerable amount of time is spent on reading, and the children work through the schemes at their own pace, with the teacher hearing children read individually as frequently as possible. In mathematics, it is again normal practice for the children to be working on different stages of either workbooks or workcards, in groups or on their own. Naturally, children's writing is at their own personal standard. Group lessons do occasionally occur; examples would be when developing a new concept in mathematics (though frequently this would be done in smaller groups); when doing a new sound for reading, and writing examples on the blackboard; or discussion lessons leading on to writing. The following description of the class organization typifies that of many of the other classes:

Don and David, first school, year 2

Basically they work individually, certainly for number work, and those that aren't capable I put the work directly into the book each day. They work from cards. I have a series of graded cards which they know which colour they're working from. Writing I suppose I tend to organise them into groups, but it's very much individual apart from when we do a handwriting lesson or follow up from a TV programme, and they're working at their own level and I hope the work's suited to that level. So Don and David in a way have their own curriculum.

One teacher, that of Maggy, Rosemarie, Hugh, Keith and Liz, provided circumstantial enrichment in mathematics by allowing these children to use a text book from the beginning of the year, whereas the rest of the class only started using it in the third term.

If a gifted child goes through the available work particularly fast, many teachers have curriculum material available, left over from their teaching of older children,

Arthur, first school, year 1

I don't need anything. I never hold a child back. I have taught older children, therefore I know the progression that they need to follow, and I can prepare their work.

However, occasionally teachers of higher classes objected if a child covered curriculum material which they felt belonged to them. This problem was avoided with family or vertical grouping,

Don and David, first school, year 2 (previous teacher of Alexandra)

I suppose things like the SRA reading lab (note 10 in Chapter 2) would be quite good with David, and comprehension things, but we don't have access to those. It's very much that's a fourth year thing, that's the third year thing, they don't do it other than in their age, which was one thing in family grouping which was much easier. I had Alexandra in a family group. I had access to the work books and things which the older children were using which she could use.

Robert, first school, year 3

The example of Robert illustrates two points. The dilemma for a teacher of providing circumstantial enrichment for a gifted child and thereby satisfying his intellectual needs, or sacrificing the gifted child's intellectual growth to soothe the social worries of another child. The second point is that there is, at times, a very fine distinction between specific and circumstantial enrichment. This particular teacher turned a circumstantial enrichment experience into a specific one.

Robert's teacher, when asked if Robert followed any particular curriculum, said that he did not. In fact, she did provide circumstantial enrichment for Robert's reading, where he was on *choosing* books, and permitted to select which books to read. But this created an element of conflict for the teacher, in that Robert's friend, Kevin, was Robert's main competition,

> I'm glad Robert has got Kevin in the class because it gives him someone of his own standard. I hope that Kevin doesn't fall behind because I think it's good for Robert to have someone doing the same as him. I'm hoping to put Kevin onto 'choosing' books soon.

But Kevin could not understand why Robert should have jumped books,

> Kevin and Robert were on the same book. Then I put Robert onto choosing books because of his [reading] test. Kevin has a history of bedwetting. When he got to the end of book six I put him onto book seven. I heard him say that when Robert had finished book six he'd gone onto choosing. I am careful not to pick Robert out as a consequence.

It was consideration for Kevin that had prevented the teacher from doing more than she did for Robert.

> I haven't given him anything because I did have this problem with Kevin and I felt I didn't want to sort of exaggerate it. If it becomes necessary, and I feel that he is becoming bored with what we are doing and needs stretching, certainly I shall have to start giving him, because I can't study the others too much, and I think Kevin now is accepting the fact the . . . but I think it was just this problem that when they were in [the previous] teacher's class they were both on the same reading book and they both reckoned that they were the top two readers, and suddenly I jumped Robert onto choosing books, and Kevin felt that in some way he'd gone back or something, so now I don't want to make the difference too obvious.

In fact this teacher acknowledged that Robert did get bored,

> I can see that at times he is bored with what we are doing but that's inevitable and something he has to put up with.

The example of Robert clearly reveals the dilemmas which a teacher can face. She may wish to provide stimulation for, and stretch, a gifted child, but at the same time she has the feelings of the remainder of the class to consider. Concurrently, she has to judge the effect that individual treatment will have upon the gifted child's personal relationships with other children. This particular teacher had made such assessment concerning Robert, whom she considered to be happy and well balanced.

> Oh I think Robert fits in pretty well. I wondered when he first came in how it would be because I am always very aware of bright children, I must say that straight away because I do feel that they do need to be stretched to the full, and I'm aware, wondering whether I am giving as much stretching as I can, but on the other hand without singling them out too much. I felt this more with Ken than with Robert because he seems well balanced and integrated and whatever you do he's quite happy to do and he isn't any problem.

Robert's teacher turned what would normally have been classified as circumstantial enrichment into specific enrichment. One morning she was observed to hear Robert read twice from his book. She then talked with him at some length about planets, distances and so on, while they both looked at an encyclopaedia together. Robert was the only child in the class to use Ladybird comprehension cards, on which he worked industriously. This would be classified as specific enrichment.

Although specific and circumstantial enrichment are discussed separately, there were occasions when both types of enrichment were available in one class.

Mary, first school, year 3

There was a single instance of specific enrichment for Mary, and that was when she brought her cello into school, and gave the whole class a lecture on how it worked, what the bow was made of, and explained all the parts of the instruments. This she did with total confidence, and then played a piece of music which the rest of the children used for musical drama.

In contrast, the teacher's method of using the reading scheme, which was described in Chapter 2, appeared to create a situation where Mary was in all probability held back, rather than enriched. However, in mathematics she worked with her friend on a Fletcher book which was two books in advance of the rest of the class.

Rosemarie, first school, year 4

Rosemarie was occasionally allowed to demonstrate her extraordinary ability at story telling. This she did at the end of one afternoon while the author was observing. The whole class were completely spellbound during a story which lasted for approximately ten minutes. The plot was original and complex, with descriptions of people and places which were detailed and vivid. As the teacher said, when Rosemarie started a story, she seemed to have little idea of where it was going. It developed as she told it, and if she had an inconsistency in the plot, she realized it, and altered the story accordingly.

Jim, first school, year 3

Jim was extremely interested in drama, and organized a play over several break and lunch times. He asked the teacher for permission to perform it one afternoon. The subject was a haunted house where some of the actors dreamed about vampires and ghosts. The play lasted approximately fifteen minutes, and included three boys and six girls in the cast. The story and production had been directed by Jim, and it was impressive to see the result of such organizational leadership. His interview revealed some of the problems that he had overcome.

Interview with Jim

R-I enjoyed watching that play. Do you often do plays like that?

J-Not really, I just make plays up.

R-And people always want to join in do they?

J-Not really, but they love doing it once I've told them how to do it. They think it's quite good.

R-But you have to persuade them first?

J-Yeah. Well how it all started was when I was thinking about William Shakespeare, and I thought I hope I grow up to be like him, so I thought I wonder if I could do a play myself, so all that night I was thinking of trying to do a play and the next day I'd thought of it and I wrote it all down, and then on Monday I got all the people and there was one too many so I had to make another space.

R-How long did you take doing the play?

J-About three weeks.

R-Did you rehearse every playtime?

J-Yeah, and that one didn't seem to last very long after three weeks so I made up another one and they all thought it was their idea and they all kept doing it themselves, so I made up another one about kidnappers and that seems to be the best play I've done so far.

R-But you weren't doing that today at playtime?

J-We always do it at lunchtime playtime.

R-Is it always the same people that you have?

J-Yes.

R-Do you find them difficult to organise?

J-Yes because a lot of the time we have a bit of an argument or something about the play about the clothes and things we're going to have and where we're going to get all the equipment and that's all we seem to argue about.

R-Why should that cause an argument?

J-'Cos we never know where we're going to get the clothes and then we can't do too many rehearsals 'cos it's raining and then they all go away from the play. When I think we've got really good at it I try and get the clothes and things.

R-It's up to you to get those is it?

J-Yeah, but some of the children who are in my play said that they'd let them borrow some of their dressing up clothes. That's nice of them. We could go up to Nottingham to do do our play at the Royal Theatre. If anyone wants to join in they can tell me and I make another space.

The four examples (including Robert) offered above indicate the somewhat transitory nature of specific enrichment as it is used here. They tended to be *one-off* occurrences. It is interesting that the three examples described in this section all came from the same school. It is possible, therefore, that these teachers have developed a flexibility of organization and awareness of the interests of their children, to allow the children to demonstrate special talents or interests to each other. In addition. Rosemarie's teacher made considerable effort with Maggy to provide enrichment which will be described below.

There are two notions which are implicit in provision of enrichment and individualized work. The first is that the work that is done has to be recorded in some way, the second that the gifted child has to be willing to do work that is different from the other children. For some of the children there were problems in these areas.

For most teachers, proof that work has been done is shown in the recording of it. This recording may present a difficulty, especially for the younger children, when doing enrichment work. Roedell and Robinson mentioned the gap that may exist for some gifted children between their intellectual and physical development, thereby limiting the completion of tasks which the children are able to conceptualize (Roedell and Robinson, 1977). Axon reported the difficulties encountered in the development of SCCEP (Schools Council Curriculum Enrichment Pack) for younger pupils, where the children still have manipulative difficulties, at times exacerbated by the speed of their mental processes (Axon, 1979). This is illustrated in the case of Alexandra, where the arduousness of writing resulted in frustration on the part of the child,

Alexandra, first school, year 4

I suppose I do stress quite a bit Don's actual writing, having seen the problems that Alexandra [brother and sister] had, as well I suppose I'm more aware of it. I felt she became frustrated because she'd got all the ideas but whenever she wrote it always looked such a filthy mess. (Previous teacher)

Although some teachers can be extremely flexible and imaginative in their expectations and suggestions for the replacement of writing, other teachers would find difficulties of this sort impossible to overcome; and therefore individualization of the curriculum may be limited, and the opportunity for enrichment may not be made available to the child. The teacher of Hugh made a definite, but unsuccessful, attempt to overcome the problem of the boy's writing difficulty by using a tape recorder.

Hugh, first school, year 4

In expressing himself in creative writing I think he has the ability but he's handicapped by his writing problems, which are pretty severe and they affect also the speed at which he writes. It isn't just a question of untidy writing, it's a question of forming the letters in such a way and holding the pencil in such a way that it takes him a very long time to write down his thoughts. But on the other hand he is able to carry over a story that he started perhaps two days before. He can open his book and know exactly where he was in that story and continue it. I think at the present moment he's held back in time, but eventually this may improve. I did try giving him a tape recorder and saying "If you'd like to speak your story as you think it into the tape recorder" and he was just totally confused. It made him feel shy, so that wasn't any help.

It is important that enrichment work be presented to an audience. This is emphasized by Renzulli, who stated that it was essential that the high school children who had been through his enrichment programme reported their results or discoveries. He felt that this should be done to an authentic audience, and he suggested a variety of forms in which it could be done, including a lecture, or a letter to the local newspaper (Renzulli, 1977). It may not be necessary for the work to be presented in written form. There are other methods available, such as making a video or giving a lecture. Flexibility concerning presentation of work on the part of teachers of gifted children with writing difficulties would appear to be necessary.

Several teachers reported problems stemming from the reluctance of gifted children to interest themselves in enrichment work. Ken's reluctance to do special work was noted from the beginning of his school career,

Ken, middle school, year 1

In the past he hasn't wanted to do anything special, even when he was capable of it. He could read when he came to school and we tried to get him to do Ladybird work cards writing sentences, but he wanted to do the filling in simple words like the others though we knew he could do the other work. (Headteacher)

His previous teacher was faced with his conflicting needs, of being the same as his classroom peers and yet needing intellectual stimulation,

> I did find problems with Ken because in some ways he didn't want to do, as his other teachers said, he didn't want to be singled out to do different work, but on the other hand if I gave him the same work to do he'd go home and say "I could do all that and I'm bored" and his mother would come in and say, but he'd never say it to me, he'd just do it. So I started giving him more difficult work, and then if he came across something he couldn't do he'd just burst into tears, so you were stuck with, you didn't know quite what to do, and I did find him a difficult child. He used to sit there and rock and look unhappy sometimes and I didn't quite know why. I didn't find him an easy child to get to know, and that probably made it more difficult. (Previous teacher)

However, once Ken was in the middle school, he was quite prepared to work on mathematics that was far in advance of the rest of the class, but this may have been because of the arrival of Ann in the school, who did the same work as he.

Maggy, first school, year 4

Maggy's teacher had made considerable effort to provide specific enrichment for Maggy, but she had failed because of the child's reluctance to co-operate. In the first place she had attempted freedom of choice of individual work,

> I've often given her a choice of things that she can do, but she doesn't always like that sort of freedom, she is worried by it. If you say "Well if you don't want to do that you can choose something else", she says, "Oh it doesn't matter" and gets all embarassed about that. I found this with reading books because she'd been through the scheme and she'd been through a number of other books that are supposed to extend their reading vocabulary, and then I said, "There is the whole of the library and there are some other books around the school, go and choose one". She just didn't know where to begin to choose. That kind of freedom seemed to worry her quite a lot. Very complex child.

Observation showed that the type of books she chose from the school library were Enid Blyton ones, yet her parents stated to the teacher that she chose Shakespeare at home, which she learned by heart. The teacher had also attempted to do specific projects, using the child's own interests,

> With Maggy I've tried, because of her interest in insects, I did try to let her catch some insects and look at them with a magnifying glass and put them in a tank and then perhaps pursue that with drawings or finding out more about them and how they live, and it didn't seem to

> pay off at all. She wasn't that interested. And I've found that within things we do that she copes quite well but not to the extent of needing something totally different from the other children, but I think again sometimes that's because she's afraid of being singled out and being apart from the others. I think it would have to be done very subtly, and I think maybe I've found it difficult to choose something that she could do. She seemed to almost reject such an idea.

It would be difficult to know if the reason for Maggy not wishing to participate was because the teacher had not found a topic that particularly interested her, or if it was because she did not wish to appear different from the other children. According to her teacher, the concern with her peers, and her appearance in their eyes, was revealed in class discussions.

> I think she is hiding her talents in order to be with her peers. When P.C. ... came she obviously understood, but when he asked her a question she giggled and wouldn't answer, as though she thought others would laugh at her if she got it right and knew the answer, and didn't want to let her own standard down and get it wrong.

The teacher had then considered using some purpose made enrichment materials belonging to the headteacher. However, she had come up against difficulties with her colleagues concerning which children should use the materials and how to identify the appropriate children. In a final attempt to involve Maggy in an activity commensurate with the teacher's judgment of her ability, she had suggested that Maggy work on some special history work cards using an encyclopaedia that Maggy's father had found for her.

Maggy's teacher had made every effort to provide the child with enrichment. She considered that Maggy was gifted, and wished her to be stimulated and achieve her potential. She was also the teacher of Liz, whom she did not label as gifted, although she acknowledged her considerable artistic ability. She had not made any special provision for this talent.

Liz, first school, year 4

> We had the Art adviser come in about Liz because we felt that she needed extra in that field. She did some drawings of skeletons at the Museum which impressed him. They were extremely good for her age. He said that whereas in the past he would have suggested that she develop all areas in art, he would now suggest that she concentrate on that area in which she shines. He gave some suggestions which I haven't been able to follow up.

The difference in effort which the teacher made for the two children may have been because of her different perceptions concerning their giftedness, or because of lack of expertise in art as a subject.

Inherent, therefore, in enrichment provision is the assumption of the willingness of the child to work independently of the classroom peers. Also the child has to be stimulated by the activity, and comfortable with it. Hugh's reluctance to work with the tape recorder seemed to be an instance of not being comfortable with the opportunity offered. Jim's disinclination to do enrichment work appeared to be limited to certain areas alone,

Jim, first school, year 3

I therefore was quite prepared to stretch him and give him different work, more advanced work. This he didn't enjoy at all, he much prefers to work along with the children at his table. I produced different work for him, cards with comprehension, and he did it, but he didn't do it very happily, and didn't do it particularly well. Could he have someone to do it with him, well that was fair of course, but I found even then, and they took it outside, there was a lot of larking about going on, he didn't really achieve any more being given harder work. Emotionally he'd still like to be seven [his actual age] ... he likes to do what everybody else is doing.

However, when there was an appearance of having the same work as the other children, then Jim was quite willing to comply with what the teacher set him,

If I'm doing language things, or work cards I've got them at different levels. I give him ones that are more difficult. If they are doing formal number work in their formal number work books, his work card is the hardest, and I do the work cards that go along with 'Fletcher'. So I always do the work cards that go with his ability, his ones are at the back of the box, and he does comprehension cards that are much more advanced. He would hate me to say you're doing comprehension now and the others are all doing a picture, he wants to be doing what the others are doing, and I often have to chivvy him to do the easiest work. The only work that he enjoys doing at his own level which is Fletcher because everybody around him is doing Fletcher.*

There were other areas of the curriculum where he did seem prepared to work on his own. For example, he was the only child in the class who was off the reading schemes, and onto his own choice of reading book. But, observation indicated that his motivation was not very high, in that he was on the same book *Winnie the Pooh* for at least one month, with little observable progress. Science was a subject which did interest him. During his interview he said that he particularly liked going to visit the Natural History and Science Museums. He had gone into a class project in science in greater depth than the other children.

* Fletcher is a mathematics scheme.

I got a lot of stuff on time, and Jim went further with that stuff than anybody else. I do know that the stuff is available. Yes there are pieces of equipment that I would like to have in the school. For one thing he was very interested in light and colour and I would have liked to have had a spectrum. I don't know where I could get held of one unless I go out and buy one.

The problem of reluctant participation by the children in some of the enrichment experiences provided seemed to be less prevalent with the provision of circumstantial enrichment. Most of the children who were disinclined to do specific enrichment activities mentioned above, quite contentedly worked on higher mathematics or reading books.

There were three first school children for whom no special provision was made. In Karl's case the teacher did not consider him to be gifted,

Karl, first school, year 2

T-He does the same curriculum as the rest of the class.
R-Is there any curriculum material that would be useful?
T-No. The opposite, because I am concerned that in primary education that social education is more useful than anything that is subject orientated. I could push him in number work, but that wouldn't be good.

Ricky had only just gone up to his class, being slightly younger, and was catching up with, but had not yet overtaken the rest of the children. Benny's first headteacher would have organized withdrawal for him, but she considered that the teacher he had at the time was excellent and was stretching him sufficiently. According to this teacher Benny did the same curriculum, but the teacher's expectations of the standard of his work was higher than for the other children.

Benny, first school, year 4

I make his work twice as hard. I expect more. In project I expect him to do what the others do, and then some extra. The only special curriculum is providing extra books. His ability is still probably not tapped yet. (First school teacher)

Benny was the child who brought his own books into school. This teacher jokingly said that she felt that he did this in case she did not provide him with adequate work. The comment was retrospectively substantiated by Benny during his interview at the end of the first year in middle school.

Interview with Benny

B-I think in a way this is a better school [than the first school]. I think mainly because there's more work for us to do, and that's better because there's more work and before there wasn't much work, we just had this list on the board of about six things to do and when we'd finished that we just had to wait for about ten minutes before we got any work because the others were all waiting to be marked. But here you have a timetable and if you've finished you go up to be marked, and then you have something else to do like when you're on an English book you finish an exercise like in comprehension you go onto another exercise which keeps you busy.

R-You used to bring books in that were nothing at all to do with what you were doing in school.

B-Yes. It was that if I did finish the work obviously and we had to wait, as I said, for about ten minutes, it was something to read.

A great deal of individualized learning that happens in first school classrooms occurs in groups or with the whole class working on the same books but on different pages. This means that instructions can be given to the whole class, or several children at one time. Once a child is doing work that is peculiar to that child, then it may be assumed that, initially at least, he will need, and possibly demand more instruction and teaching time. The question of teacher time allotted to the gifted child as compared with the rest of the class will be discussed in the next chapter.

The emphasis on individualized organization of learning programmes in first schools seems highly conducive to the presence of some enrichment for gifted children. However, some of the gifted children were indisposed to differential treatment as compared with their peers. This emerged as a difficulty less often with the use of circumstantial rather than specific enrichment. There was a tendency for the former to occur mainly in mathematics and reading, and occasionally in other English work. This tendency may be attributed to the abundance and richness of materials available at most levels in those curriculum areas, though some teachers with fourth year children did mention a lack of reading materials suitable for their gifted children.

In first schools only three children had no enrichment programme provided. Two children had the opportunity of breadth enrichment, as used in the conventional sense, of studying additional topics to the rest of the class. These were Maggy, who refused to be involved; and Robert, when his teacher used his choice of reading books to expand his knowledge of the topics he chose. The small amount of provision of breadth enrichment may be a result of the dearth of enrichment materials for gifted children in first schools, especially for projects. Most of the enrichment subject matter that has been developed has been aimed at the middle school level, as mentioned above. Possibly this is because of the general use of individualized learning methods at first school level. The strong approval reported by Ogilvie (op cit) by first school teachers for enrichment may well be considered partly due to the ease with which it can be incorporated into the organization of most first school classrooms. A busy teacher,who may well be lacking in expertise in the subject which interests a particular gifted child, would probably have great difficulty in providing material for one child, especially at the top of the school. This situation may be relieved in a combined first/middle school, where curriculum materials can be borrowed from the teachers of the middle school, and the child can use books from the middle school library (provided the opportunity is made available). Actual depth enrichment, as in the conventional use of the term, only occurred with Jim in the project on 'Time'.

Specific and/or circumstantial enrichment appeared to occur regardless of the label *gifted* or *non-gifted*. The only child who was considered to be non-gifted, and who did not have enrichment was Karl. His teacher did most of her teaching in a didactic manner, and therefore individualized work would have been difficult to incorporate into her system of classroom management.

Enrichment in Middle Schools

In middle schools, as in first schools, there were a few classes where both specific and circumstantial enrichment were provided, and other classes where only one form of enrichment was observed. Thirteen of the twenty middle school children had some enrichment. On the whole the pedagoguism in middle schools is more didactic than in first schools. Therefore, there is less opportunity for individualized work, except in classes which use published mathematics or reading schemes, and/or do project work. These will be discussed below. The number of children per class tends to increase in middle schools, therefore there is less opportunity for individuated teaching. The specific and circumstantial enrichment in three middle school classes will be described.

Christopher, middle school, year 3

Christopher had had personal lessons with the headteacher for algebra in previous years. The headteacher considered Christopher to be absolutely brilliant, in that he was able to do several steps of a problem mentally, although he was reluctant to write each step down as he saw little relevance in doing so. A local lecturer had also done an individual project with him. However, the year in which he was observed, his specific enrichment programme consisted of differentiated homework provided by his teacher,

> He does special work for me in English, more traditional English language written work, rather sophisticated grammar that we can't really teach children of his age, it doesn't mean anything to them.

Christopher's teacher taught using a whole class method, apart from occasionally in mathematics, when the class was divided into two groups, plus one remedial group. The teacher (who was a mathematics specialist) often provided sheets from which the more able group worked on their own, while he went over the examples with the rest of the class. This teacher's ideology seemed to be implicitly anti-individualized teaching, as indicated in his statement,

> I have to drill them in order to teach them how to obey instructions. They can't follow written instructions the way that the eleven plus child could. I think it's bad teaching in the infants, being allowed to do what they want to do. I have to go over the whole work with them or else there would be tears because they can't follow basic written instructions.

When Christopher finished his work, which he was observed to do twenty minutes in advance of anyone else in the class, he was given further similar examples to do. This would only be considered as enrichment if the examples extended the child's knowledge rather than repeated the work already completed.

Hank and Benny, middle school, year 1

Benny, in contrast to when he was in first school (see above), was given considerable specific enrichment. This appeared to be mainly in order to fill his time, because he inevitably finished the class work in advance of the rest of the class. He also received circumstantial enrichment in SMP (Mathematics) and SRA (Reading) where he was ahead of the other children.

> Benny always finishes immediately which is very difficult in a varied class. Benny does have a special curriculum if he finishes quickly and does other things. SMP is its own curriculum and SRA English he is ahead of the others. He does . . . a maths game that the head gave me.

The speed at which Benny worked, and the way in which specific enrichment occupied him can be observed in the following extract of a lesson. It illustrates the difference between teachers in their treatment of children who finish their work quickly. Benny was given new and special work to do while Christopher (see above) was given more of the same work. The extract also compares two gifted children in the same class, Hank and Benny, both of whom had been labelled as gifted, but whose standard of work production diverged noticeably.

> The children do a test on the four rules of number. Benny is quickly way ahead of all the others except one girl. Benny is the first to finish. He does it very obviously making a noise turning over the paper and then getting his reading book out *Paddington Goes to Town* (a book which is more suitable for children of about seven years of age). The teacher goes to Benny and tells him to start his English.

Benny goes to the teacher to talk about the English.

Hank is lagging behind the other children.

Benny goes to the cupboard to get blotting paper and talks to a boy as he does so.

Hank tries to get help (along with various others) but the teacher says he has to think about it (his first attempt to get help).

Benny talks to the teacher about glasses.

Benny puts up his hand.

Four children finish the work, which is ten minutes after Benny.

Eight minutes later twelve children have finished. When they do so they read their reading books. (Difference of treatment compared with Benny, despite the fact that there is twenty minutes of lesson time left).

The teacher asks the author to help Benny with something he is finding difficult. It is turning nouns into adjectives.

The teacher has started to mark the tests and calls Benny out to correct something. He has misread a six for a five because of bad printing. Benny stands up as the teacher passes and shows her that he has finished. She puts him on to the next bit.

Approximately eight children have not finished. Hank is looking worried and is trying to get help from his next door neighbour. (He has tried conventional means, and now turns to illicit methods).

Hank is still on the test, and is now rocking backwards and forwards, playing with the pencil on his desk. (A cry for help which is visible to the teacher).

T-Have you finished Hank?

H-No. (Under his breath) I'm stuck.

T-If you're stuck Hank go onto the next one.

T-Tells off Hank for talking to a boy.

Benny comes back up to the teacher because he has finished.

T-I suggest you have a little read now.

Hank is still doing the test.

Hank puts his chin down and thumps it on the table. He jiggles his jaw around. He gets his reading book out. (He has given up).

T-Have you finished Hank? How many more have you got to do?

H-Well, just the bottom ones and they're hard.

T-Two more minutes then.

Hank puts the sheet down and starts reading. (Refusal to comply with the teacher's request, but does an acceptable activity).

T-Aren't you going to do any more then? They're a bit hard are they? (Teacher's acceptance of Hank's refusal).

Sandy and Vicky, middle school, year 1

Sandy and Vicky had a definite combination of specific and circumstantial enrichment. Their science teacher dealt with their questions on an individual basis after lessons,

> When teaching them one would pick them both out. Vicky asks particularly good questions, to such an extent that one needs to answer them after the lesson because they are over the head of the rest of the class. She is quick at answering and confident and easy at asking the appropriate questions. (Science teacher)

Their own teacher, despite thinking that she did nothing special with them, in fact provided specific enrichment with Logi blocks and research, plus circumstantial enrichment with SMP Mathematics.

> I don't do anything special with them, though a lot of the work is individual, so in that way they work at their own level. Sandy plus another one [are the only two] . . . on Unit 2 in SMP maths. She is the most able in maths. She has a logical mind. Vicky puts in punctuation as she writes it. Topic work is individual and I try to stretch them with questions to make them think. I get out Logi blocks and try to make them think differently, do special setting with them. When they answer questions in class I come back at them to make them think more and give reasons. When they have finished their work early they can go into the Quiet Room and do research. When I hear them read I ask them questions about comprehension. They don't ever seem bored.

The three classroom examples provide illustrations of the variety of enrichment which was provided for the gifted children. They also showed the different interpretations by teachers of similar types of enrichment, such as giving additional work to a child who finishes before the rest of the class.

Topic or project work[1] were mentioned by three teachers of eight gifted children as a method used to stretch or extend their gifted children. In fact, observation indicated that a total of ten of the classes were doing one or more projects.

The categorization of topic work as a form of enrichment would be dependent on the teachers' treatment of it, as they seem to vary in their conceptions of project work, and their modus operandi of organization. The question of whether project work in a particular class could be termed enrichment would be dependent on the extent of individualization of that work, and consequent opportunity for the gifted child to work at his or her own independent academic level. The following teacher implied that Angela did work at her own level,

Angela, middle school, year 4

> The curriculum she follows is the same as the rest of the class, although when we do projects she does something more academic.

Geography and history lends itself to children working to their own ability.

Many different methods of project organization were observed, not all of which complied with the notion of enrichment. For example, the teachers of Peter; Angela; Tony and Mandy; and Dennis, had the whole class doing the same work off the blackboard; or the children summarized what the teacher said, which was then put into a project book. Lilo and Kathy's teacher had a pile of books, with work cards attached to each one. These cards varied in ability level according to the reading requirements of each book. Unless a card was made which was academically suited to the gifted child, then this would not comply with the definition of enrichment. The teachers of Sylvia, Les, George and Laurence; Ann and Ken; and Jo and Nicholas, provided a pile of books on a project subject, and allowed the children to choose and work with the ones that interested them. This may be closer to what might be considered to be enrichment, although to be categorized as such the books would need to be of a suitable academic standard.

Ann and Ken, middle school, year 1

"Topic" is the main area in which we can stretch them because we have lots of stretching topic books. It is only "Topic" that keeps them going at their own level. It can happen that they repeat at secondary school. If they are gifted they have to put up with a lot of repetition which is a shame because they are the cream of the country.

'Project' work was therefore an area of the curriculum which was claimed by three teachers to stretch their gifted children. Renzulli differentiated clearly between project work and enrichment, which he felt should be qualitatively different in the instructional process. The ultimate type of enrichment, he claimed, should aim for original research using appropriate investigative techniques in an area which was of interest to the child. Renzulli was discussing enrichment at high school level, though most of what he said may be considered appropriate for children from the third year of middle school (Renzulli, 1977). Observation indicated that the amount of extension provided by many of the teachers may be considered to be limited. As in first schools, this may be because of the extra demand made on the teacher in the preparation of project materials, plus an expectation that if the children are gifted, they will produce work of an exceptional standard without being given extra initially. What would seem like an excellent opportunity of enrichment by depth or breadth, when the whole class was involved in project work, in fact did not necessarily appear to be used as such.

There was a particularly interesting finding in mathematics. Nine of the children in five classes worked on SMP, KMP (notes 6 and 7, Chapter 2) or a scheme developed by a teacher. When these schemes were used, the gifted children had the opportunity of working in advance of the rest of the class, as indicated by the fact that at least one child in each class did so. In another six classes involving eleven children mathematics was done with the use of books, such as the *Alpha Beta* books. In all but Ann's and Ken's cases the classes were normally divided into two groups, and the gifted children worked with approximately half of their class on the identical or nearly identical page. Ann and Ken were the exception in that they were permitted to progress through the book at their own speed, though this could create problems for subsequent teachers unless they also operated with this individualized system,

Ann and Ken, middle school, year 1

They work on 'Alpha'. They can then go at their own individual pace. The middle group keep together because they need more teaching, though I let them go on of course. Some need a great deal of help. It is a matter of looking at them as individuals. If they get ahead in maths it's difficult for the next teacher unless they have extra help. It is inevitable that they will have some of their time wasted. This applies to highly intelligent children as well.

Their teacher was finding that the two children were progressing so fast that they were going to run out of work, and she was going to have to go to the teacher of the next class to get appropriate books.

Although the 'Alpha' scheme was being used in Angela's class, and although her teacher stated that she did harder work than the rest of the class, observation indicated that she was doing the same work as a small group. The rationale that this teacher had for not allowing anyone to work too far in advance was as follows:

Angela, middle school, year 4

(About Alpha mathematics books) It assumes streaming. Where one has different abilities one has to go over it together because it is so difficult. Possibly one could allow Angela and a few others to do it alone, but there is no point in going over hard things several times individually.

Angela was obviously considered by the group of girls with whom she worked to be more able than themselves, because they consulted her when they were in difficulties.

It would appear that the extent of circumstantial enrichment in mathematics, in the form of working in advance of the rest of the class, was partly dependent on the scheme followed, as the materials provided both structure constraints and limitations upon the teachers' thinking. The mathematics curriculum which consisted of individualized and self-marking work cards, which also attempted to be as self-explanatory as possible, seemed to be more conducive for the teacher in encouraging self-paced work than a curriculum presented in book form. Many of these points were made in the Cockcroft Report, which stated that specific provision should be made for mathematically able primary school children. It was considered inappropriate that they should only be allowed to work through books or workcards on their own and/or be given extra examples of the same type of problems. It was suggested that they should be allowed to make more rapid progress through the syllabus, combined with more demanding work related to it, and that they should have the opportunity to develop powers of generalization and abstraction (G.B., DES, 1982).

Straker stated that children who are able mathematically should be provided with opportunities to investigate topics outside the normal mathematics curriculum. Her book contains a variety of sources for stimulus materials to be used for such topic work. The investigation by pupils would be preferable in small groups in order to encourage interaction and discussion, but at the same time permit the development of individuals within the group (Straker, 1982). This form of enrichment was not observed in any of the research schools.

SRA is similar to SMP in that it is a scheme intended to improve reading skills, and uses work cards at several ability levels. The children work through these cards at their own speed. The scheme also includes some class activities. The advantages for gifted children with the scheme are the same as those mentioned in the discussion concerning mathematics above. SRA was observed in use in three classes (Jo and Nicholas had already finished it). In two classes Benny and Lilo were working ahead of the other children. The use of SRA can only be a form of circumstantial enrichment if the gifted are permitted to progress more rapidly than the other children. In Tony and Mandy's class extensive advancement was prevented, as the two children were used as monitors.

Tony and Mandy, middle school, year 3

All the children are doing SRA cards including what turn out to be the monitors, who finish first.
Sharon puts her hand up, Mandy goes and says, "Are you stuck?" and then helps her.
Gary has his hand up.
Mandy is going around the class giving out people's cards and special coloured crayons. When someone puts up their hand they are attended to by Paul, Mandy or Tony, who have their names on the boxes of crayons, and whose duty it is to find the relevant answer card.
Mandy helps Rachel.
M-T Rachel's got a problem and I can't sort it out.

The teacher gives the card she was about to put away to Mandy who puts it back in the box.

Mandy then goes back to help Sharon.

Angela calls Mandy over to get her help on a question.

The teacher asks Mandy to put a large pile of cards back in the box.

M-the author-I like doing this

After Mandy has done the cards, Angela calls her over to help again.

Sharon asks Mandy to help her with some of her work that she got from the remedial teacher.

At another school, children of the same age were observed to do two cards during a lesson, and the children helped themselves from the box. The lesson was very smooth without the use of monitors, and quiet enough for the teacher to have a small group out for conversation. The use of gifted or able children as monitors in this way raises the question of the relative importance of their intellectual development or the development of their social skills. As monitors they are in a position of responsibility, and they have the opportunity to use this position in a constructive manner. However, there are other opportunities within the social life of the school for these skills to be developed in a way which may be considered to have a less dampening effect on the intellectual advancement of the children.

Scrutiny of the data indicated that out of a total of twenty middle school children (excluding Geoff and Adrian) there were seven children in three classes for whom no enrichment was observed to be provided. In these cases the teachers themselves raised several issues which they considered to be important, such as holding gifted children back academically, boredom on the part of the children, and the repetition of work.

Angela has already been discussed, and was provided with enrichment according to her class teacher in geography and history project work. But Angela's French teacher taught in an extremely didactic manner. During her interview, she raised the question of the extent to which gifted children should be held back by the academic standard of the rest of the class,

Angela, middle school, year 4

[Her French] is very good. You only have to tell her something once and she remembers it. She initially had a handicap because when she arrived at the school the others had done two terms. Instead of being left behind she caught up and overtook them. *She would be fluent by now if she could go at her own pace* (author's emphasis). She only glances at the work for a test each week and always gets full marks, every little accent is correct. She is a gifted pupil as you have probably guessed. (French teacher)

Mandy and Tony's teacher stated that she was aware that some of the work was too easy for the children. The question of boredom was also raised by some teachers,

Pat, middle school, year 3

> I find that I give them so much to do I don't think he's bored. I aim at his standard rather than the others. He rarely finishes the work completely because he just gets more to do.

Pat's teacher was fairly confident that the boy was not bored. The next teacher had more complex feelings regarding the subject,

Sylvia, Les, Laurence and George, middle school, year 3

> There are some children who are impatient because they are aware and because they are bored, and as soon as that arises it is an indicator that you are not doing the right things for them. Sylvia is a case in point. I very often feel that I'm not giving her what she needs. That's it partly, but what I'm expecting of her is what she doesn't want. I feel that it's better for her that she should be doing one thing or another, because I realise that there are things that she should be doing. She's all right with me, but I found that with other people on the staff it creates tension, and she will refuse something, really obstinate. I haven't come across that but [mentions three women teachers] they've all said the same thing about her. They cannot get her to do things that they want her to do, because she's so obstinate. She's not like that with me, but I've realised that there are a lot of things that she won't do as well as she could because she's not involved. She just does them, but she feels that it's not what she ought to be doing.

It would appear that Sylvia gave her teacher an impression of not being totally satisfied, and therefore not working as well as she might. This teacher was very keen on gifted children following the same curriculum as the rest of the class, but extending it,

> I would say that [the curriculum] is a matter of *extension*. I would prefer it that way. I like to feel that they are doing what the others are doing in the same context that the others are doing it, but carrying it that much further themselves. I think that there are arguments for saying that they should have a special curriculum, but I like to feel that they are tackling the problems that other children are tackling but with their own abilities taking them perhaps a stage further.

However, from what he said about Les, this extension could be interpreted as repeating work already done, but with a different emphasis or interpretation.

> Whereas Les may know this while thinking that he ought to be doing something else, will make the best of it, because he's matured to that extent. He realises "Oh well, it's something that I've done before, but I can get something out of it by doing it". He's actually said so when I've tackled him on something that he's done in maths for instance, he's said, "Well, I've done it before, but I haven't actually done it in quite that way, but I did see that there was something to be got out of it". With him I make a point of asking him if it's something that he's thoroughly happy about because he's one of those who I don't want to be bored, he must be active.

The teacher appeared to differentiate between Sylvia and Les with regard to boredom, and was more concerned that Les should not be bored. This may have been because Les was more co-operative in doing work that was not what he wished to be doing. There would seem to be two factors within the teacher's rationalization of not making an enrichment provision for his gifted children, one being that there were several bright children in the class (it was a streamed class), and the other that they should not be treated differently for social reasons.

> They can have social problems I think, and they could certainly have problems if they were not extended, if they're bored. I think very often it depends on the way the class is organised. I'm fortunate in having several bright children who support each other. There are some bright children I have had in the past who ... because other children recognised them as being different, and treat them differently, and not always in a way that's good for them. Not in a theoretical sense but they give them a feeling that they are not normal. We're normal children, and he's something different, and one can expect him to be different, which is not always good for a child. *A child who is gifted should not be treated as though they are gifted.* (author's emphasis)

The teacher seemed to feel that if the gifted children were treated differently in their curriculum from the other children that it would lead to social difficulties on the part of the gifted children, which he used as a rationalization for not making special provision for the children. He also took into consideration the emotional problems of the children, and treated them accordingly,

> It very much depends on how they are emotionally, and how they get on with other children ... he's [Laurence] a skiver, a born skiver. He'll get away with it and enjoy it. I ought to, but I don't to the same extent, I don't put the same pressure on him that I would do on Les, because they're two different types. In some ways I think that Laurence deserves the pressure but I realise that the emotional difficulties that

he has, pressure's not the best thing for him. He ought to have more than he's got, but he can't stand a lot of pressure.

This particular teacher was extremely aware of the children as individuals, and appeared to have a complexity of dilemmas concerning the treatment of the children. He did not wish the children to be bored – but he wanted them to be extended – and it depended on what the other children in the class were like – and on the emotional status of the child involved. The teacher's perceptions of giftedness were extremely complex and comprehensive, and he had obviously thought about each individual child. His policy concerning the gifted children doing the same curriculum as the whole class was observed. However, it was not obvious that the abilities of the children necessarily 'took them a stage further' as the teacher had hoped.

Returning to the gifted and non gifted groups, three of the children who had been delabelled as gifted did not receive enrichment, Pat, Mandy and Tony. As with Karl in the first school, the teachers concerned taught in a very didactic manner. Mandy and Tony's class were doing a project, but it was organized in a way that appeared to prevent the children from doing their own research.

The fact that children in first and middle schools who were not labelled by their teacher as gifted were still given the opportunity of enrichment, emphasizes the circumstantial element of the provision. It was there for all children who were able to benefit by working faster than the other children. This need not mean that it was necessarily restricted to, nor particularly appropriate for the gifted children.

To conclude, in an LEA where no official policy exists for educational provision for gifted children, the main method which is available to teachers is enrichment, unless there is an intra-school withdrawal group.[2] Several points can be delineated from the descriptions of the enrichment provided for the children in the sample.

On the whole, the provision of specific enrichment was negligible, and circumstantial enrichment predominated. Teachers who used schemes which were individualized in their ideology were more able to provide opportunity for the children to be extended, particularly in first schools. However, for children to progress at a faster pace than the rest of the class is not necessarily the optimum position. Breadth enrichment, where children extend their knowledge of an area, is also favourable. This would be particularly suitable in project work, but it was not observed to take place. For able children to be able to make the most of project work, their study skills need to be developed. Extensive reference materials (not necessarily in the school) need to be made available for the children. The burden of providing suitable work for the gifted children is lessened in project work if the children have the relevant skills, and materials on which to use those skills. Many of the teachers questioned the suitability of the work that they were providing for their gifted children, as stated by Bennett,

To understand classroom learning is to understand children's progressive performances on tasks teachers assign to them. To understand the degree to which teaching prospers learning it is necessary to question the degree to which work assigned is appropriate to the pupil and to explain any shortfall in optimal appropriateness (Bennett et al, 1981, page 23).

Notes

1. The teachers appeared to use the words topic and project interchangeably. Project work is a teaching method in which a topic is approached from a number of angles. Ideally, it can cut across traditional subject divisions and involve pupils actively in the solving of problems. A single project may be studied by just one child, a whole class, or an entire school. Its study may be periodic, for example once a week for a term, or take up most of the child's time over a set period.
2. Intra school withdrawal groups did not exist in the LEA in which the study was conducted.

5   Gifted Children in the Classroom

The previous chapter considered the transactional setting in which the interaction between teachers and gifted children occurred. It looked at the educational provision that was made for the gifted children which was similar and dissimilar to that of their classmates. This chapter is concerned with four main areas. The first is the interactions between teachers and gifted children compared with those between teachers and the other children. As indicated by Garner and Bing, teachers do not necessarily distribute their contacts with children in the class equally (Garner and Bing, 1973). The second is the allocation of contacts between children and the intentions that the teachers stated that they had concerning the distribution of their time. As stated by Withall, the intentions that a teacher has with regard to distributing attention are not necessarily carried out in practice (Withall, 1956). The differentiation of disciplinary contacts with gifted children as compared to the other children is followed by a study of the concentration of the gifted children on written tasks.

The data for this chapter consist of three main types: a numerical count of the interactions that occurred between teachers and children; interviews with teachers; and transcripts of lessons, thereby combining quantitative and qualitative data (see the Appendix).

Figures 12 for first schools and 13 for middle schools show the interactions that took place between the teachers and the gifted children in the form of the number of interactions which occurred with the gifted children above or below the mean for each class.[1]

The analysis of the data indicated that teachers and gifted children tended to have more interactions than the mean number of interactions for the whole class. That is to say, gifted children tended to have a greater number of contacts with their teachers than average. This tendency for gifted children and teachers to interact more frequently was found to be significant for first and middle schools (at the levels of $p < 0.01$ and $p < 0.001$ respectively). However, within the general tendency there was also considerable variation between the individual gifted children. This ranged from -4.9 below the mean to $+30.4$

Figure 12   The number of total, teacher-initiated, child-initiated, and disciplinary
interactions between teachers and gifted children above or below the
mean of the class in first schools

Year Name		Total interactions	Teacher-initiated interactions	Child-initiated interactions	Disciplinary interactions
1	Arthur	+2.7	0.0	+2.7	0.0
2	Ricky	−0.5	+0.6	−1.1	−0.2
	{ David	+1.1	+1.9	−0.8	+0.6
	{ Don	−4.9	+0.9	−5.8	−0.4
	Karl	+15.5	+1.8	+13.7	−0.5
	{ Rita (1)	+5.0	+1.4	+3.6	+0.9
	{ Rita	+1.5	+0.2	+1.4	+1.4
3	Robert	+16.8	+16.2	+0.6	+9.3
	Mary	+3.0	+1.4	+1.5	−0.3
	{ Jim-morning (2)	+8.4	+0.9	+7.5	+0.5
	{ Jim-afternoon	+9.2	+1.3	+7.9	−0.1
4	[Maggy	+5.3	+8.0	−2.3	−0.5
	Hugh (3)	−1.3	+1.0	−2.3	−1.4
	{ Rosemarie	+3.3	−1.0	+2.7	−1.5
	Keith	+0.3	+2.0	−1.3	−1.5
	[Liz (4)	−0.4	−0.4	0	−0.2
	Benny	+30.4	+6.0	+24.1	−0.2
Level of significance		**	***	*	

(1) There were different numbers of children in the morning and the afternoon.
(2) Jim had a different teacher in the morning and the afternoon.
(3) Hugh was absent during one of the interaction observation periods.
(4) Liz was absent for two of the interaction observation periods. The total of the number of
interactions available for her is therefore low, and the reliability of her scores is more
questionable than those for the other children.

Wilcoxon matched-pairs signed-ranks test, one tailed, significant at levels of *$p < 0.05$,
**$p <$ to 0.01, and ***$p < 0.001$.[2]

above the mean in first schools, and −4.9 below the mean to +25.6 above the
mean in middle schools.

The data were further analyzed to show the interactions that were initiated
by the teachers with all their children as compared with the gifted children.
The tendency for the number of interactions occurring with the gifted children
to be above the norm for the class was found to be significant for first and
middle schools (at the levels of $p \leqslant 0.001$ and $p < 0.001$ respectively).
However, the range of scores among the group of gifted children was
considerable. An attempt will be made to account for some of these variations
later.

There was an overall and significant tendency for the gifted children in
both types of schools to initiate more contacts with their teachers than the
norm for their class (at the level of $p < 0.05$ for both first and middle schools).
Furthermore, there were some interesting differences in the ratios of the

Figure 13   Number of total, teacher-initiated, child-initiated, and disciplinary interactions between teachers and gifted children above or below the mean of the class in middle schools

Year Name		Total interactions	Teacher-initiated interactions	Child-initiated interactions	Disciplinary interactions
1	Sandy	+7.1	+6.5	+1.6	+0.8
	Vicky	+1.1	+2.5	−0.4	−0.2
	Peter	+15.3	+6.8	+8.5	+3.1
	Ann	+11.3	+9.2	+3.2	+1.1
	Ken	+2.3	+2.2	+0.2	−1.9
	Lilo	+14.9	+8.2	+6.7	+1.6
	Kathy	+7.9	+3.2	+4.7	+0.6
	Benny	+23.1	+10.9	+12.5	+1.7
	Hank	−4.9	−2.1	−2.7	−1.2
3	Laurence	+2.2	+2.8	−0.7	+1.6
	Les (1)	+1.2	−0.2	+1.3	−0.4
	George	+25.2	+11.8	+13.3	+7.6
	Sylvia	−0.8	−0.2	−0.7	−0.4
	Jo	+3.3	+3.2	+0.1	−0.6
	Nicholas	+1.3	−0.8	+2.1	+1.4
	Mandy (2)	+3.5	−1.7	+2.7	−0.4
	Tony	−2.1	−1.6	−0.6	+0.4
	Pat	+3.1	+3.1	0.0	0.0
	Christopher	+25.6	+9.3	+15.3	+8.2
4	Angela	+5.0	+5.1	−0.1	−0.1
	Dennis	+1.7	+2.0	−0.4	−0.1
Level of significance		***	***	*	*

(1) There was a long gap in the observation of this class while the teacher was ill. On his return the author was reluctant to do much interaction observation as the teacher was still weak. The reliability of the scores for these children is therefore questionable, though supported by transcripts.

(2) Mandy was absent for some of the observation time.

Wilcoxon matched-pairs signed-ranks test, one tailed, significant at levels of *p < 0.05, **p < 0.01, and ***p < 0.001.[2]

teacher-initiated/child-initiated interactions between first and middle schools. In first schools both types of interaction were almost equal. The mean of teacher-initiated interactions with all children was 91.7, and the mean of teacher-initiated interactions with all children was 78.1. In middle schools the teacher-initiated interactions with all children were approximately two and a half times as frequent as the interactions initiated by all the children in the class (the means being 114.4 and 43.6 respectively). This probably reflects the overall pedagogical differences between first and middle schools. As children become older they are expected to conform to more rigorous procedures and rules of interactive conduct. They are also gradually socialized into more passive pupil roles. This pattern applies to the gifted children as much as to the rest.

When a comparison is made between the percentage of teacher attention available for all children, if distributed equally, and the percentage of time[3] occupied by or with the gifted child, there are some interesting results, as shown in figures 14 and 15 for first and middle schools respectively.[4] In first and middle schools the total percentage of interactions was greater for the gifted children than might have been expected if the teacher divided her contacts equally among all the members of the class. In first schools the interactions with the gifted children were 3.8 per cent greater (significant at the level of $p < 0.01$) and in middle schools 5.4 per cent greater (significant at the

Figure 14   *Teacher time available per child, total teacher/gifted child interactions, teacher-initiated/gifted child interactions, and gifted child-initiated/teacher interactions given as percentages for first schools*

Year	No. of children in class	Name of gifted child	Teacher time available per child	Total interactions with gifted child	Teacher initiated interactions with gifted child	Interactions initiated by gifted child
1	22	Arthur	4.5%	6.9%	0.0	6.9%
2	20	Ricky	5.0%	4.6%	7.1%	3.9%
	21	{ David	4.8%	5.2%	6.5%	4.2%
	21	{ Don	4.8%	2.8%	5.6%	0.7%
	22	Karl	4.5%	9.4%	5.3%	19.1%
	31	{ Rita (1)	3.2%	19.4%	10.0%	36.4%
	19	{ Rita	5.3%	6.7%	5.7%	7.2%
3	24	Robert	4.2%	9.9%	14.0%	4.7%
	24	Mary	4.2%	6.6%	6.5%	6.8%
	26	{ Jim-morning (2)	3.8%	12.9%	5.5%	23.7%
		{ Jim-afternoon		16.7%	6.8%	32.1%
4	24	⎡ Maggy	4.2%	7.1%	10.9%	0.0
	24	⎢ Hugh (3)	4.2%	3.3%	5.2%	0.0
	24	⎨ Rosemarie	4.2%	6.0%	5.0%	8.9%
	24	⎢ Keith	4.2%	4.3%	5.9%	1.8%
	24	⎣ Liz (4)	4.2%	2.9%	3.0%	0.0
	33	Benny	3.0%	17.1%	7.6%	28.1%
Mean			4.5%	8.3% (5)	6.5% (5)	10.9% (5)
Level of significance				**	***	

(1) There were different numbers of children in the morning and the afternoon.
(2) Jim had a different teacher in the morning and the afternoon.
(3) Hugh was absent during one of the interaction observation periods.
(4) Liz was absent for two of the interaction observation periods. The total of the number of interactions available for her is low, and the reliability of her scores is more questionable than those for the other children.
(5) Equivalent of 17 classes.

Wilcoxon matched-pairs signed-ranks test, one tailed, significant at the level of **$p < 0.01$, ***$p < 0.001$.[2]

Figure 15   Teacher time available per child, total teacher/gifted child interactions, teacher-initiated/gifted child interactions, and gifted child-initiated/teacher interactions given as percentages for middle schools

Year	No. of children in class	Name of gifted child	Teacher time available per child	Total interactions with gifted child	Teacher initiated interactions with gifted child	Interactions initiated by gifted child
1	32	{ Sandy	3.1%	6.9%	8.8%	5.3%
	32	{ Vicky	3.1%	3.7%	5.3%	2.6%
	31	Peter	3.2%	7.4%	5.9%	10.9%
	31	{ Ann	3.2%	9.2%	8.3%	15.4%
	31	{ Ken	3.2%	4.3%	4.4%	3.8%
	35	{ Lilo	2.9%	8.9%	6.9%	17.8%
	35	{ Kathy	2.9%	6.0%	4.4%	13.3%
	35	{ Benny	2.9%	12.5%	10.4%	15.6%
	35	{ Hank	2.9%	0.8%	1.4%	0.0
3	33	⌈ Laurence (1)	3.0%	6.6%	10.5%	0.0
	33	| Les	3.0%	4.9%	2.6%	8.7%
	33	| George	3.0%	44.4%	34.2%	60.9%
	33	⌊ Sylvia	3.0%	1.6%	2.6%	0
	24	{ Jo	4.2%	7.1%	7.7%	4.8%
	24	{ Nicholas	4.2%	5.4%	3.3%	14.3%
	34	{ Mandy (2)	2.9%	7.8%	2.4%	30.0%
	34	{ Tony	2.9%	1.7%	1.1%	2.3%
	31	Pat	3.2%	8.6%	8.6%	0.0
	29	Christopher	3.4%	17.3%	9.8%	76.2%
4	36	Angela	2.8%	9.9%	10.3%	0.0
	27	Dennis	3.7%	5.1%	7.5%	3.1%
Mean			3.2%	8.6%	7.4%	13.6%
Level of significance				***	***	**

(1) There was a long gap in the observation of this class while the teacher was ill. On his return the author was reluctant to do much interaction observation as the teacher was still weak. The reliability of the scores for these children is therefore questionable, though they are supported by transcripts.
(2) Mandy was absent for some of the observation time.

Wilcoxon matched-pairs signed-ranks test, one tailed, significant at the level of **p < 0.01, and ***p < 0.001.[2]

level of p < 0.001). The gifted children received significantly more contacts started by the teacher (at the level of p < 0.001 in first and middle schools). However, the gifted child initiated contacts were not significant in first schools whereas they were in middle schools (at the level of p < 0.01).

The percentages highlight further aspects of the different school experience that some gifted children would appear to have in terms of their interactions with their teachers as compared with that of the 'average' member of the class. This point will be expanded below.

These results coincide with those of Good et al. However, their study was concerned with older children in America. They found that,

> student achievement level influenced the quality and quantity of classroom interaction. High achievement students ... were more active participants, received more teacher contacts, and generally obtained more positive feedback than low achievement students ... High achievement students initiated more comments and questions and they received more open questions, process questions, and product questions. They also called out more answers, initiated more contacts with the teacher, and received more total response opportunities (Good et al, 1973, page 79).

By contrast, the ORACLE study of Galton et al indicated that the interactions between the teachers and children in three achievement groups was almost identical. They stated that,

> while the weaker pupils are more likely to be helped individually than the other two groups, the teacher's attention is equally divided between all three achievement groups. No single group is either favoured or discriminated against (Galton et al, 1980, page 65).

In the ORACLE study the children were allocated to the three groups of high, medium and low ability according to the results of tests of basic skills.

The divergence in the results of the ORACLE study as compared with Good et al and the present study may be embedded in the variation in research methodologies. ORACLE and Good et al were comparing children of three levels of ability, low, medium and high achievers. The present study looked at particular members of the last group, a select category within the group of high ability. While ORACLE designated their pupils to achievement groups according to the results of pre-tests and Good et al allocated the children according to a list of expected achievement supplied by the teacher, this research used children that had been labelled by the school and/or teacher as gifted. It seems likely that it is teacher perception of ability that directly affects the quantity of teacher initiated interactions. ORACLE would not necessarily have revealed this aspect, as their methodology selected a cross section of children which may not have replicated the ability groups as perceived by the teachers. Secondly, Good *et al* counted all the interactions that took place between the teachers and all the children. ORACLE was interested in eight particular children per class, but the teacher did not know which ones. In this study the teachers knew that the interest was in a specific child or children, but did not know that the contacts between themselves and all the children was being counted. It may therefore be considered that the data were distorted by researcher presence, although the ignorance of the teachers concerning what was happening should have partially compensated.

There are two conclusions which may be reached concerning the interactional pattern of the classroom by examination of the differences between the present and Good et al's research compared with that of ORACLE. That teacher awareness of which children are being observed affects the behaviour of the teacher and/or that the perception of the teacher about the academic ability of the children concerned is an important factor in interactional sequences.

The discussion now turns to the two groups of gifted children which were developed in Chapter 2. The gifted were children labelled by their present teacher as gifted; and the non gifted were children who had been decategorized by their present teacher, but had been considered gifted by their past teacher or were considered gifted by the school as a result of labelling by their headteacher or the educational psychologist.

Figures 16 for first and 17 for middle schools compare the interactions between the teachers and the two groups of gifted children, gifted and non gifted. There were no significant differences at the first school level, but in the middle schools the tendency for teachers to initiate interactions with the gifted as opposed to the non gifted group was significant (at the level of $p < 0.05$). At middle school level, then, there would appear to have been a difference in the interactive behaviour of teachers between those children whom they perceived to be gifted and those whom they had delabelled as gifted. This raises the question of the relationship between the number of teacher-gifted child interactions and the delabelling of some children. For example, did those children become delabelled because they interacted less with the teacher and were less obvious to her? Or were there fewer interactions because they were treated in the same way as other non gifted children? Or did they behave differently because at this time they were being perceived differently from earlier in their educational careers? Perhaps those children who interacted more with their teachers were more likely to be labelled as gifted initially.

The discussion so far has concentrated on the interactions between teachers and the gifted children as a group, measured in terms of the numbers of interactions that took place. However, the data indicate that there was considerable diversity of interaction within this group of gifted children. The following sections will examine this diversity in some detail, concentrating on the differences between teachers and differences between children. A considerable variety of data will be drawn upon, particularly that of classroom observation, to expand and illuminate what has been mentioned so far.

The quantitative data presented above was collected at times of intensive teacher-children interaction. The qualitative data, on the other hand, was gathered from a variety of classroom situations, when the focus of attention was specifically on the gifted child rather than the total class.

Figure 16 Teacher/gifted child interactions, above and below the mean of the class, and percentages, for gifted and non-gifted groups in first schools

Name of gifted child	No. of total interactions between teacher and gifted child above/below mean of class	No. of teacher-initiated interactions above/below mean of class	No. of gifted child-initiated interactions above/below mean of class	Total interactions with gifted child	Teacher-initiated interactions with gifted child	Interactions initiated by gifted child
Gifted						
Arthur	+2.7	0.0	+2.7	6.9%	0.0	6.9%
Ricky	−0.5	+0.6	−1.1	4.6%	7.1%	3.9%
David	+1.1	+1.9	−0.8	5.2%	6.5%	4.2%
Don	−4.9	+0.9	−5.8	2.8%	5.6%	0.7%
Rita (1)	+5.0	+1.4	+3.6	19.4%	10.0%	36.4%
Rita	+1.5	+0.2	+1.4	6.7%	5.7%	7.2%
Robert	+16.8	+16.2	+0.6	9.9%	14.0%	4.7%
Jim-morning (2)	+8.4	+0.9	+7.5	12.9%	5.5%	23.7%
Maggy	+5.3	+8.0	−2.3	7.1%	10.9%	0.0
Rosemarie	+3.3	−1.0	+2.7	6.0%	5.0%	8.9%
Benny	+30.4	+6.0	+24.1	17.1%	7.6%	28.1%
Hugh	−1.3	+1.0	−2.3	3.3%	5.2%	0.0
Non Gifted						
Karl	+15.5	+1.8	+13.7	9.4%	5.3%	19.1%
Mary	+3.0	+1.4	+1.5	6.6%	6.5%	6.8%
Jim afternoon (2)	+9.2	+1.3	+7.9	16.7%	6.8%	32.1%
Keith	+0.3	+2.0	−1.3	4.3%	5.9%	1.8%
Liz	−0.4	−0.4	0.0	2.9%	3.0%	0.0

The differences between the gifted and non gifted group were not significant.

(1) There were different numbers of children in the morning and in the afternoon.
(2) Jim's morning teacher considered Jim to be gifted, his afternoon teacher perceived Jim to be non gifted.

Teachers' Intentions Regarding Their Distribution of Time

The analysis of the teachers' priorities in terms of how they aimed to distribute their time and attention in the classroom clearly indicated four distinct groups of teachers. These were teachers who saw themselves as primarily concerned with the less able children; or middle ability children; those whose standards were formed by the more able members of the classroom; and those who described themselves as consciously attempting to divide their time equally among all the children.

Figure 17   Teacher/gifted child interactions, above and below the mean of the class, and percentages, for gifted and non-gifted groups in middle schools

Name of gifted child	No. of total interactions between teacher and gifted child above/below mean of class	No. of teacher-initiated interactions above/below mean of class	No. of gifted child-initiated interactions above/below mean of class	Total interactions with gifted child	Teacher-initiated interactions with gifted child	Interactions initiated by gifted child
Gifted						
Sandy	+7.1	+6.5	+1.6	6.9%	8.8%	5.3%
Vicky	+1.1	+2.5	−0.4	3.7%	5.3%	2.6%
Peter	+15.3	+6.8	+8.5	7.4%	5.9%	10.9%
Ann	+11.3	+9.2	+3.2	9.2%	8.3%	15.4%
Ken	+2.3	+2.2	+0.2	4.3%	4.4%	3.8%
Lilo	+14.9	+8.2	+6.7	8.9%	6.9%	17.8%
Laurence	+2.2	+2.8	−0.7	6.6%	10.5%	0.0
Les	+1.2	−0.2	+1.3	4.9%	2.6%	8.7%
George	+25.2	+11.8	+13.3	44.3%	34.2%	60.9%
Sylvia	−0.8	−0.2	−0.7	1.6%	2.6%	0.0
Jo	+3.3	+3.2	+0.1	7.1%	7.7%	4.8%
Christopher	+25.6	+9.3	+15.3	17.3%	9.8%	76.2%
Angela	+5.0	+5.1	−0.1	9.9%	10.3%	0.0
Non Gifted						
Kathy	+7.9	+3.2	+4.7	6.0%	4.4%	13.3%
Benny	+23.1	+10.9	+12.3	12.5%	10.4%	15.6%
Hank	−4.9	−2.1	−2.7	0.8%	1.4%	0.0
Nicholas	+1.3	−0.8	+2.1	5.4%	3.3%	14.3%
Mandy	+3.5	−1.7	+2.7	7.8%	2.4%	30.0%
Tony	−2.1	−1.6	−0.6	1.7%	1.1%	2.3%
Pat	+3.1	+3.1	0.0	8.6%	8.6%	0.0
Dennis	+1.7	+2.0	−0.4	5.1%	7.5%	3.1%
Level of significance	*				*	

Wilcoxon matched-pairs signed-ranks test, one tailed, significant at the level of *p < 0.05.[2]

It will be seen that many of the teachers recognized the discrepancy between their intentions with regard to which children they hoped to concentrate their attention upon and the practicalities of the classroom situation (Berlak and Berlak, 1981; and Pollard, 1980). The teachers appeared to recognize the dynamics of the class, the tensions and dilemmas present which affected their interaction, and the consequent possible unfulfilment of their intentions.

The first group of five teachers were those who taught Maggy, Hugh, Rosemarie, Keith and Liz; Peter; Laurence, Les, George and Sylvia; Angela; and Jim's morning teacher. They intended to concentrate on the less able children in the class, especially in terms of individual help, because these were the children who were seen to have the greatest need.

Teacher of Maggy, Hugh, Rosemarie, Keith and Liz, first school, year 4

I tend perhaps to give my attention to the other end of the spectrum [from the gifted] with individual help. I have those who need my help close to me, and those who don't further away.

At the same time the teachers were well aware of the more able children,

Teacher of Peter, middle school, year 1[5]

Well there's three children, when we're doing English work they're on sentence makers so I try to talk to the rest of the class first and get them working, and then go and see what they're doing, and I know at the moment I do spend quite a lot of time with those 'cos I feel that it's important to get them going. I sort of fluctuate really. But I always try to keep the bright ones with something to do. When they've finished their maths work they do SMP cards and SRA cards which are graded, and they're on a particular colour, because I don't like to see them just sitting there reading a book or something. I mean if there's only five minutes left and it's not worth starting anything else.

The following teacher had an A-stream class, but preferred mixed ability teaching provided that the remedial children were removed.

Teacher of Laurence, Les, George and Sylvia, middle school, year 3

Well, that's always a problem [the distribution of time]. I think it very much depends on pressure. Some years you don't feel that there's pressure and you can organise your time very much more. Where it becomes difficult is when you have in a class ... where there are intelligent children also a number that need a lot of individual help. I prefer to have a mixed group, for social reasons, but it doesn't help if you have to give a lot of time to a very few, so in the mixed group I think it is useful to have children who are very weak excluded for remedial purposes ... because proportionately they take up so much more of your time, and they need it, they deserve it. I believe that the weak ones really should have more of your time and that's what tends to happen in class, that you can forget the needs of the good ones.

This teacher was aware of the ease of allowing the more able children to get on by themselves because of their ability to do so.

> You know that they can get on by themselves, and you know that they can cope with anything that you can give them to do, and you tend to throw things at them because you know they can cope with it, but perhaps not give them enough of your own time. Not helping them necessarily, but letting them know you're interested in what they are doing, that's where I feel that perhaps I don't do enough, but it varies from year to year.

He then discussed the yearly variations of the individual classes and the ability levels of the children within the classes.

> This year I've had what are supposed to an A-class ... only a third of those children are really 'A's and some out of those are high fliers, but the rest are good, average or below, and it's the low ones this year who have taken most of my time. So when you organise your time to help children it depends. The year before last I had a mixed group in which I had one or two really good children, but they were so tranquil as a group, the whole class went so smoothly, that you could distribute your time just as you wanted to. It depends to some degree on what has gone before, some years you feel that the children are so much behind what you expect them to be for their age that you have to put a lot of pressure on them to help them catch up, and in that case a bright child can get lost a little bit because you're trying to maintain your standard with the others, and you don't notice the gap so much with the bright ones.

He then brought the question down to the reactions of individual teachers as well as the number of children in the class.

> It's a bit a matter of awareness and of pressure, and I think that individual teachers react very differently. The pressure in numbers is a great thing, and I'm very much in agreement with a small class environment of family groups and those schools are marvellous, because they all help each other, but the stronger ones don't seem to be handicapped. The kind of atmosphere makes progression seem a natural thing, and the older ones expect to take part in it too and progress themselves.

It would appear that this group of teachers intended to concentrate their attention on the less able children, but remained aware of the gifted children and attempted to keep them occupied.

The second group of two teachers, which included the teachers of Nicholas and Jo; and Sandy and Vicky, were concerned that the middle ability children should not be forgotten as a result of focussing on the bright or remedial child.

Teacher of Nicholas and Jo, middle school, year 3

> Over the week they all get a fair bit [of time]. It happens as it comes. If one concentrates on the bright child, and drag the tail with you, one can miss the average child. One has to watch this. The great mass can be missed.

Sandy and Vicky's teacher had been a remedial teacher and had been instructed by the headteacher to give more attention to the non-remedial children.

Teacher of Sandy and Vicky, middle school, year 1

> I try to give attention to table four [remedial table]. The headteacher had told me to give more attention to the rest of the class and give them occupying things. It is difficult to talk to everybody because they are not on the same wavelength, and don't understand.

At the same time as attending to her less able children, this teacher was conscious that the standard of the whole lesson should not be brought down and that she should attend to the middle ability level,

> With this class there is such a large range of ability that sometimes when one is trying to do something with the class one has to ignore the slower children on the remedial table. I can't give them so much attention or I find that the others miss out. I have to concentrate on the middle lot. *I have to be careful not to bring the lesson down to their level.* On the other hand I have to make sure they understand. There is a lot that they can't do. (Conversation in the classroom)

The prominence that this had for the teacher was made apparent by her repetition of the emphasized sentence later in the conversation. However, she considered that gifted children should have special attention because of the use that they could be to society,

> I would think that we should offer the equivalent benefit to gifted children as to remedial children. We should concentrate on gifted children more because they will be of benefit to us. (Conversation in the classroom)

The third group consisted of three teachers, those of Benny and Hank; Lilo and Kathy; and Pat. They did not state that they aimed to give more of their time to the more able children, but, for example, one teacher considered gifted children to be entitled to as much time as the remedial child,

Teacher of Benny and Hank, middle school, year 1

I feel that a lot of time is spent on remedial children, and not enough on the gifted. I would like to see more done for them, especially as there is a tendency to get bored leading to bad behaviour.

The other two teachers reported that they tried to bring the standards of the whole class up to the level of the most able, whch is reflected in the following quotation from one of the teachers,

Teacher of Pat, middle school, year 3

I aim at his [Pat's] standard rather than the others.

The final group of four teachers, which included the teachers of Don and David; Ann and Ken; Mary; and Robert, were concerned to distribute their time equally among all the children, as with the following teacher, who was conscious of both ends of the ability spectrum,

Teacher of Ann and Ken, middle school, year 1

[I distribute my time] according to need. One has to be very careful not to spend too much time on the backward ones. I try to give the bright ones a fair amount of attention.

In the first schools time allocation was closely involved with hearing children read. The following teacher had a reading rota which enabled her to give individual attention to all the children,

Teacher of Mary, first school, year 3

I teach in a class situation, but not a lot of that, in a group situation and according to the needs of the children. There are children who demand a lot of time, but I try to make notes of children who need to be sorted out, and need individual attention, but of course the larger the class the more difficult it is. By starting with a different group for reading each day, at least you know that whilst they're working as a group, that first group, they're all going to get their individual attention, so working that rota helps, subject-wise and child-wise to give particular children particular attention on a particular day.

Robert's teacher heard her very poor readers every day,

Teacher of Robert, first school, year 3

You obviously try to give an equal amount of time to every child, but whether one does or not is very difficult. I try with reading, I do think reading is important, and the poor readers ... I usually try to hear every day of the week, whereas the better readers, I really do try and spend a bit of time with those ... if I look at my reading register I do see those every day of the week because I do feel that that is important.

So this teacher concentrated in part on the less able children, whilst her more able children appeared to get less individualized attention in reading, but this was in order to enable them to speed ahead,

The others I will often have two readers each side of me, which isn't a good idea perhaps, but on the other hand I do feel that they ought to get on with their reading and get on to new reading books and it's just a question of you can't hear every child read every day on their own, and also listen to their little bits of chat.

She clearly felt herself to be pulled in several directions,

So I do with number and reading spend a little bit more time with the slow ones, but on the other hand perhaps it depends how one's feeling, if you have a guilty day and you feel oh dear those slow ones aren't getting on, and so one ... then you spend more time with them, and then you suddenly feel oh dear the red table are ready to go onto something else, so you forget about those. It's very difficult, you try obviously to spend time with everybody, and I do try.

This teacher was also conscious of the needs of her gifted child,

I'm always aware of Robert and what he's doing, and I sort of feel, is he doing something that is sort of worthwhile and stretching him and keeping him occupied and whatever? Sometimes I have to think he's getting on and he's got through several reading books, and he's doing the Ladybird work cards, he's learnt his tables, and this sort of thing. After seven or eight weeks I can't work miracles.

Remarks such as 'I can't work miracles' and 'There never seem to be enough hours in the day' epitomize the problems that first school teachers had concerning hearing their children read as frequently as possible, plus the scarcity of themselves as a resource for all their children. This was further illustrated by Don and David's teacher,

Teacher of Don and David, first school, year 2

There never seems to be enough hours in the day. Even when I only had thirteen in the class when there was a chicken pox epidemic, there still seemed to be days when I didn't get round to everybody. It's just impossible I think. I try desperately to hear them read every day. More often than not it doesn't work, so the ones I don't hear the previous day I hear the next day, or certain children that I feel are at a crucial stage, just on to another book, or just ready to start another book, I would perhaps give extra time to, or a particularly good reader or one that's very confident I might not hear for two days, and then I'd hear half a book from, but I do try desperately to hear them every day, in some form or other. It might not be necessarily from their reading book, like this morning it was from their 'Breakthrough' folders, hearing their sentences. Some days I manage it quite easily, and other days I don't.

There was a feeling from this group of teachers of considerable pressure and consciousness of the probable impossibility of fulfilling their intention of providing for each individual on an equal basis as much as they could have liked.

Generally, the teachers seemed to have priorities concerning how they would like to distribute their time among the children in the class, which placed them into four groups. The differentiation of their opinions concerning their apportionment of their time appeared to be based on considerations of factors such as the range of ability present, and the needs that particular groups or individuals had of their time. Many of the teachers were aware that in relation to the exigencies of the classroom, their best intentions, or priorities, were likely to be diverted.

When the stated priorities of the four groups of teachers are compared to the interaction scores of the gifted children above or below the mean for their class, there are some interesting results.[6] There did appear to be a tendency for the teachers who were particularly concerned with high standards to have a greater mean number of interactions with the gifted children above the class mean. The mean of interactions for this group was +8.8. What was perhaps more surprising was that the next highest mean was for the group which was particularly occupied with the less able child, the mean for this group was +5.3, although this category did include several negative scores.

To examine the intentions of the teachers in isolation would misrepresent the total situation, though in fact many classroom interaction studies do concentrate solely on the teacher. The interactions between teachers and children are reciprocally influenced by the teachers and the children. It might be expected that the teacher generally controls the procedures and consequent allocation of interactions, but at the same time the children also have an element of control, albeit possibly less consequential than that of the teacher. For example, contributing factors could be other competition for interaction in the class; the willingness of specific gifted children to speak or make contact with the teacher; and personality variation among the children, such as introversion and extroversion. It was possible to observe two children, Jim and Benny[7], with two different class teachers. The interaction scores of these two children were similar with different teachers, indicating relative stability in the quantity of interactions that they had from teacher to teacher. Therefore, it is necessary to look at the influence of specific children on the interactions, in order to give a comprehensive perspective of reciprocal interactions in the classroom.

The Dynamics of Reciprocal Interaction

This section will examine individual children and their apparent influence on the interactions that took place. Children who interacted less with their teacher than the mean for their class will be considered, as well as children at the opposite extreme. The behaviour of children will be discussed in varying classroom situations, such as queues and question and answer sequences.

Surveillance of the children with negative interaction scores revealed that all but one, Ricky, were members of classes containing more than one gifted child. The initial assumption might be that in classroom situations, where competition existed for possible interactions with the teachers, and where there was a tendency for gifted children to do well in acquiring access to the scarce resource of teacher contact, then the presence of more than one gifted child resulted in greater competition, with one or more of the gifted children doing less well in it. However, all these children also appeared as negative in figures 12 and 13 under child initiated interactions, which indicated that these children started fewer contacts with their teachers than the mean for their class. When their attitude to school is related to their low child initiated interactions, a definite picture emerges. The WAYG was available for twenty of the gifted children (see the Appendix). Two of the dimensions related to attitude to school – like school versus do not like school, and like school work versus do not like school work. The comparison of positive or negative feelings concerning school with child initiated interaction scores above or below the class mean is given in figure 18. It would appear that those children who had negative feelings about school also initiated significantly fewer interactions with their teacher than the mean for their class, and vice versa.

The question of whether these children disliked school because they did not interact with the teacher, or whether they did not interact because they disliked school, is debatable. One group consisting of Maggy, Hugh and Liz (who was absent for some of the data collection) appeared to boycott their teacher, as their initiation of interactions was zero. On the other hand, they interacted among themselves a great deal, and may therefore not have required as much contact with their teacher.

A serious problem in illuminating the interactive behaviour of the children with low or negative contact scores is that by definition there is little observable material, because the children are silent or relatively silent. However, occasionally a child's low interactive contact could be related to specifically observable behaviour. One such child was Ricky, whose interaction scores

Figure 18   Positive and negative feelings for school and scores of gifted children in initiation of interactions with the teacher above and below the mean for the class

		Schools and School Work	
		Positive	Negative
Initiation of	Above the mean	10	0
Interactions	Below the mean	4	6
Total number of children		14	6

Fisher exact probability test, two tailed, $p < 0.01$

(figure 12) were below the mean of the class, and reflected the low number of contacts that he started with his teacher. In the following extract it can be observed that his *queue* behaviour contributed to this,

Ricky, first school, year 2

The children are doing mathematics workcards, and are going to the teacher to have them corrected in order to go on to the next card. They form a queue at the teacher's desk.

Ricky goes up several times to the wrong part of the queue. Eventually he joins the queue. He stands at point A in the plan, and allows several children to push in front by remaining at the same spot.

Teacher

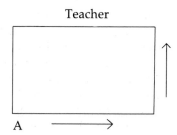

A

Six children push in front of Ricky.

Ricky leaves the queue and goes to collect a card. He is now six places further back from when he started. He still stays at the same corner. Another child pushes in. Ricky does not move around the tables as the queue moves forward. Eventually Ricky reaches the teacher. He does not have an answer written down. He goes to his desk to do it. He returns to the queue. The teacher pulls him out with three other children to use as birds so that another child can count their legs. Ricky does not go back into the queue, but returns to his desk and fiddles with his card.

Ricky rejoins the queue at the correct place, then works his way backwards to corner A, leaving a gap for other children to push in. The children talk about how many cards they have done. Some children have done six cards, Ricky has done one.

The teacher sends Ricky back to his desk for his card. He rejoins the queue at the back. Seven children push in front of him.

Although this type of behaviour was repeated on other occasions, Ricky was observed to act *normally* by going to the back of the queue, and advancing until he arrived at the teacher.

The motivation that some of the gifted children had concerning their work was also revealed in their queue behaviour, in that they pushed into the queue, or went to the opposite side of the teacher from the queue, thereby gaining the attention of the teacher more quickly. Many of the gifted children finished their work faster than the other children. This resulted in more contacts with the teacher because of her looking at their work, and possibly giving them more work. This was exemplified by Arthur, who finished his work quickly and therefore contacted the teacher twice, about his work, as compared to many of the other children, who only completed one piece of work.

Arthur, first school, year 1

The children are doing mathematics from the blackboard. Arthur takes his book up to the teacher because he has finished the work in approximately one minute (addition sums). The teacher gives Arthur some different individual work cards (addition sums).
A-Ian-I have to do some sums.
Ian gets his work marked.
Ian-A-I can do some cards with you now.
A-Ian-Three and three's easy, six.
Ian-A-You're not allowed to do these, they're too easy.
A-Ian-I can.
Arthur is working at twice the speed of Ian, and is picking out the easy sums.
Arthur goes to the teacher when he reaches the bottom of the page, and pushes into the queue.

The overall differentials in speed of work and classroom competence of gifted pupils in the classroom resulted in greater teacher/gifted child interactions in other situations. For example, when the teacher asked questions, the children who knew the answers were obviously in a better position to make a sensible response. For simpler questions, most of the children were potential respondents, but as soon as the questions became harder, the teacher was limited in her choice of respondents, with the gifted child sometimes being her sole possible choice. This may be because the gifted children were the only children in the class to have the knowledge, or because they responded more quickly because of their greater speed of thought or were better able to recall the knowledge. This is shown in the following lesson where the teacher was writing a story on the blackboard for the children to copy, and asking them questions concerning the next sentence as she did so. Frequently Robert was the only child who knew the answer to the question.

Robert, first school, year 3

T-Can anyone tell me anything about the word "knew"?

R-It's got a k in front of it.

T-That's right (and she gives an explanation). As she writes the words on the board she says them out loud, so does Robert rather loudly, some children say it softly.

T-Be careful when you write the word 'people' because it's spelt differently.

R-(CO)*-I know how to do it.

T-I know some of you can do it.

T-Who knows how to spell the word "who" Shelley? (Robert has his hand up)

R-(CO)-The chalk's going double.

T-Yes, I know, it does that sometimes.

T talks about the sentences.

R-(CO)...

T-Sorry?

R-There's seventeen words in that sentence.

T-Yes, it's a long one. That's quite possible Robert.

T-What sort of tools would Jesus have laid down?

R-(only hand up) Carpenters' tools.

T-What sort of tools would they be?

R-Saws, hammers, nails.

Kevin-(CO)-Screwdrivers.

R-Drivers? (pun on drivers)

T-I don't know that they would have screws in those days.

T-Anyone have a go at spelling Nazareth?

Robert is the only child with his hand up.

T-All right Robert.

R-NAZERETH

T-Good, almost.

T-Do you remember where Jesus went?

R-CO-Jerusalem.

T-No.

R-CO-Caperneum.

T-Yes, good.

T-Class. I don't suppose you remember the name of the lake, we haven't mentioned it lately?

R-Galilee (only child with his hand up).

* Calls out

The element of *calling out* in the above extract was observed to be fairly typical, and could be partly attributed to the keenness of the gifted children to answer, and also to the fact that some of them had a *repartee* with the teacher which appeared to allow them to converse with the teacher on relatively equal terms. It would seem in the following extract that Jim followed the conventions when answering a question addressed to the whole class, but called out when the remarks were addressed to. the teacher on a personal basis. The lesson included both Jim and Mary's classes, and was about a television reading programme.

Jim, first school, year 3

Mary (gifted child in another class) comes in hand in hand with her friend.

Boy-(CO)-It's always Grandpa Gripe who gets caught in traps.

T-Well perhaps it's because it serves him right because he's a grumpy old chap.

J-(CO)-Yes perhaps it does.

T-Grey, greasy, gravy made grandad grumpy.

J-(CO)-and repeats what the teacher has said half way through.

T repeats the sentence, and then the whole class repeat it.

T-I have lots of questions.

J-(CO)-Oh good.

T asks a question.

J-(CO)-You're racking our brains this time.

T-Yes, I am racking your brains this time.

Boy-Wrong answer.

J-(Hand up)-ooh-Grotto.

T-Well done. (There is only one other child who has his hand up among all the children in the two classes).

T asks a question.

Ten children answer who have their hands up and get the answer wrong, finally Mary gives the correct answer.

T-Good girl. Give her a clap.

T-I think I'll get loads of grubs and greens brought in. (The children bring items into school beginning with the sound given in the programme).

J-(CO)-You'll get lots of food beginning with "gr".

T-How long would it take to get to Australia in a boat?

Five children give the incorrect answer.

J-Three weeks. (This is acknowledged by the teacher as correct).

Calling out in question and answer situations and pushing in in queues both resulted in a decrease of interactions between teachers and other children, and an increase in those interactions with the gifted children.

Repartee could, especially with older children, border on what might be considered as cheekiness in different circumstances, but was considered acceptable, and encouraged by the teacher of Jo,

Jo, middle school, year 3

At the end of the lesson, as the children leave the classroom, a boy says to the teacher,
B-She won't go out with Jo.
The teacher smiles.
T-Jo-I saw your mother at lunchtime.
Jo-Where, tell me where?
The teacher smiles.
Jo-I want to know where you saw her. Tell me. I'll be naughty.
T-I told her what a naughty boy you are and she's going to beat you when you get home.
The total conversation between the teacher and Jo was lively and cheerful.

Christopher, middle school, year 3

Christopher was the gifted child who had the highest number of interactions with the teacher above the mean for his class. These were equally divided between teacher and child-initiated contacts. His case will be examined in more detail because he illustrates many of the points mentioned in this section, including knowledgeable response to questions, calling out, and behaviour which deviated from that expected of the class. His teacher considered Christopher to be demanding of attention, and stated in the interview that,

To say that he is attention seeking is an understatement. I try to stop it by anticipating and going to him first and getting his things ready. He lives in a closed world...and this tends to make Christopher very self-centred. He can't appreciate other people's point of view.

Christopher received some of his attention by behaving in a *conventional* manner, such as being keen to answer questions, though usually when he put up his hand it was accompanied by a squeaking noise, or he made a remark about the question, which was presumably to gain the attention of the teacher.

T-What is irrigation?
Christopher puts up his hand – OH easy.
C-It's where you get water up with – and locks to send to places like

> Australia where there isn't any.
> T-Why is irrigation a good thing?
> C-Because it helps grass to grow in an area and the cattle and if the lakes dry up the poor fish die etc. etc. (one or two people laugh because he is carrying on and on very fast).

The way in which Christopher extended the answer here was an example of how once he acquired the audience, he would frequently hold on to the floor. He was also observed many times to finish his work in advance of the other children which involved him approaching the teacher with it.

Christopher gained further attention using non-conventional methods such as calling out, which he tended to do in two ways. The first was work orientated, where he wanted information or to answer a question. The second was what might be interpreted as mishearing what was said, or attention seeking. The frequency with which it occurred would seem to indicate the latter explanation.

> T-Class. Before we do maths this morning we'll do English. Don't say I haven't marked it.
> C...
> T-All right Christopher?
> C-You haven't marked it.
> T-What did I just say Christopher?

The final method was one that he used at the beginning of practically every morning and afternoon session. The teacher took the register with the children standing up. Christopher always took this opportunity to read a book, and was the only child in the class to do so. He inevitably did this in a way which verged on insubordination, thereby challenging authority, which might be interpreted as a method of obtaining recognition. For example, when he was meant to be standing at his desk, he would be slouched right over the desk, reading his book. The following extract is typical of the responses he received to his behaviour from his classroom peers and his teacher.

> The teacher takes the register. He tells off two girls.
> Children-Stand up Christopher.
> Lucy-T-He won't stand up.
> Christopher stands up. Two minutes later ...
> T-Stand up children. The longer it takes the longer you'll be standing.
> Christopher stands kicking the chair and making a noise.
> The teacher tells the class off for taking a long time.
> T-Stand up David (Christopher lolls on top of his desk)
> T-Christopher, you'll get a thick ear in a minute.

This section has examined aspects of the interactions between teachers and gifted children, and an attempt has been made to give some explanation for the higher levels of interaction by teachers with these children. Examples were given from individual cases to illustrate various ways in which this appeared to occur. Those children who deviated from the general trend were also examined. It was emphasized that the contacts between individuals were dynamic, and not entirely dependent on the teacher alone, or on the child alone, and the interactions occurred within the environment of the classroom, where many people were present. The next section turns to the discipline of gifted children as compared with the other children.

Gifted Children and Classroom Discipline

As the gifted children generally had more interactive contact with their teacher than the norm for the class, it might be expected that they also had greater disciplinary contacts. Figures 12 and 13 for first and middle schools respectively, given the censorious contacts for gifted children as compared with all children. It can be seen that there were no significant differences in this area between gifted children and other children in first schools, but in middle schools there were considerably more disciplinary contacts with the gifted children (significant at the level of $p < 0.05$).

Some of the extracts from the previous chapters and from the previous section, including those that referred to Robert and Christopher, indicated that there was an element of behaviour, by some of the gifted children, which diverged from that normally expected in the classroom in terms of the norms and expectancies concerning classroom interaction between teachers and children. Examples were, pushing into queues, calling out and so on. Observation revealed many occasions when there was differentiation of discipline for the gifted children. The most obvious was when other children were rebuked for calling out, but the gifted child, who did so frequently, was not. There were occasions when a gifted child and another child were performing identical observable actions, and the gifted child was not told off, whereas the other child was. As pointed out by Hargreaves et al

> ... teachers often ignore deviant acts which are "trivial" on the pragmatic grounds that intervention would disrupt the time-flow of the lesson (Hargreaves et al, 1975, page 240).

The present study would appear to extend beyond the findings of Hargreaves et al, who further discussed the concept of 'avoidance-of-provocation' more in terms of pupils labelled as deviant being regarded negatively by their teachers. The teachers wished to avoid confrontation with these particular pupils, and therefore raised their personal intervention threshold. In the present study, the same phenomena occurred, but apparently for different reasons. The actions of the teachers in situations where they were able to choose to intervene, as a result of mis-behaviour, will be discussed.

The example of Ann which follows shows identical action by two children, resulting in differential discipline,

Ann, middle school, year 1

The author needs a pair of scissors. Ann goes to look for some in a cupboard which is on the other side of the room, together with Stephen (this was an action which was not requested, but was done voluntarily). The teacher enters the room.

T–Why are you not in your place Stephen? You know you should be in your place. What should you be doing? You know what you should do on a Tuesday.

While the teacher is saying this, Ann closes the cupboard door and returns to her desk. She is not rebuked by the teacher despite the fact that she was doing exactly the same as Stephen.

There were further occasions when other children were rebuked or punished for talking, and the gifted children were not, even though they were talking at the same time. There appear to be several possible interpretations of this. The first one might be that because of the reputation of the child, the teacher made an assumption that the talking concerned work. The following child was highly respected and liked by the staff as a very hard working and responsible pupil. The quotations are from notes made on two separate occasions.[8]

Angela, middle school, year 4

Angela and a girl are talking. Someone else who is talking at the same time gets a punishment from the teacher. The teacher sees Angela and a girl talking. She has just two seconds previously given a punishment of copying out work to another child who was talking. She looks at Angela, but ignores the talking.[9]

It was observed that teachers ignored chatting when it came from specific children, which may have been affected by the presence of the author. An alternative explanation could be in terms of teacher strategies for maintaining order. Different children may require different levels of admonition to ensure conformist behaviour. When there are several lawbreakers the teacher, knowing this, may apply sanctions to those whose co-operation is most difficult to attain. In the following example there were five gifted children present. Maggy, Liz and Hugh sat at the same table (the same group who did not initiate contacts with the teacher).

Maggy, Liz, Hugh, Rosemarie and Keith, first school, year 4

The class are doing creative writing. Rosemarie has written three-quarters of a page, Keith has written just over a page, and has finished. There is continual chatting from Maggy's table, but when a girl makes a noise getting up from her chair the teacher turns round and says "ssh". The teacher then tells another child off for talking and fussing.

Hugh has written one and a half lines, Maggy six lines, and Liz nine lines.

Maggy-Hugh-Hold your breath as long as you can without killing yourself.

Maggy, Liz and Hugh tuck their jumpers around the back of their chairs.

Keith has finished his story and is drawing a picture, Rosemarie is on her second page.

The teacher tells off the class, so now there is silence for a short time. Liz starts talking.

The teacher does a general "Ssh" sound. Hugh and Liz ignore this.

T-Liz-I said no talking.

Hugh carries on whispering.

The teacher tells off two boys for talking, and a girl's table, *not* Maggy's table.

Maggy passes air and the children at her table giggle loudly. The teacher looks but says nothing. She sends a girl to the 'Quiet room' for talking.

The girl mouths-It wasn't me.

Maggy starts coughing.

T-You need a drink of water Maggy?

Maggy-No thank you. (Maggy started coughing because she was giggling).

The way that Maggy had of deflecting an incident which might have led to punishment was repeated on other occasions,

> T-You're forgetting what I said about no talking (points at Maggy's table) I don't want to hear what you're saying about Brownies. That sort of talk is for playtime.
>
> The teacher carries on helping Keith. Maggy and Liz continue to talk just as loudly. The teacher turns to them.
>
> Maggy quickly stands up with a tissue to her nose.
>
> T-How are you getting on? How many pages have you done?
>
> Liz-I'm on my third.
>
> T-Good, well done. How about Maggy?
>
> Maggy-I need another tissue.
>
> T-Well, we have plenty of those. Go and get one.
>
> Maggy, Liz and Rosemarie are chatting. The teacher ignores this, but tells off a boy for sharpening a non-school pencil, not working, having a school pencil in his drawer, putting a book in the wrong place, and not working when the teacher is not at her desk.

In a similar way to Maggy's sidestepping trouble, some children had developed techniques of adapting nonconforming behaviour to that which was acceptable to the teacher. For example, Tony frequently spoke to his next door neighbour, but quietly behind his hand. It was obvious enough to be noticed, especially when the room was silent, but was never remarked on by the teacher.

Tony, middle school, year 3

Concentration/distraction transcript (see the Appendix)
The class are writing about their topic in complete silence.
Tony speaks to his next door neighbour behind his hand.
Tony has a conversation about pictures in a book. The teacher looks at them but ignores the conversation.
The two boys are talking about what they are writing.
The teacher looks at them, but ignores them.
The two boys are the only children in the room who are talking. The teacher passes right by them, but ignores their talking.

Presumably the teacher assumed that the conversation was about work, though other children in the class were not allowed to speak.

Finally there was an aspect of expectancy of responsibility and honesty from some of the gifted children by the teachers, epitomized by Ann's teacher during a games lesson.

Ann, middle school, year 1

Ann is limping, she is sent into the classroom to get something to keep her warm as she is no longer doing games. Later another child is sent in to get dressed because he has been naughty. A boy is sent to accompany him because the teacher stated that she did not like the children to be in the room on their own as things disappear. No one was sent to accompany Ann.

A final point from figures 12 and 13 that needs to be mentioned is the increase in significance levels for disciplinary contacts for gifted children from first to middle schools which occurred despite the differential discipline. The majority of the gifted children did not deviate far from the mean for their class, apart from Christopher and George. it would therefore be incorrect to imply any general tendency on the part of these gifted children to become increasingly disobedient or indisciplined as they grew older, indeed ten of the children received no chastizing contacts at all.

It is possible that the lack of response by some teachers to the misbehaviour of some gifted children was caused by the presence of the author. To make an accurate and valid assessment in this area, research would need to be conducted in a situation where the teachers were unaware of the researcher's particular interest in the gifted child.

Concentration and Distraction

This section is concerned with the level of timed concentration versus distraction of the gifted children. The results will be compared with other research. Gifted children with very good or very bad concentration will be examined, followed by a consideration of the differences between the gifted and the non gifted groups.

Figure 19 for first and middle schools shows the distraction time for the gifted children in situations where the whole class were involved in individual, and relatively silent, written work.[10] It was not possible to time other children in each class. In this case, therefore, there is no indication of how far the gifted children aligned with, or deviated from, the norm for their specific class. It was frequently noted, when timing distraction, that the teachers were the most distracting influences in the class, in that they frequently spoke in normal voices, or walked around the room, which sounded very loud in the silence.

Figure 19 indicates that the concentration of gifted children was greater in middle schools compared with first schools, the mean distraction percentages being 20.7 per cent in middle and 33.1 per cent in first schools. There does not appear to be any other comparable published material with which to make direct comparisons concerning what the expected concentration level could be for writing activities. However, there have been three studies concerning classroom task involvement during normal lessons. Boydell observed mathematics lessons in six informal junior classrooms (Boydell, 1975a); Galton et al observed classes which spanned almost the total junior school curriculum for eight children in each of fifty-eight classrooms in nineteen schools (Galton et al, 1980); and Poppleton reported a study of two open plan classrooms (Poppleton, 1975). Boydell found that the average task involvement was 70 per cent when the time spent waiting for the teacher was excluded. Galton et al gave a total distraction figure (page 95) of 24.7 per cent using similar distraction criteria as that used in this study. Poppleton found that when working on projects the children interacted with each other for 25 per cent of the time, which included task and non-task related interactions. She also found that more interaction occurred when the children were working individually than when they were working in pairs or small groups.

In this study concentration/distraction were recorded only during involvement in writing tasks, therefore it might be that the concentration levels here obtained are artificially high when compared with studies that were measuring complete lessons. The gifted children in this study would appear to concentrate slightly better in the middle schools and slightly worse in the first schools than those children in the Galton et al and the Boydell studies. The relatively

Figure 19   *The percentage of time gifted children were distracted while performing written tasks in first and middle schools*

Child	Total time measured	Time distracted	% of total time distracted
FIRST SCHOOLS			
Arthur	15 mins	5 mins 8 secs	34.2%
Ricky	18 mins	2 mins 9 secs	11.9%
David	15 mins	6 mins 46 secs	45.1%
Don	5 mins	22 secs	7.3%
Karl	45 mins	10 mins 3 secs	22.3%
Robert	5 mins	10 secs	3.3%
Mary	13 mins	4 mins 25 secs	39.1%
Jim	13 mins	5 mins 22 secs	41.2%
Maggy	10 mins	3 mins 5 secs	30.8%
Hugh	15 mins	8 mins 26 secs	56.2%
Rosemarie	14 mins	6 mins 8 secs	43.8%
Keith	13 mins	59 secs	7.6%
Liz	16 mins	10 mins 18 secs	64.4%
Benny	29 mins	14 mins 40 secs	51.7%
Mean			33.1%
MIDDLE SCHOOLS			
Sandy	37 mins	16 mins 16 secs	44.0%
Vicky	18 mins	2 mins 10 secs	12.0%
Peter	26 mins	2 mins 32 secs	9.7%
Ann	38 mins	7 mins 42 secs	20.3%
Ken	24 mins	3 mins 25 secs	14.2%
Lilo	32 mins	2 mins 25 secs	7.6%
Benny	9 mins	6 mins	66.7%
Hank	21 mins	15 mins 30 secs	73.8%
Kathy	21 mins	49 secs	3.9%
Laurence	12 mins	1 min 25 secs	11.8%
Les	33 mins	6 mins 19 secs	19.1%
George	7 mins	1 min 45 secs	25.0%
Sylvia	22 mins	4 mins 2 secs	18.3%
Jo	34 mins	9 mins 45 secs	28.7%
Christopher	29 mins	4 mins 46 secs	17.6%
Mandy	20 mins	2 mins 59 secs	14.9%
Tony	20 mins	2 mins 55 secs	14.6%
Pat	25 mins	41 secs	2.7%
Nicholas	32 mins	5 mins	15.6%
Angela	34 mins	7 mins 1 sec	11.5%
Dennis	15 mins	1 min 23 secs	9.2%
Mean			20.7%

poorer concentration of the first school children may be attributed to the younger age of the children. There are also considerable pedagogic differences between first and middle schools, with different expectations of the children.

However, further analysis of figure 19 shows that there were very large variations between individual gifted children of from 3.3 per cent to 64.4 per cent distraction in first schools, and 2.7 per cent to 73.8 per cent distraction in middle schools. The emphasis for the remainder of this section will be on the observed activities of those children who were at the extreme of high distraction.[11]

Hugh had difficulty writing (Chapter 4) and appeared to prefer to read rather than to do the allocated task, which in the following case was creative writing.

Hugh, first school, year 4

Concentration/distraction transcript
Class activity: creative writing.
The class is almost silent.
9.47 Start time.
20 secs-Playing with rubber and looking at clock and running across the room.
51 secs-Flicking through the pages of a reading book. He starts to read. A girl comes over and tells him he should not be reading. He talks to Liz and Maggy.
2 mins-Chats to Liz.
20 secs-Talks to Maggy and Liz.
25 secs-Talks to Maggy and Liz.
T-Hugh, Are you getting lots of ideas down.
H-Yeah. He starts writing.
Silence in the room.
1 min 45 secs-Reads his book, and is completely engrossed.
1 min 50 secs-Talks to Liz. Plays with the cover of the book.
He reads the book. A girl tells him he should not be reading his book, and he starts writing.
1 min-Talks to Liz
10.02 Finish time.
Total-15 minutes. 8 mins 26 secs distraction (56.2%)

Hugh's distraction from the assigned task resulted in extremely poor output, however his concentration was good when reading his book, which was a task which would have been considered appropriate on a different occasion. Hank was another child whose concentration was very poor. This was also revealed in the extract concerning the mathematics test (see Chapter 4).

Hank, middddle school, year 1

Concentration/distraction transcript
Class activity-Spellings in a spelling book
The class is silent.
5 mins 25 secs-Talking to his next door neighbour about a test that they

have had, and other subjects. He chews his pencil, dreams, fiddles, looks around the room, bites his pencil, shakes his head around. The next door neighbour tells him to start working.

2 mins-Talking to next door neighbour. Other children in the class are finishing. Hugh flaps his paper in the air.

3 secs-Playing with next door neighbour.

1 min 40 secs-Talks to next door neighbour, scribbles on desk, jumps pen up and down on the desk.

1 min-Stands up and fiddles with his chair.

1 min 35 secs-Talks to his other next door neighbour, jumps up and down when his next door neighbour returns from seeing the teacher.

10.52 Finish time

Total-14 minutes. 12 mins 10 secs distraction (86.9%)[12]

In Jim's case his poor output of work appeared to be connected to his sociability. All through the lesson from which the following extract is taken, Jim was having a lively conversation with the other children at his table. The children were writing about a class outing and the room was reasonably quiet.

Jim, first school, year 3

Concentration/distraction transcript

Class activity: writing about a class excursion that took place on a previous day.

General silence

9.34 Start time

15 secs-Talks about spelling to next door neighbour and then notices the teacher looking at him and stops.

11 secs-Looks around at the others.

25 secs-Laughs at what someone says, and says he has to rub it out.

35 secs-Discussion as follows:

J-What happened to your finger?

B-Nothing.

J-Why have you got a plaster on then?

T-I hope you're talking about your day out. (Two children are sent out of the room for talking – differentiation of discipline)

40 secs-Paul talks to Jim.

J-Shut up.

P-Why?

J-You know you're not supposed to be talking.

They then play together with their fingers.

1 min 46 sec-Talks to next door neighbour. Paul asks for help with a word, and Jim shows him which one it is in his work book.

T-Right Jim. Can you bring your work to me and show me what you've done.

9.41 Timing of distraction was temporarily stopped while Jim was with the teacher.

Jim's teacher stated during her interview that she felt that Jim was not performing as well as he might and was easily distracted. The request to see his work was presumably an attempt to redirect his attention to it, yet two of the other children were moved in similar circumstances.

> T-Good, that's a good beginning. What are you doing sitting chatting. It could be good enough to go on the wall, but you're wasting time.
> General silence
> 9.42 Restart time
> 20 secs-Talks to a boy
> 30 secs-Watches the teacher. Plays with a rubber.
> 40 secs-Asks for the rubber (the teacher is watching him) and throws the rubber in the air. Drops the rubber.
> 9.48 Finish time
> Total-13 minutes. 5 mins 22 secs distraction (41.2%)

Despite the amount of time that Jim was distracted from the official task, the work that he was producing was sufficiently good for the teacher to suggest that it might go on the wall. Bennett and Bennett et al indicated that 'time on task' or 'active learning time' is a strong indicator of pupil achievement (Bennett, 1978; Bennett et al, 1981). The majority of the children in this sample were noted by their schools for their achievement in terms of output, being in advance of the other children, and/or the speed of their work. In some cases where their distraction level was high, this might be considered remarkable, as the time which they spent on the task was shortened, which is perhaps a further indication of the peculiarity of gifted children and the diversity of ways in which they can cope with and relate to the lesson activities. Benny has already been mentioned, where his activities during an SMP lesson were not related to the task at hand, and yet he was ahead of the remainder of the children. Another example was David, who once he actually sat down to do the work finished it very quickly. He was noted for the length of time it took him to change after physical education. The previous day he was the last to change, taking over fifteen minutes. The following extract was not a timed concentration/distraction transcript. The times are included in order to show the contrast between the time spent dressing and the time on task.

David, first school, year 2

11.20   The children start changing after P.E. When they are dressed David and four others, including Don, are supposed to do work cards about letter sounds.

11.28   David is still getting dressed and is looking at the work another child is doing. He then helps two other boys with their work. He moves over to the teacher's desk where he is asked what a word is by a boy.

11.35   David has finished dressing, and is the last child to do so. He stops to chat to a boy on the way to the teacher's desk to get a pencil. He talks to another boy about what the boy is doing, which is what David is supposed to be doing. He then looks for a card.

The teacher asks David what he is doing. He cannot find his book. The teacher tells him to look in the tray. It is there, though it should not be.

11.40   David settles down to work.

There is a discussion at the table about what words they have on their cards.

11.50   David finishes and takes his book up to the teacher.

T-David-When do we get capital letters?

D-At the beginning of a sentence.

T-That's right. Good boy.

David is given a star.

David was the last child to start his work, but when he did begin, it only took him ten minutes, while other children took a whole lesson. It may be that he knew he could finish the work quickly and did not bother hurrying to start. But once the children had finished their 'work task', they were allowed to play (with sand, puzzles, lego and so on). By not finishing, David was reducing the time that he had to play. Another day he had to do his mathematics in the afternoon (which was free activity time) because he had not started the work in the morning. On that occasion he took two minutes to do the work. Some very recent work, which is still in progress at the University of Lancaster, concluded that 57 per cent of tasks given to children were not matched with the attainment levels of the children. It was suggested that many high attainers were able to finish their work very quickly and spent a lot of time on routine activities rather than developing their abilities. It was also found that teachers were less likely to identify tasks as too easy rather than too hard, and were not adept at noting children who were marking time (Bennett and Desforges, 1982; Desforges and Cockburn, 1982). It is possible that it was for those reasons that David was occupying himself by socializing, and helping other children with their work.

A lesson

The following extract of a lesson illustrates many of the points already discussed. The 'star' of the observation is George. Two other gifted children, Sylvia and Les, are also mentioned. The lesson includes examples of the difference in concentration between gifted children in identical circumstances; differentiation in discipline for George and other children; repartee between the teacher and individual children; and the sociability of George.

George, Sylvia and Les, middle school, year 3

The class are doing a page in their mathematics books. Sylvia and Les get on with the work. George walks around the class showing a picture from a Sunday supplement to the children.

*T-Now, I don't want to moan at people on a nice sunny Monday morning, but I shall do so if people don't get on (holding George by the back of the neck jokingly).

George has his hand up.

T-I'll be with you in a moment. I just want to help Elsie. Is it something quick?

G-Yes. (He has no ruler)

George carries on chatting and jokingly thumping people on the head.

T-Go and see if there's a ruler on the mathematics table.

George finds one which is a metal tape. He wanders around the class bending it and chatting to other children.

Sylvia is working hard.

George puts the ruler in the position of his penis, it droops. He is standing in front of the class at the back of the queue of children waiting to see the teacher.

Les is working.

George pretends to play billiards with the ruler.

Les is working despite the fact that three girls around him are chatting.

Sylvia is slightly distracted by George playing billiards on her desk.

George returns to his desk and is mucking around with a jacket on his head.

Les turns round to talk to a boy very briefly.

George talks to someone in the front of the class, and then to a boy at the back of the class.

There is now a class lesson for those children who do not understand.

George is sitting at his desk facing the boy behind him.

*T-George-Would you mind getting on without being a nuisance (gently).

Teacher asks a question.

T-Boy-I didn't think you were listening when I was explaining the first part. Now will you please listen Robert (sharply). While the teacher is talking one can hear George's voice chatting and he is shaking the metal ruler. He drops the ruler and it makes a lot of noise. He picks it up and wraps it round his head.

T-George-What was your guess (about the length of the wall)? George is trying to touch the ceiling with the ruler.

*T-George-(shouting)-Do that again George and you're in trouble. We had enough of that last week.What page are you on?

George-Page 72.

T-Well get a move on. You ought to be on 'Alpha' by now.

The teacher goes round the class seeing individual children.

T-Boy-Oh marvellous, jolly good.

T-Boy-Oh get that answer you sausage.

T-Sylvia-Check those some time or other.

A boy asks Sylvia a question.

George has turned round and is chatting to the boy behind him.

T-Girl-Does that mean I mustn't be cross with you all day because it's your birthday? Well happy returns love.

Paul-(CO)-It's my birthday today.

George throws the ruler like a spear to a boy behind. The teacher looks but says nothing.

George now chats to a boy about a pen which he had loudly claimed back from another boy.

Sylvia is chatting to a boy, her first distraction.

George has put something on a boy's chair which hurt him.

*T-George-Just get on with your work George.

George-I didn't put it there.

T-Just get on with your work.

Les turns round to watch the boy who is clutching his leg.

Sylvia is still chatting to the boy, apparently about work.

T-Boy-(semi-shouting)-Well it would help if you would listen.

George is still playing around with the boy behind.

Les turns round to talk to a boy.

Sylvia and the boy are definitely talking about work.

The teacher is helping two girls.

A boy has his hand up and George is talking to him.

The teacher goes to help the boy, and blames him for something.

George puts his arms up in the air as though he has got a goal.

George is looking at his pen. He goes to a boy to look at the boy's watch.

End of the lesson.

This extract from a lesson highlights several points. One of the most important is the differences between gifted children. George spent the entire lesson socializing with his classmates and playing around, while Les and Sylvia concentrated on the allocated task. Despite George's active distraction and misbehaviour, only the third of the four interactions that could be interpreted as disciplinary (they have been asterisked in the text) was a 'telling off'. The second and fourth interactions were a reminder to get on with work, and the first was a humorous interchange. In the same lesson, other children were disciplined quite sharply. The next chapter will examine the social status of the gifted children, where it will be shown that the friendliness and sociability of George was responded to favourably by his classmates. The extract also highlights the heterogeneity of gifted children within the tendency for gifted children to have more interactions with the teacher than the mean number of interactions for the whole class.

Boydell surmized that in a class containing forty children an individual child could expect to have three thirty second individual contacts with the teacher per hour if the contacts were divided equally among the children. She suggested that inequality of the spread of contacts resulted in differential experience of the classroom for children (Boydell, 1975b). Boydell also pointed out that in a study carried out by six observers of six teachers, 70 per cent of teacher contacts with children were individuated (Boydell, 1974), and therefore presumably excluded the majority of the children. Boydell also considered that a combination of individuated and inequal contacts may well result in deprivation for some children. Jackson and Lahaderne stated that,

> For at least a few students, individual contact with the teacher is as rare as if they were seated in a class of a hundred or more pupils, even though there are actually only thirty or so classmates present. For others, the teacher's presence is the same as it might be if there were but a handful of classmates in the room (Jackson and Laharderne, 1967, page 274).

It has been shown that the quantity of interactions was generally favourable for the gifted children. Therefore if favourable classroom experience can be equated with teacher child contact, then gifted children tend to have good experiences with consequent deprivation for other children. This has serious implications for some of their classmates which will be considered in a broader educational context.

In Chapter 1 the various political, philosophical and economical arguments with regard to gifted children were explored. One of the main arguments against the various forms of special educational provision for gifted children is that these children are already advantaged. At the time of economic difficulty, the allocation of scarce resources to gifted children cannot be justified when other children in need may be thereby deprived. This rationale has encompassed all types of educational provision requiring economic resources. Further, in the controversy concerning special classes for gifted children, it has been suggested that one result would be a lowering of standards for those children left behind. In other words, stress has been laid on the intellectual value that the presence of the gifted children has for the other children in the normal classroom. The results of the present research should lead to a re-assessment of the educational approach to gifted children in that, in terms of contacts with the teacher, the presence of the gifted children may be considered to be disadvantageous for the other children in the class because of the occupation of the teacher by the gifted child. Prescriptions concerning this problem will be explored in the concluding chapter.

Having indicated the possible effect on classroom peers of the presence of a gifted child, the next chapter will examine the perceptions by the peers of the gifted children.

Notes

1. The positive and negative figures for each gifted child were assessed as follows:
   (a) The interactions between teachers and all the children in the class.
   (b) The interactions that occurred between the teacher and the gifted child.
   (c) The mean of the interactions with all the children.
   (d) The number of interactions that occurred with the gifted child which were above or below the mean for that class. The Wilcoxon matched-pairs signed-ranks test compared items (c) and (d) (see note 2).
2. The Wilcoxon matched-pairs signed-ranks test is appropriate here because it utilizes information about the direction of the differences between pairs (Siegel, 1956, page 75). The Wilcoxon test is more powerful than the T test, the use of which would also be appropriate. The T test may produce seriously inaccurate significance values if it is used on data which are not normally distributed, but there is no adequate test for normality of small samples and there was some evidence that the data to be analyzed here would not be normally distributed. The levels of significance from the Wilcoxon test will always be close to the true values whatever the distribution of the data. If the data are normally distributed the Wilcoxon test will have an efficiency of 95 per cent and in other circumstances it will be even better. The hypothesis that gifted children interact with their teachers more than other members of the class do, was formulated early in the study, before the data tested by the Wilcoxon method had been collected. As this was clearly a directional hypothesis a one-tailed test was appropriate.
3. The data refer to frequency of interactions, and exclude length or quality of interactions. References to time, therefore, are in terms of interaction frequency rather than actual time span.
4. The percentage of time available for all the children was calculated as $\frac{100}{N}$, N being the number of children in the class. The formula $100 \times \frac{I_A}{I_G}$ was used to give the percentages for the gifted children, I_A being the number of interactions that occurred for all the children in the class; and I_G the number of interactions that occurred for the gifted child.
5. Peter was accelerated by two years.
6. This refers to only fourteen teachers which places some limitations on the interpretations that can be made.
7. Jim had a different teacher in the morning and the afternoon. Benny was studied twice, once in first school, and once in middle school, where he was together with Hank.
8. As the incidents with Angela occurred early in the research the author was alerted to gathering more material of this kind.
9. The following note was made at the time 'There seem to be different ways of treating them, perhaps the teacher assumed that they were talking about their work.'
10. Rita's concentration was not timed because the class was taught using the method of an integrated day, and therefore there was no time which was considered to be adequately silent.
11. Classroom transcripts which refer to concentration/distraction give the starting and finishing times, plus the length of time a child was distracted, and the activity of that child while distracted from the task at hand.
12. Hank was timed on two occasions.

6   Gifted Children and their Peers

In previous chapters the concentration has been mainly, but not completely, on teachers' perspectives of giftedness and of the gifted children, plus observation in the classroom. In the present chapter the perceptions of the gifted children by their classroom peers, and the self-perceptions of the gifted children will be explored. Some reference will be made to the perceptions of the teachers concerning the social relationships of the gifted childen. Thus the multi-dimensional perspective of the study of gifted children will be completed. The data in this chapter will be related back to important ideas contained in previous chapters, such as the gifted/non gifted concept from Chapter 2 and the interactional data from the last chapter. *Primary triangulation* will be used to investigate differences and similarities between the perceptions of the peers, gifted children and the teachers (see the Appendix). As shown in the Appendix, the material for this chapter uses a number of varieties of *secondary triangulation*. An attempt is made throughout to create a detailed and comprehensive picture of the gifted children in their classrooms.

The Social Relations of Gifted Children

There is considerable conflict in the literature concerning the social relations of gifted children. Some research has found that gifted children tend to be popular (Gallagher, 1958a, 1958b, and 1975; Gallagher and Crowder, 1957; Hartup, 1970; and Heber, 1956). On the other hand, it has been shown that some gifted children, particularly those with extraordinarily advanced abilities, tend to be alienated from their peers (Gallagher, 1958a; Getzels and Dillon, 1973; Hollingworth, 1942; Lutz and Lutz, 1981; Miller, 1956; Newland, 1976; and Terman and Oden, 1947). Taylor investigated the relationship between intelligence and social status, and found there to be a significant positive relationship between mental age and social acceptance, which was significantly more positive than that between chronological age and social acceptance (Taylor, 1952).

The research in this area has been predominantly American, apart from that of Freeman and Hitchfield, both of whom looked at the perceptions of parents, teachers and gifted children (Freeman, 1979 and Hitchfield, 1973). Freeman compared the gifted children with a control group. In comparison to the control group, the parents of gifted children described them as having fewer friends, and tending to have friends who were chronologically older than themselves. This was supported by the gifted children themselves, and by their teachers. Hitchfield found the gifted children to be sociable, only two of the children in her sample said they had no friends. This was confirmed by the parents of the gifted children who described regular exchange of visits for 80 per cent of the children. There has been no comprehensive study, such as the present one, of the perceptions of the three groups — teachers, peers and gifted children — employing sociometric indices of the social relations of the gifted children.

The study of the social status and relations of gifted children is important for a variety of reasons. One of the main considerations for headteachers and teachers concerning forms of educational provision for gifted children (such as acceleration or various forms of segregation) is the effect that the provision will have on the children socially. Emphasis is also put upon the future role of gifted children in society as leaders and influencers.(Benn, 1982) There is further a stereotyped notion of gifted children being unpopular and loners, which may have been encouraged by notions put forward by the media and supported by the NAGC. Without systematic data on the social status of the gifted children in the normal classrooms, educational decisions will continue to be based on assumptions which have not been tested. Research studies which are solely concerned with the social status of children who are gifted, are in danger of making the assumption that it is the children's giftedness which is of overriding importance. Whereas, studies which are broader in perspective may reveal other factors than giftedness which may affect the social status of the relevant children. In the present study, in order to explore this possibility, peer perceptions of the gifted children in terms of academic ability will be examined to see whether the peers were aware of the gifted children's generally superior abilities. The sociometric data will also be related to the interaction data, discipline and the social attributes of the gifted children.

The sociometric questionnaire used requested all the children in each class to make positive and/or negative choices from the children in their class about *sitting next to, working with* and *playing with* (see the Appendix). These responses were used to estimate the social status of the gifted children in comparison to the other children in the class. Also used were Guess Who questions which referred to social attributes of *being hard to get on with* (question 9), and *being good at organizing* (question 13). Furthermore, the WAYG gave an indication of the self-perceptions of the gifted children on the contrasting dimensions of *well liked* versus *not well liked, friendly* versus *not friendly, good organizer* versus not *a good organizer*. Teachers' perceptions were derived from two questions on the BSAG which referred to 'companionship' and 'ways with other children'. The underlining of the phrases *good mixer* and *gets on well with others* gave a positive score. Data from interviews with the teachers and the gifted children were also used.

Peer perception of academic ability was taken to be the total of the nominations for the gifted children on questions 4, 5, 7 and 8 of the Guess Who test. To give a score for self-perception of the gifted child, the dimension 'clever versus not clever' on the WAYG, and where this was not available the ability placement (see the Appendix) were used. Whilst acknowledging that the majority of the children were considered to be academically very able, it was thought to be to see if the very fine differentiation between the labelling 'gifted' and 'non-gifted' would have any effect on the perceptions of the gifted children by their classroom peers, and/or on the self-perception of the gifted children.

The perceptions by classroom peers of whether or not gifted children created disciplinary problems were reflected in question 6 of the Guess Who, while 'being good' was shown in question 12. One of the sections in the BSAG referred to classroom behaviour, and gave an indication of whether the teacher perceived the children to be 'generally well behaved'. The disciplinary interaction scores from the previous chapter will also be used.

A comparison will be made between the gifted children in this study and the gifted children in the Freeman and Hitchfield studies, in terms of the perceptions of the teachers regarding the social adjustment of the gifted children. For this purpose the scores given by the teachers on the BSAG will be used.

As the research is interested in particular individuals in their social context, it is appropriate to use sociometry to establish the gifted children's social position within their own classroom. At the same time, it is desirable to be able to compare the gifted children across the classrooms. Different classes vary in their social networks as a function of age, group cohesion, teacher method, teacher effectiveness and so on. It is therefore not possible to compare one gifted child's sociometric score with that of a gifted child in another class without some adjustment. The children's scores, as presented in figure 20 and 21, take into account the number of choices and rejections received, plus the average number of choices and rejections of the class. A standard deviation score was calculated for each gifted child.

Figures 20 for first schools and 21 for middle schools give the *sitting standard deviation scores* (S-SDS), *working standard deviation scores* (W-SDS), *playing standard deviation scores* (P-SDS), and *total standard deviation scores* (T-SDS) for the gifted children. It will be noted that Adrian (football) and Geoff (music) are included, but they are excluded for discussions of academic perception, as there was never any question of them being considered to be academically gifted.

It was hypothesized that there would be a positive correlation between the different sociometric measures, but it was not initially certain whether 'sitting next to' would be associated with 'working with' (as a more academic and classroom based notion) or 'playing with' (which is taken to refer to the social and playground environment).

Figure 20   Standard deviation scores of the gifted children for sitting with, working with, playing with, and total in first schools

Class	Child	Sitting SDS	Working SDS	Playing SDS	Total SDS
1	Arthur	1.8	2.45	0.71	1.83
2	Ricky	0	−0.6	−0.5	−0.37
2	David	−0.11	−0.71	−0.88	−0.6
2	Don	−0.11	0.71	−0.25	0.15
2	Karl	1.0	1.25	0.27	1.04
2	Rita	0.43	0.5	0.2	0.5
3	Robert	−0.2	−0.5	−0.33	−0.44
3	Mary	0.89	1.3	0.5	1.0
3	Jim	−0.71	0	−0.57	−0.53
4	Maggy	−0.09	0.44	−0.13	0.04
4	Hugh	0.27	0	0.38	0.24
4	Rosemarie	0.73	0	0.38	0.4
4	Keith	−0.09	1.0	1.5	0.76
4	Liz	0.73	1.0	1.0	0.92
4	Benny	−3.75	−0.75	−2.8	−2.67
4	Vi	1.4	−0.67	0.75	0.8
4	Alexandra	0.6	2.17	−0.75	0.8

Figure 21   Standard deviation scores of the gifted children for sitting with, working with, playing with, and total in middle schools

Class	Child	Sitting SDS	Working SDS	Playing SDS	Total SDS
1	Sandy	0	1.0	0.9	0.59
1	Vicky	0.77	0	0.9	0.59
1	Peter	0.22	−0.57	−0.22	−0.17
1	Ann	−0.73	−0.4	−0.5	−0.5
1	Ken	−0.09	−0.1	−0.5	−0.17
1	Lilo	−0.63	0.29	−0.75	−0.4
1	Kathy	−0.25	−0.57	1.13	0.2
1	Benny	−3.67	−2.5	−2.5	−3.11
1	Hank	0.33	0.5	0.67	0.5
3	Laurence	0.33	−0.8	−0.44	−0.35
3	Les	−0.17	1.0	−0.11	0.18
3	George	2.00	0.4	1.33	1.47
3	Sylvia	0.33	0.4	−0.11	0.18
3	Adrian	1.33	0.4	2.00	1.65
3	Jo	1.13	0.57	1.00	1.00
3	Nicholas	1.63	2.43	1.57	2.05
3	Mandy	−1.13	−0.57	−0.57	−0.8
3	Tony	0	0.29	−1.0	−0.2
3	Pat	0.6	1.27	0	0.77
3	Christopher	−3.89	−3.83	−3.0	−3.9
4	Angela	0	0.4	1.57	1.0
4	Dennis	1.13	1.5	1.13	1.5

The matrices of the correlations between the different sociometric standard deviation scores are given in figures 22 for first schools and 23 for middle schools. All the correlations are significant and positive, which supports the initial hypothesis that the social status of the gifted children would be similar on the different sociometric measures. It can be seen from the figures that in both first and middle schools the correlations between S-SDS and P-SDS were greater than those between S-SDS and W-SDS. Therefore, S-SDS appears to be more related to the social and playground environment than to the academic or classroom environment.

Figure 22 *Matrix of correlations between sociometric standard deviation scores for first schools*

	Working SDS	Playing SDS	Total SDS
Sitting SDS	0.4302**	0.5224**	0.7761***
Working SDS	(17)	0.3596*	0.6677***
Playing SDS	(17)	(17)	0.5926***
(17 cases)			

Significant at levels of * $p < 0.05$, ** $p < 0.01$, *** $p < 0.001$ (l-tailed test – Kendall Rank Correlation[2])

Figure 23 *Matrix of correlations between sociometric standard deviation scores for middle schools*

	Working SDS	Playing SDS	Total SDS
Sitting SDS	0.4959***	0.6327***	0.6572***
Working SDS	(23)	0.4385**	0.6585***
Playing SDS	(23)	(23)	0.7273***
(23 cases)			

Significant at levels of ** $p < 0.01$, *** $p < 0.001$ (l-tailed test – Kendall Rank Correlation[2])

Figure 24 *Number and percentage of gifted children with positive, zero and negative standard deviation scores in first and middle schools*

	First Schools				Middle Schools*			
	Sit SDS	Work SDS	Play SDS	Total SDS	Sit SDS	Work SDS	Play SDS	Total SDS
No. above 0	9	9	9	12	12	14	11	14
% age above 0	53%	53%	53%	71%	52%	61%	48%	61%
No. at 0	1	3	0	0	3	1	1	0
% age at 0	6%	18%	0	0	13%	4%	4%	0
No. below 0	7	5	8	12	8	8	11	9
% age below 0	41%	29%	47%	29%	35%	35%	48%	39%

* Includes Adrian and Geoff

Figures 20 for first schools and 21 for middle schools show that the gifted children were heterogeneous with regard to sociometric choice. The lowest SDS score was −3.9 for Christopher and the highest +2.45 for Arthur. Figure 24 gives the number and percentages of gifted children with positive, zero and negative SDS in first and middle schools. It would appear that generally more gifted children were chosen than rejected in all areas of the sociometric choice, apart from 'play SDS' in middle schools. If a hypothetical level of *superior* or *inferior* social status were to be taken as one standard deviation above or below the mean, then a total of four gifted children had inferior social status (Benny, Mandy, Tony and Christopher) whereas seventeen gifted children had superior social status for one or more of the sociometric SDS. The names of the children with superior social status have been emphasized in figures 20 and 21. Some of these children will be discussed in the sections that follow. It is not possible to go into detail about such a large number of children, so three out of the seventeen children have been selected who illustrate some interesting and contrasting points. These are Karl, Jo and Nicholas.

Karl, first school, year 2

Karl's sociometric SDS were more than one standard deviation above the mean for 'sitting' and 'working with', but somewhat lower for playing with. His teacher stated during the interview that Karl was socially unaware, selfish, unwilling to help others and self-indulgent. When asked what the other children thought of the child, the teacher said,

> They don't think much of him. They ignore him mainly. He is on the same table as some motivated children. They accept him, but the others ignore him. They don't laugh at his jokes.

In class Karl was observed to be seated at a table where there was considerable social interaction, in which he participated. But during playtimes Karl was observed to spend some of his time sitting on a bench by himself or talking to the teacher. He had a reputation amongst the teachers for asking them unusual and personal questions when they were on playground duty. Occasionally Karl would talk to older children. He frequently had a book with him, which he read or showed to passing children. During his interview he stated that he sat on the bench at playtimes and his friends did not seem able to find him. In answer to the sociometric question concerning 'playing with' he put himself. When questioned about this he said that he liked to walk around the playground with himself.

Karl was not socially isolated in the classroom, although seen to be so by his teacher. He spent much of his playtimes on his own, but he also did play or talk with other children. The case of Karl illustrates two points. That sociometric data may be inadequate, in that according to his sociometric scores Karl was popular, but observation indicated that he was frequently isolated in the playground; and that teachers can misinterpret the social relations of the children. The latter point is further illustrated in the cases of Jo and Nicholas.

Jo and Nicholas, middle school, year 3

Jo and Nicholas were in the same class and were friends. All three of Nicholas's SDSs were more than one standard deviation above the mean. His work SDS was the highest for all the gifted children in the middle schools. Jo's SDSs were lower than Nicholas's for all three of the sociometric areas measured, but were more than one standard deviation above the mean for sitting and playing. However, their teacher's perception of the social relations of the two boys was the reverse, as stated in her interview,

> They get on very well [with other children]. Perhaps better with Jo than Nicholas, but Nicholas does not live on the estate and Jo has joined the scouts. Nicholas is more separated. They are no trouble socially.

Jo thought that the other children considered him to be quite nice. Nicholas answered as follows,

Interview with Nicholas

> R-What do you think the other children think of you?
> N-Well lots of people when I go home with them and their mum comes along they say "Oh look, he's the brainy one" (laughing).
> R-Do they do that for Jo?
> N-Yes.

Indeed, they both had many nominations on the 'Guess Who' for academic ability. When asked who Jo would like to be in the class, he responded that he would like to be Nicholas.

Interview with Jo

> I just like him, I'd like to be him. I've always wanted to be in someone else's mind to see my actual body, to see what my face looked like, to see when I'm walking around 'cos I can't see and you can see other people, but you can't see your own.

In the playground they were observed to be part of a large group of boys who met regularly at playtimes.

The relationship between the sociometric data and perceptions by class-room peers, the gifted children and the teachers about the social status and social attributes of the gifted children were studied in more detail. Also an assessment was made of how far the three groups agreed in their perceptions. No hypotheses were formed prior to the collection of the data that are relevant to these areas, so 2-tailed tests are used.

Figures 25 and 26 for first and middle schools respectively give the matrices for the correlations between the sociometric data and perceptions of social status and attributes. None of the correlations in the first schools were significant.

The first interesting point is that there were no significant correlations between the sociometric data and self-concept of 'well liked' in first or middle schools. This would appear to indicate that the gifted children as a group were relatively unaware of their own social status. This finding contrasts with that of Gallagher who found bright elementary school children particularly able to predict their own social status (Gallagher, 1958). Livesley and Bromley stated that children's self-perception develops with age, particularly from the age of eleven onwards. Possibly the majority of the gifted children in this study were too young to assess their own social status (Livesley and Bromley, 1973).

The lack of significant correlations between the sociometric data and the first school teachers' perceptions of the social status of the gifted children as measured by the sociometric questionnaire gives some indication of a similar lack of awareness. This indicates that the teachers were unable to judge how the classroom peers placed the gifted children socially in terms of sociometric choice. However, in the middle schools the correlations between total SDS and both teacher assessments were significant (at the level of $p < 0.05$), that

Figure 25   Matrix showing correlations between sociometric data and perceptions of social status and attributes of gifted children in first schools

Sociometry	Peers		Self			Teachers	
	Hard to get on with	Good organizer	Well-liked	Friendly	Good organizer	Good mixer	Gets on well
S-SDS	0.0541	0.0894	0.2493	−0.3631	0.1254	−0.0615	0.2000
W-SDS	0.0761	0.3302	−0.2243	−0.2381	0.1284	0.0155	0.2476
P-SDS	−0.0858	0.0147	−0.1427	−0.2602	−0.4957	0.0456	0.2891
T-SDS	0.0107	0.2501	0.0519	−0.3528	−0.0735	−0.0303	0.2118
No. of children	(16)	(13)	(14)	(9)	(10)	(14)	(14)

Figure 26   Matrix showing correlations between sociometric data and perceptions of social status and attributes of gifted children in middle schools

Sociometry	Peers		Self			Teachers	
	Hard to get on with	Good organizer	Well-liked	Friendly	Good organizer	Good mixer	Gets on well
S-SDS	−0.2502	0.5289**	0.1497	0.6325	0.4536	0.3341	0.2780
W-SDS	−0.3018	0.2722	0.2429	0.6325	0.2520	0.4931**	0.3405
P-SDS	−0.3742*	0.6649**	0.1571	0.7071	0.6928*	0.3663	0.4167*
T-SDS	−0.2628	0.4529*	0.2429	0.6325	0.3712	0.4344*	0.4111*
No. of children	(21)	(16)	(9)	(5)	(8)	(22)	(22)

Significant at levels of *$p < 0.05$, **$p < 0.01$ (2-tailed test – Kendall Rank Correlation[2])

between play SDS and 'gets on well' was significant (at the level of $p < 0.05$), and that between work SDS and 'good mixer' was significant (at the level of $p < 0.01$). Thus there are indications that the middle school teachers were better able to assess the social status of the gifted children amongst their peers compared with the first school teachers. This finding is important in terms of the research already mentioned concerning the popularity of gifted children, where teacher assessment was generally used.

The negative and significant correlation between those gifted children whom the peers found 'hard to get on with' and the play SDS (at the level of $p < 0.05$) indicates that gifted children who were so perceived were not chosen as playmates.

The correlations between peer perception of the gifted children as good organizers and the sociometric SDS referring to play environment, sitting SDS and play SDS, were significant (at the level of $p < 0.01$) and total SDS (at the level of $p < 0.05$.) Play SDS also correlated significantly with gifted children's self-perception of themselves as good organizers (at the level of $p < 0.05$). It could be that the gifted children received positive sociometric choices because of their good organizational ability, or that they were allowed to organize because they were well perceived socially. It is interesting that in first schools the direction of the correlations between sociometric data and self-perception of the gifted children as good organizers was opposite to that in the middle schools. Although this negative correlation was not significant, a first school and a middle school child will be discussed in order to highlight the factors at work in this context.

Two case studies of gifted children nominated as good organizers

There were two children, Jim and Adrian, who were nominated most frequently as being good organizers. Both children perceived themselves as being good at organizing, but Jim had negative play SDS. Jim will be remembered from Chapter 4 as the child who organized the play which was performed in the classroom. In the light of the sociometric data, his description of how he organized it will be re-examined. In the following extract from his interview (which was quoted in Chapter 4) it appears that there was an element of friction between Jim and his peers. First he had to persuade them that they wanted to do the play,

Interview with Jim, first school, year 3

R-I enjoyed watching that play. Do you often do plays like that?
J-Not really, I just make plays up.
R-And people always want to join in do they?
J-Not really, but they love doing it once I've told them how to do it.

They think it's quite good.

R-But you have to persuade them first?

J-Yeah. Well how it all started was when I was thinking about William Shakespeare, and I thought I hope I grow up like him, so I thought I wonder if I could do a play myself, so all that night I was thinking of trying to do a play and the next day I'd thought of it and I wrote it all down, and then on Monday I got all the people and there was one too many so I had to make another space.

R-How long did you take doing the play?

J-About three weeks.

R-Did you rehearse every playtime?

J-Yeah.

Then in order to ensure that he remained as the director, Jim changed the play,

J- ... and that one didn't seem to last very long after three weeks so I made up another one, and they all thought it was their idea and they all kept doing it themselves, so I made up another one about kidnappers and that seems to be the best play I've done so far.

R-But you weren't doing that today at playtime?

J-We always do it at lunchtime playtime.

R-Is it always the same people that you have?

J-Yes.

There also appeared to be some quarrelling.

R-Do you find them difficult to organise?

J-Yes because a lot of the time we have a bit of an argument or something about the play about the clothes and things we're going to have and where we're going to get all the equipment and that's all we seem to argue about.

R-Why should that cause an argument?

J-'Cos we never know where we're going to get the clothes and then we can't do too many rehearsals 'cos its raining and then they all go away from the play. When I think we've really got good at it I try and get the clothes and things.

R-It's up to you to get those is it?

J-Yeah, but some of the children who are in my play said that they'd let them borrow some of their dressing up clothes. That's nice of them.

During morning and afternoon playtimes, when the play was not being rehearsed, Jim was observed to wander around the playground, mainly on his own, but chatting occasionally to other children or to the teacher on duty.

Adrian, who was in middle school, had the highest play SDS and peer nomination as good organizer of the total sample. He was the gifted footballer, and he organized a large group of boys to practise football in the playground with a tennis ball. He stated in his interview that the small ball was used because it demanded greater skill and therefore improved his ability.

These two children perceived themselves as good organizers, and were perceived by their peers as such. Jim had negative play SDS whereas Adrian had positive play SDS. Jim therefore illustrates the direction of the correlation between self-perception as good organizer and play SDS which was negative in first schools. Adrian illustrates the positive correlation between sitting SDS, play SDS and total SDS with peer perception of good organizer in middle schools.

A final point is that in both first and middle schools the correlation between peer perception of the gifted children as good organizers and the self-perception of the gifted children as good organizers was significant (at the level of $p < 0.05$)[3]. Gifted children who considered themselves to be good at organizing were also perceived to be such by their peers. The use of the observation data here is important and allows some unpicking of the unclear and apparently contradictory aspects of the correlations.

In the previous chapter some indication was given of a tendency for there to be more interaction between the teachers and the gifted children than the mean of interactions for the class. It was also suggested that this could lead to *inter-actional deprivation* for other children, which was considered to be educationally disadvantageous. Unfortunately there is little research on this area generally – therefore, in the absence of informed opinion, the hypothesis was formed that there would be a negative correlation between interaction scores and sociometric SDS. In other words, those children who dominated the interactional scene would be more likely to have negative sociometric SDS. The rationale behind this hypothesis was that if the teacher is a scarce resource in the classroom, and if it might be the case that first school and younger middle school children are still dependent on the teacher emotionally and academically, then monopolization of that teacher by a minority sector of the classroom population could be assumed to negatively affect the rest of the children. This may not be the case solely for gifted children, but may also be true of socially disturbed, remedial, or handicapped children who take up inordinate amounts of the teachers' interactions. However, in this case the concern is with the gifted children.

Figures 27 and 28 give the matrices of the correlations between the inter-action scores (total, teacher initiated and child initiated) and the sociometric scores (sitting SDS, play SDS, work SDS and total SDS) for first and middle schools. It can be seen that, apart from three, all the correlations are indeed negative, thereby supporting the hypothesis generally. In first schools the only significant, negative correlation is that between sitting SDS and teacher-initiated interaction score (at the level of $p < 0.05$), thereby indicating a tendency for children who receive more than the mean number of interactions from their teacher for their class to receive negative choices from their peers for sitting next to. There are several possible explanations for this relationship. It may be that children who are always answering questions give their neigh-bours a feeling of academic inferiority; or sitting next to children who interact frequently with the teacher means that the teacher's attention is directed to that

Figure 27   Matrix showing correlations between sociometric and interaction data for first schools

	Total interaction score	Teacher-initiated interaction score	Child-initiated interaction score
S-SDS	−0.1651	−0.3889*	0.1366
W-SDS	−0.1756	−0.2778	0.0098
P-SDS	−0.3173	−0.2747	−0.1159
T-SDS	−0.1723	−0.3187	0.0481
(15 children)			

Significant at level of *p < 0.05 (1-tailed test − Kendall Rank Correlation[2])

Figure 28   Matrix showing correlations between sociometric and interaction data for middle schools

	Total interaction score	Teacher-initiated interaction score	Child-initiated interaction score
S-SDS	−0.3148*	−0.2093	−0.3309*
W-SDS	−0.3496*	−0.2732*	−0.2830*
P-SDS	−0.2400	−0.1501	−0.2413
T-SDS	−0.2500	−0.1304	−0.2415
(21 cases)			

Significant at level of *p < 0.05 (1-tailed test — Kendall Rank Correlation[2])

area of the classroom, which may be considered 'dangerous' for those who prefer not to participate; or possibly a child will have less chance of participating if he wishes to.

The correlations for the middle schools are slightly different. Both sitting SDS and working SDS correlate signficantly and negatively with the total interaction score (at the level of $p < 0.05$). They also correlate significantly and negatively with the child-initiated score (at the level of $p < 0.05$). Only work SDS correlates significantly and negatively with the teacher-initiated interaction score (at the level of $p < 0.05$). These differences in the middle schools may be accounted for by the differences in teacher-initiated and child-initiated interactions between first and middle schools. In first schools the interactions which were initiated by teachers and children were almost equal, whereas in middle schools the teachers initiated interactions two and a half times more frequently than did the pupils. The correlations between sitting SDS and interaction scores may be accounted for similarly, in that in middle schools children who frequently initiated interactions with their teachers were more noticeable to their peers.

The overall indication is that, in middle schools particularly, there was a tendency for children who interacted with their teachers more than their peers to receive negative choices on the sociometric questionnaire, especially for 'working with'. This tendency was not revealed in first or middle schools for 'playing with', and therefore appeared to be limited to the classroom environment, as might be expected.

There are several possible explanations for the negative relationship between sociometric choice and interaction score. The gifted children may be isolated by their classmates in the classroom, and therefore build up a more interactive relationship with their teacher on the basis of academic ability, or social rapport; those children who interact a lot with the teacher prevent their peers from interacting and therefore are perceived negatively; or the peers may not wish to sit next to or work with the gifted children because they are perceived as academically more able. The question of how far the gifted children were perceived as academically able will be discussed in the next section.

Perceptions of Academic Ability

There was a difference between first and middle schools in perceptions by the classroom peers of the academic ability of the gifted children. The nominations on the 'Guess Who' which referred to academic ability averaged 10.35 and 26.3 nominations for first and middle school gifted children respectively. The age group peers would therefore appear to have been aware of the academic ability of the gifted children, and increasingly so in middle schools. It may be that gifted children in first schools, being younger, have had less time to build up a 'gifted' or 'academic' reputation. Also, the perceptual awareness of first school children, concerning their peers, with regard to their academic ability, may be less well developed than that of middle school children. In middle schools, expectations of classroom conduct are more formalized, and deviance from formal patterns may be more noticeable. Also, there are changes in pedagogic style, middle schools tend to be more didactic, with children working as a cohesive class, which may make the children more aware of the abilities of the other members of the class. The awareness of academic success and failure based on correct and incorrect responses is probably heightened by the middle school age, and the children are therefore more able to make comparisons between themselves and others in terms of academic ability (Nash, 1973.)[4] Also teachers may be using more comparative assessment between children in class.

The peer perception of children as academically able may make the children less willing to place themselves in a situation, such as working or sitting with, a child who will 'show them up' in an unfavourable light in class. The greater awareness of the middle school children with regard to the academic ability of the gifted children may partially account for the differences between first and middle schools found in the previous section concerning the relationship between the sociometric and interaction data.

Figure 29 for first and middle schools together, gives the significance levels

Figure 29 Matrix showing correlations of perceptions of academic ability for first and middle schools together

	First Schools			**Middle Schools**		
	Peers Guess Who	**Self Clever**	**Teacher Gifted/ non gifted**	**Peers Guess Who**	**Self Clever**	**Teachers Gifted/ non gifted**
Peers Guess Who		0.1647	−0.0408		0.3692*	0.0820
Self Clever	(15)		0.0983	(19)		0.0455
Teacher Gifted/ non-gifted	(15)	(15)		(19)	(21)	

Significant at level of * p < 0.05 (2-tailed test Kendall Rank Correlation[2])

of correlations for perceptions by peers, gifted children and teachers of the academic ability of the gifted children. The differentiation between the gifted and non gifted groups is reintroduced at this point, in order to assess whether the label *gifted* made a difference to the perceptions by the peers and the gifted children of the academic ability of the gifted children. It should be stressed that all the children were perceived as academically able by their classroom peers, as indicated above. Only two children (Karl and Rita) in first schools, and two children (Kathy and Laurence) in middle schools had zero scores with regard to academic ability on the Guess Who. The question was whether the gifted children, who were labelled as gifted by their present teachers, would be perceived as more academically able than the non-gifted group.

Figure 29 shows that there were no significant correlations between the teacher labelling of gifted/non gifted and peer perception and self-perception of academic ability. However, there was a significant correlation between peer perception and self-perception in middle schools (at the level of p < 0.05) which was not repeated in the first schools. The differences between first and middle school children in the peer perception of the gifted children and the gifted children's self-perception concerning academic ability may be attributed to a developmental stage. According to Livesley and Bromley, for children aged between seven and ten years

> Ability and achievement seem to be important values ..., living as they do in a competitive world where physical and mental skills are important indices of status ... Judgements of [intellectual aptitudes and abilities; achievements and skills] occurred ... frequently in descriptions of peers ..., thus demonstrating a close link between ego-development and person perception (Livesley and Bromley, 1973, page 154).[5]

It appears that the peers and the gifted children did not distinguish between the teacher groups of gifted and non gifted. However, as Gage points out, teachers have a cumulative effect, each teacher affecting what occurred with the preceding teacher (Gage, 1978). Therefore, the fact that a previous teacher considered a child to be gifted, whereas a present teacher did not, cannot be presumed to eliminate the effect of past teachers. Also, the teachers used two category sets of academically able and gifted; whereas the children used one category set, that of academically able.

The fact that the gifted children in middle schools had similar perceptions of their academic ability to those of their peers, as against the teacher's gifted/non gifted categorization, might indicate that the reference point for self-perception was based more on peer rather than teacher perception. This point will be explored in greater detail because of its relevance to the literature of the 'self-fulfilling prophecy' as developed by Rosenthal and Jacobson (1968). The self-fulfilling prophecy claimed that teachers' attitudes and expectancies of children affect the performance of those children, presumably by the teachers communicating their attitudes to the children, or, as shown in this study, by handling them differently in some way. There would therefore be expected to be an effect on the children's self-perception. In this study the self-perceptions of the gifted children seemed to be affected more by their peers than by their teachers. Teacher perception does not appear to be definitive in the formation of gifted children's self-perceptions; and in the classroom it is likely to be a three-way process between teachers, peers and gifted children, which will also be affected by the perceptions of the parents. However, more conclusive evidence would be needed to establish the points made here.

Perceptions of Discipline

In the previous section it was shown that there was a tendency for there to be a negative correlation between sociometric choice and high interaction scores of the gifted children. This indicated that gifted children who interacted more with their teachers than the mean for their class had lower social status, especially in middle schools. The tendency appeared to be limited to the classroom situation. This section will examine whether perceptions of the gifted children in terms of discipline were also related to social status.

In the previous chapter it was shown that in first schools the gifted children did not receive significantly more disciplinary contacts from their teachers than the mean for their class; whereas in middle schools they were censored significantly more than the mean for their class (figures 12 and 13). It was also pointed out that there appeared to be an element of differential discipline in favour of the gifted child, and that many of the gifted children were not chastised at all during the period of observation, whereas a small minority were well above the mean for their class.

Figures 30 for first schools and 31 for middle schools give the correlations

Figure 30   Matrix showing correlations of sociometric data with peer perception and
teacher perception of the gifted children in terms of discipline and
disciplinary interactions in first schools

	Peers		Teachers	
Sociometry	Gifted child in trouble	being good	Generally well-behaved	Disciplinary interactions
S-SDS	−0.2921	0.3880	−0.1088	−0.0597
W-SDS	−0.2933	0.6049**	0.0000	−0.0500
P-SDS	−0.4155*	0.2430	0.1721	−0.3548
T-SDS	−0.3148	0.5770**	0.0000	−0.1667
No. of children	(16)	(16)	(14)	(15)

Significant at levels of * $p < 0.05$, ** $p < 0.01$ (2-tailed test − Kendall Rank Correlation[2])

Figure 31   Matrix showing correlations of sociometric data with peer perception and
teacher perception of the gifted children in terms of discipline and
disciplinary interactions in middle schools

	Peers		Teachers	
Sociometry	Gifted child in trouble	being good	Generally well-behaved	Disciplinary interactions
S-SDS	−0.2306	−0.0437	0.3097	−0.1275
W-SDS	−0.4809**	0.1049	0.5056**	−0.2604
P-SDS	−0.3680*	0.1304	0.4141*	−0.1135
T-SDS	−0.3924*	0.3099	0.4484*	−0.1849
No. of children	(21)	(21)	(22)	(21)

Significant at levels of * $p < 0.05$, ** $p < 0.01$ (2-tailed test − Kendall Rank Correlation[2])

between the sociometric SDS and the classroom peers' perceptions of the gifted
children 'getting into trouble' or 'being good', teacher perception of the gifted
children being 'generally well behaved', and the disciplinary interaction scores
of the gifted children above or below the mean for the class.

All the correlations between the sociometric SDS and peer perception of
the gifted children 'being in trouble' were negative in both first and middle
schools. In first schools the correlation with play SDS was significant (at the
level of $p < 0.05$) and in middle schools the correlations with work SDS, play
SDS and total SDS were significant (at the levels of $p < 0.01$ and $p < 0.05$). It
would appear that gifted children who were perceived by their classroom peers
as 'getting into trouble' were less likely to be chosen on the sociometric
questionnaire and therefore had lower social status. This is further supported
by the correlations between the sociometric SDS and peer perception of the
gifted children 'being good', all of which were positive in first schools, and

only one was negative in middle schools, that with sitting SDS. Two of the correlations were significant in first schools, those with work SDS and total SDS (at the level of $p < 0.01$). In middle schools all the correlations between the sociometric data and teacher perception of the gifted children being 'generally well behaved' were positive, that with work SDS was significant (at the level of $p < 0.01$) and those of play SDS and total SDS were also significant (at the level of $p < 0.05$). There were no significant correlations between the sociometric SDS and the disciplinary interaction scores, but all the correlations were negative.

The general picture given by the data is that those gifted children who were perceived by their peers as 'getting into trouble' were likely to have low social status; and those gifted children who were perceived by peers and teachers as 'being good' were likely to have high social status.

It would seem important at this point to examine the extent of agreement between the perceptions of peers and the teachers concerning the behaviour of the gifted children, and how far their perceptions were supported by the disciplinary interactions observed in the classroom. Figures 32 for first schools and 33 for middle schools give the relevant correlations. In first schools the significant negative correlation (at the level of $p < 0.05$) between peer perception of the gifted children 'being in trouble' and teacher perception of the gifted children being 'well behaved' indicates that there was some agreement between the perceptions of the peers and the teachers. The correlations of the data concerning the perceptions of the gifted children by the peers and teachers with the discipline interaction scores are in the expected direction, but they are not significant. In middle schools the correlation between teacher perception of the gifted children being 'generally well behaved' and peer perception of the gifted children 'being in trouble' is significant and negative (at the level of $p < 0.01$), and peer perception of 'being good' significant and positive (at the level of $p < 0.05$). This suggests that the perceptions of the peers and the teachers were similar with regard to the general behaviour of the gifted children. The significant and positive correlation between peer perception of the gifted children 'being in trouble' and the disciplinary interaction scores (at the level of $p < 0.05$); and the significant and negative correlation between teacher perception of the gifted children being 'generally well behaved' and the disciplinary interaction scores (at the level of $p < 0.05$) indicates a close alignment between the perceptions of the teachers and the peers with the disciplinary interactions that occurred.

In general terms, it appears that the perceptions of the classroom peers and the teachers were similar with regard to the behaviour of the gifted children; and that how the gifted children behaved was relatively important for the peers in terms of sociometric choice.

Some of the children who were perceived by their peers as 'getting into trouble' will now be studied. In first schools four gifted children were nominated in this category, namely, David, Karl, Maggy and Benny. Only Benny had a very high number of nominations, seventeen. In middle schools

Figure 32 *Matrix showing correlations of peer perception and teacher perception of the gifted children in terms of discipline together with disciplinary interactions for first schools*

	Peers		Teachers	
	Gifted child in trouble	**being good**	**Generally well-behaved**	**Disciplinary interactions**
Peers – in trouble		−0.1972	−0.5993*	0.0323
Peers – being good			−0.1665	−0.0738
Teachers – well-behaved	(13)	(13)		−0.1101
Disciplinary interactions	(14)	(14)	(14)	

Significant at level of * p < 0.05 (2-tailed test – Kendall Rank Correlation[2])

Figure 33 *Matrix showing correlations of peer perception and teacher perception of the gifted children in terms of discipline together with disciplinary interactions for middle schools*

	Peers		Teachers	
	Gifted child in trouble	**being good**	**Generally well-behaved**	**Disciplinary interactions**
Peers in trouble		−0.4126*	−0.6722**	0.4192*
Peers being good	(21)		0.4075*	−0.1765
Teachers well-behaved	(20)	(20)		−0.4277*
Disciplinary interactions	(19)	(19)	(21)	

Significant at levels of * p < 0.05, ** p < 0.01 (2-tailed test – Kendall Rank Correlation[2])

five children were mentioned, including Laurence and Mandy who had few nominations; George who was nominated twenty-nine times; Benny, whose score had increased to twenty-four; and Christopher who was mentioned nine times.[6]

Case studies of George, Benny and Christopher

The three children who had an extremely high number of nominations on the 'Guess Who' for 'getting into trouble' were George, Benny (in his first and his middle school) and Christopher. They will be examined individually.

George, middle school, year 3

George's typical classroom conduct was illustrated in the lesson extract at the end of the previous chapter, where he was shown to spend the majority of his time walking around the classroom misbehaving. He was clearly aware of his misbehaviour, and in his interview state that,

Interview with George

> I always seem to be in trouble, don't know why, but if someone talks he [the teacher] says "George is that you?" . . . reputation like Miss. B. reckons I'm famous in the staff room.

This self-perception was supported by his peers, and he had the highest number of 'Guess Who' nominations in the total sample of gifted children, which he anticipated in his interview,

> R-What do the other children think of you?
> G-Naughty. You know that green paper you gave us with the "who is the naughtiest" [Guess Who] um I bet they all put me and . . . [another boy].

He also had the second highest disciplinary interaction score of the total sample of gifted children [the highest was Christopher]. Yet, in the BSAG his teacher put him as 'generally well behaved'.

At the same time George's answer to the question 'who would you like to be in the class?' was revealing,

> G-I think I'd like to be Adrian [the gifted footballer] now, 'cos he plays for . . . [a local club], he's a terrific footballer.
> R-Is he?
> G-Yeah, very good. He plays for . . . and er I'd like to be able to, you know, just settle down a bit more, get on with my work like Les [gifted child in the same class].
> He never stops.
> R-You'd like to be able to do that?
> G-Yeah.
> R-Why can't you?
> G-I know I can do it, I just can't sit down and concentrate.
> People go "George come here and look at this" and I go.
> I haven't got the sense to say no.

The extract shows a desire on George's part to improve his conduct and settle down to work.

George's sociometric scores were in excess of one standard deviation above the mean (indicating high social status) in all but 'work SDS'. The lower level of sociometric choice for working may be because he did very little work, and indeed was rarely seated at his desk. His classroom time was spent socializing with the other children. During playtimes he was part of the group who played football with a tennis ball (organized by Adrian). Out of school he stated that he spent much of his time with several school friends 'having a good time', as shown by the extract from his interview,

> G-We play football a lot, and we play up the top of our road where there's a little bit of wasteland. We play on the front of it which is all grass, ... and there's a couple of people across the road there who say "clear off, we're trying to have a peaceful afternoon". So we just sit down and don't take any notice of them, and er they may threaten to call the police up, but before the police got time to come up we're gone, and er we have quite a good laugh really.

George appeared to be aware of social status, as indicated by the fact that he was the only child during the field work who asked the author if the sociometric questionnaire was going to be used to rank the children in popularity. He was the boy in Chapter 4 who was mentioned as being reluctant to go to public school because he wished to stay with his friends and go to the local comprehensive school.

George is interesting because his case is contrary to the group patterns indicated by the correlations already discussed. He had high social status, yet his interaction scores were among the highest, and he was regarded as 'getting into trouble' by his peers, yet he was not perceived as a disciplinary problem by his teacher. The variance between the group patterns revealed by the correlations and individual patterns shows the importance of examining individual cases.

Benny, first school, year 3, and middle school, year 1

Benny had the lowest social status of the total sample of gifted children. In first school his total SDS was in excess of two standard deviations below the mean, which had further decreased in middle school, where it was in excess of three standard deviations below the mean for the class. His interaction scores were the highest of all the first school, and the third highest of all the middle school gifted children. He perceived himself as fairly well-liked, but was regarded by 46 per cent of his middle school class as 'hard to get on with'. Playground observation was deceptive, in that he was invariably surrounded by a group of four or five boys whom he appeared to organize in their games. This gave an impression of good social relations, but in fact he was rejected sociometrically. There appeared to be several reasons for this rejection. The first was that he seemed to have a negative attitude towards his classroom peers, as shown in the following extract from his first school interview,

Interview with Benny in first school

B-I go to ... [NAGC Saturday Club].
R-What's at ...?
B-It's a place for doing things like talks, and painting and things.
R-What sort of children go there?
B-I think it's a place for sort of clever children.
R-Are you a clever child then?
B-Well I've sort of crept in [he put himself as clever in the WAYG the following year].
R-What do you do there?
B-They have talks every week, and I go to those, and they have a newspaper, and I do that.
R-What are the children like?
B-Nice. I've got seven or so friends here, but there I've made eleven or twelve.
R-Are they nice?
B-Yes, they're nicer than the children here because they seem to understand me. The children here talk a different language.
R-Did you say that first, or did your mother?
B-My mother said it first.
R-What do you really think?
B-I agree with my mum. The children here are awkward because they cause fights because they can't talk. I've stopped fighting, though I used to do it ... I don't play with anyone out of school because I don't like the children in the area, they are always fighting. So I play with grown ups.

Secondly, he seemed to be more interested in having many friends, though in the extract from his middle school interview that follows he refers in passing to depth of friendship, and he also compares the first and middle schools.

Interview with Benny in middle school

R-How are you getting on with other people now?
B-I'm making friends a bit more easily now, and the friends that I've got are much more closer friends than I had before. If I compare with my first year at ... [first school] I only made about four friends. Now at this school in the first year I've got about ten friends I made immediately, well not immediately, but gradually made, and then I made friends with some other people, and I've got generally more friends.
R-In what way are they better friends?
B-Well, before, some of my friends at ... [first school] were fair weather friends in a way because if ... they were friends one minute

> and then they wouldn't be friends, if someone didn't have a football or something when we were going out to play they wouldn't be friends with that person any more, and they would be friends with the person who had the football, but now friends at this school are not really friends like that.

The impression given by these two extracts is of a boy who had many friends; was concerned with having quantities of friends; and had, what might be termed, a snobbish attitude towards his classroom peers, which may have been encouraged by his home. In the interview with his first school teacher she revealed that an attempt was made to keep him out of the playground. The school had encouraged him to go home at lunchtime in order to alleviate the problems that he caused by fighting. She also considered him to be popular with the boys.

> He likes to help others and have responsibility. He tidies the library at 1 p.m. in order to keep him out of the playground. If there is a fight he is usually involved. The children look up to him because he is the top of the class and is the one to follow. They know that they can get him into trouble, and they do. He is not altogether liked. He is popular with the boys, but not with the girls. (First school teacher)

Benny's perception of the fighting was slightly different from that of his teacher,

Interview with Benny in first school

> I used to fight a lot. I don't fight anymore, I try and stop the fights by separating them, and then I get involved and get into trouble.

His aggression became worse in the middle school, as revealed by an interview with his middle school headteacher,

> His behaviour to other children is appalling. His physical size is large. He became a bully. His intelligence is rammed down our throats by the mother ... He finds it difficult in play to accept that others are intellectually equal and others will try to make games of theirs and expect to be leader. They gang up on him now and he has developed bad traits, kicks and punches in the stomach ... He went up to a child and punched him in the stomach. I went into it. He told the boy he'd been waiting for him. It appeared that he'd been waiting over a week because there had been half term in between. The boy had called him names over a week ago. I have got a soft spot for him. (Middle school headteacher)

Benny's aggressive behaviour in the classroom resulted in drastic action according to his middle school teacher,

Last week someone bit him, so he had a feel of what it was like. At times we have him without shoes so that he doesn't hurt when he kicks. (Middle school teacher)

Benny perceived himself as clever, and was perceived by many of his peers as academically able. He received more nominations on the 'Guess Who' for academic ability than any other first school gifted child. He also had the highest BSAG score of any first school gifted child, which was reduced in the middle school.

It would appear in Benny's case that his low social status was caused by a combination of factors, such as slight 'snobbishness' and physical aggressiveness. The extent of the contribution to his social status by his very high interaction score and his academic ability is difficult to ascertain.

Christopher, middle school, year 3

Christopher was similar to Benny in his interaction and sociometric scores. He had the highest total interaction score for the middle schools, and the second lowest sociometric total SDS, which was more than three standard deviations below the mean for his class. He also received more disciplinary contacts than any other middle school gifted child. This was suggested, in the previous chapter, to be the result of deliberate action on his part, apparently to gain attention. He was perceived by himself and by his peers as being academically able, and he had a high BSAG score. In the playground Christopher was observed to be completely isolated. Every playtime he read a book at the top of some steps which separated him slightly from the main playground. During his interview he stated that he was called a bookworm by some of his peers.

Interview with Christopher

R-What do the other children think of you?
C-I don't know.
R-You've never thought about it?
C-They call me a bookworm though.
R-Do they?
C-Yeah, and Vic and David at the playground sat down reading with me, and David was kind of ripping the kind of thing and I hit him, and David said "that's not a good bookworm" or something, that was it. When David went away Vic said "now we have two bookworms minus two" or something like that, and he was reading *Monsieur . . . in Paris"*, and I've already read that in another class.
R-Do you think you're a bookworm?
C-I like reading a lot, I never thought you know bookworm, I like reading a lot, and I do read a lot, I like to.

Christopher was aware of his social isolation in school, and he accounted for his out of school isolation as being because there were no children from the school living near to him.

> R-Who do you play with in school?
> C-Well I don't really play with anyone. I usually just read, but sometimes I play with Rod who's in the top class, and apart from that I haven't had any friends for a long while. The last ones I had was when I was in class one [first school] when I played with some of the big girls in the top class and then they went away to ... [senior school], and I haven't had anyone since then, so now I just read a book in the playground.
> R-Have you tried to make friends?
> C-Yeah, I sometimes try to talk to people when they read at the top of those little steps.
> R-What about outside school, is there anybody you play with then?
> C-Only my brother, because we live two miles from the school and there ... anywhere near round us.

His teachers were well aware of his social isolation. His teacher stated during the interview that,

> ... the world that he lives in is a closeted world separate and apart from everything and everybody else. And this tends, you asked me how I felt about him, this tends to make Christopher very self-centred. He can't appreciate other people's point of view.
> R-What do the other children think of him?
> T-I think on the whole the children in my class are very very tolerant to him, because there's no doubt about it, he's a disruptive influence. But they've been in the same class with him for a few years now, have got used to him. In the classroom situation they will respond with a typical sort of "Oh Christopher", but they do not really apply any malice to him, which in a way is unusual, because he stands out from the rest by his own individuality and his inability to get involved in games with other children or friendships with other children.

The teacher was concerned about what would happen to him when he went on to senior school,

> R-Is he popular?
> T-He's not unpopular, but not popular either. He is a nuisance and the class are very tolerant ... I dread to think what it'll be like at ... [senior school]. Here the children are very long suffering of him because they've had him since the infants, because he does disrupt the class. They do get fed up sometimes, but they don't bully him the way they would at the comprehensive school.

The two cases of Benny and Christopher suggest that their low social status stemmed primarily from their social inadequacy or disturbance. The extent of the contribution made by their giftedness to their social inadequacy is difficult to assess.

It would appear from the examination of the data in this chapter that the social status of gifted children is affected by other factors than giftedness, such as the dominance by gifted children of the interactions in the classroom and/or the perceptions of their peers concerning the behaviour of the gifted children. The data from the BSAG will now be examined for the sample of gifted children, and related to previous research.

The Bristol Social Adjustment Guide

In recent years it has been suggested in the media that gifted children have problems of maladjustment (Benn, 1982b). This notion has been supported by the NAGC and has filtered into the schools (Maltby, 1979). The HMI survey referred to the discussion on television and in the press which associated maladjustment to general giftedness, however, they found few children whose teachers considered them to be both gifted and maladjusted. Some gifted children who were referred to as disturbed, the report suggested, were or had been having difficulty adjusting to inappropriate teaching methods (G.B., DES, 1977). Actual research concerning the emotional stability of gifted children has given the opposite impression from that popularly held, and has found gifted children to be above average in adjustment (Gallagher, 1975; Hitchfield, 1973; Shields, 1975; and Terman, 1925).

In the present study the Bristol Social Adjustment Guide was not used as an assessment of maladjustment (see the Appendix) because of the general problems of measuring social adjustment, and the particular weaknesses of the BSAG. Rather, the teachers were asked to complete the BSAG form in order to enable comparisons to be made with the previous research of Hitchfield and Freeman, and also to focus on certain phrases.

Stott, in the manual to the BSAG, suggests that a score of less that nine indicates stability or near stability, and a score of twenty plus indicates maladjustment (Stott, 1974). Figure 34 gives the percentage of children whose scores place them in the three ranges of *stable*, *unsettled*, and *maladjusted*. Three samples of children are shown. The cohort from the National Child Development Study are given at ages seven and eleven as being representative of the general population of children of that age in Britain, this was a longitudinal study of 15,496 children (Davie et al, 1972); Hitchfield's sample of gifted children at ages seven and eleven; and the present sample of gifted children in first schools, middle schools, and first and middle schools together. From the figures it can be seen that both groups of gifted children were perceived by their teachers to be better adjusted than the cohort, and that there was a rough approximation between Hitchfield's and the present sample.

In Freeman's study she did not follow Stott's recommendations, but redesignated the three categories of adjustment, which increased the number

Figure 34   Figure showing the percentage of children in each range of adjustment
according to the BSAG scores for the National cohort, Hitchfield's gifted
children, and gifted children in the present study

Stott's BSAG score	0–9 (stable)		10–19 (unsettled)		20+ (maladjusted)	
	number	%age	number	%age	number	%age
Cohort @ 7 years		67%		21%		12%
Hitchfield @ 7 years*		88%		10%		3%
Cohort @ 11 years		67%		21%		12%
Hitchfield @ 11 years*		86%		7%		7%
Sample, both schools	27	75%	8	22%	1	3%
Sample, first schools	9	64%	5	36%	0	0%
Sample, middle schools	18	82%	3	14%	1	5%

* Figures taken from tables A3.1 and A3.2 of the Appendix to Hitchfield (1973) published by
Longmans in 1974.

of children who appeared in the maladjusted group considerably. She divided
her sample of parent identified gifted children into *good*, *moderate* and *poor*
adjustment groups according to scores of two or less, three to eleven,
and twelve or more on the teacher completed BSAG. It seems likely that a
comparison of Freeman's sample of seventy gifted children with a National
cohort would again indicate that Freeman's gifted children were perceived by
their teachers as on the whole better adjusted, figure 35.

Figure 34 shows that there are some differences between the first and
middle school gifted children of the present study. More of the middle school
children, in terms of percentages, were perceived as 'stable', and more of the
first school children were in the 'unsettled' group. There could be a variety of
explanations for these differences which are not necessarily to do with the first
school children being less well adjusted. It may be that the BSAG is less
appropriate or less discriminating for use with younger children, in that
behaviour, which may be considered inappropriate at middle school level or
older, may be relatively normal for younger children. An example in the BSAG
is the question concerning 'General manner with teacher'. 'Over friendly' is
taken to be a sign of attention seeking, but many young children regard their
teacher in the same way that they would their mother or a family friend, and
their friendliness is not necessarily attention seeking. 'Shy but would like to be
friendly' is marked as unforthcomingness, but frequently first school children

Figure 35   Percentage of gifted children in each range of adjustment according to
the redesignated system of BSAG scores for Freeman's and the present
sample

BSAG score	2 or less	3–11	12 or more
Freeman's sample*	30%	47%	23%
Present sample	39%	44%	17%

* Figures adapted from the tables on pages 193 and 194 of Freeman's study.

take time to adjust to being outside their own homes, and away from their mother, and therefore they may act in a shy manner. It might be stated that teachers would make allowances, but the teachers are unaware, when completing the forms, of which phrases contribute to the final adjustment score. They are requested to note what they observe.

There was only one child who appeared in the 'maladjusted' category according to Stott's recommended scoring.

Hank, middle school, year 1

Hank scored more than twenty on the BSAG, indicating that he was perceived by his teacher to be maladjusted. His scores were predominantly in the under-reaction section. His records from the first school were littered with phrases such as 'He still exists in his own world'; 'His absorption in his own world makes him unreceptive to advice or suggestion'; 'Hank's behaviour now frequently shows up in comparison with that of most of the other children ... He still does not conform to the general standard'; 'Great imagination'. The comment on transfer to a new school was, 'Highly intelligent but rather strange boy. Very much one on his own and still in a dream world – a mixture of immature behaviour and conversation of an adult level. Dislike of physical activity!' His present teacher described him during the interview as,

> ... a little vacant ... a little eccentric at times. Hank is very much a scatter brain. He is often late to school. He forgets his work when he takes it home because he's been slow. He fiddles and fidgets with pencils a lot. His desk is always a tip. He didn't bring his folder for four weeks when the student came to work with gifted children.[7] In the end I had a quiet word with the Head and next week he brought it in.

The teacher seemed to ascribe much of Hank's *problems* to the mother's over-protective attitude.

> He's gained a lot of confidence in swimming. At the beginning of the year Hank came into PE and stood. The girls undressed and dressed him at the beginning and the end. When the mother takes him swimming the mother undresses him, towels him down, sits him on her lap like a baby and powders him. The brother is younger and bigger than Hank. She is having trouble distinguishing between them and finding identity [for Hank] as the older child. When Hank is late it's because the brother wants to go to the loo. I have asked mother to make sure he gets here at the right time because he is being allowed to be different.

Presumably the teacher did not consider eccentricity to be a *good* thing. Hank's painting was extremely unusual and slightly abstract, and perhaps reflected some of his difficulties. However, his teacher did not like his concentration on one subject.

> I haven't seen giftedness even in his art work. There is always conflict in pictures of animals and insects. He can't be very original in his thinking because he always leads back to the same.

The concentration in his painting on animals was because of his keenness for bird and animal watching as stated in his interview,

Interview with Hank

R-What do you like doing best out of school?
H-Well I really like bird watching.
R-Do you do it very much?
H-Yes.
R-What do you do?
H-I sort of get a little guide out of my pocket and I look and then I wait for the bird, the bird will be around the air, and when it pops down I look at my guide quickly to see what bird it is and I usually record it when I get home.
R-Do you use binoculars?
H-I used to use binoculars, but mine are broken. I've got a telescope which I use sometimes.
R-What sort of things do you do at weekends?
H-At weekends I usually do bird watching, practising my violin, drawing and recording my sights, and I'm also an animal watcher. I've got two main bird guides ... and I've got a guide of animals.
R-Do you go out by yourself to do your bird watching?
H-Usually, but sometimes I do it when we're shopping. I find the birds round the town like sparrows and I find different kinds of pigeons like wood pigeons.

His interest in animals appeared to distract him from his school work.

R-What do you want to do when you leave school?
H-Something about animals. I'd rather be a park owner, somehow a sort of nature park owner or reserve.
R-What do you like doing best in school?
H-I like a bit of science and nature study. We're doing an insect project at the moment.
R-What about maths, how do you get on with maths?
H-Not very well. I'm not very good at mathematics.
R-Why's that?
H-Well really I don't really know why I'm not good at mathematics.
R-Do you like maths?
H-No. Sometimes I'm a bit of a day dreamer.

R-What does that mean?

H-While I'm meant to be thinking about one thing, I seem to be thinking about something else.

R-What sort of things do you think about?

H-Mainly animals, I just sort of go off, and how they're getting on and how the animals live, and I sort of go off all the maths and English and my work I have to do.

R-It's a funny thing to day dream about animals, do you see pictures of them in your head?

H-Yes. I see pictures of the rarest bird which I know off by heart, the . . ./kestrel. There are only eight or ten nests have been recorded so far, there might be less than a million left.

R-A million's a lot.

H-Yes, but it isn't when you get to the animal world. Rabbits are starting to go down too.

Hank's behaviour in a mathematics lesson was shown in the concentration section of the previous chapter, where he spent the majority of his time dreaming, chewing his pencil, fiddling, and talking to his next door neighbour.

In the sociometry Hank received positive choices, though his score did not deviate markedly from the mean. In the playground he normally stood on the steps close to the classroom and watched the other children. He did not perceive himself as well-liked or popular, as confirmed in his interview.

R-Do you play with your brother very much?

H-Not often, 'cos he's usually off at parties.

R-Why's that, does he go to that many?

H-Well, he's rather popular at school.

R-Are you?

H-Not much.

R-Why's that?

H-Well I've come to a new school and there's children who don't know me. It takes a very very long time, about over a year for popularity to grow.

R-What school did you go to before?

H-The first school.

R-And are there different children at this school from the ones you were with in your first school?

H-Well I had the same children that are in my class, but there have been some added and some taken away.

R-Would you like to be popular?

H-Not much, 'cos I like staying at home drawing.

Hank had accounted to himself for his lack of popularity, though his logic was strange, because he had been with the same children for several years.

Hank had come up from the first school with very high NFER scores, and a reputation for being bright, an excellent reader, and an imaginative though untidy writer. At home the parents were keen that he should be good at mathematics, but his first school reports indicated a gradual decline in that subject. In middle school he puzzled his teacher and headteacher because they could see no indication of him being academically exceptional, which was exaggerated by his getting very little down on paper. In his interview he stated that he did not like school work and found it boring,

> H-... Well, I don't like doing work.
> R-What's wrong with it?
> H-Well it seems to be a bit boring.
> R-In what way?
> H-Well when you keep on doing work and keep on doing work you sort of get bored.
> R-Is there any sort of work that wouldn't bore you?
> H-Bird watching and animal watching and writing down the results.

Hank appeared to be retiring into himself, and rejecting the conformity of classroom expectations of the production of written work. He also appeared to be restricting his interests entirely to the natural sciences.

Hank's teacher accounted for his problems by referring to his home background. In Chapter 3 reference was made to Lacey's psycho-socio-cultural resources concept, which fitted the teachers' conceptualizations of the home backgrounds of the gifted children, especially with reference to social class (Lacey, 1970). The problems of all the children who were perceived by the teachers to be in the 'unsettled' and 'maladjusted' groups according to their BSAG scores, plus Vi who attended a family consultation clinic, were accounted for by the difficulties that the children had at home. A brief description of these accounts will be given.

Vi's father had a terminal illness, and the mother pressurized the child. Maggy's parents pressurized her. Hugh had moved home frequently, and had at one time lived in very poor surroundings. He had had unfortunate experiences at a very formal nursery school where he had been forced to write. This was given as an explanation for his writing difficulties once at school. Benny was from a one parent family, and the mother was very dominating. Laurence was an adopted Asian boy, who had had traumatic experiences at a private school. Christopher was from a one parent family, where he was over-protected by the mother and grandmother. No material was available to substantiate the impressions given by the teachers. It is interesting that so little reference was made to any problems that may have been related to, or caused by the school.

Social Class and Gender

No anticipatory hypotheses were formed regarding differences in social class or gender, apart from that the boys would be more likely to be perceived negatively with regard to discipline. There was a significant correlation between gender and peer perception of 'being good' (at the level of $p < 0.05$), which indicated a tendency for gifted girls rather than gifted boys to be perceived as good by their peers.[8] No significant correlations were found for any of the data with regard to social class.

Discussion

Considerable emphasis in this chapter has been placed on statistical material. It should be treated with caution for two reasons. Firstly, because of the division in the analysis between first and middle schools, the sample numbers are small, which is further exaggerated by some missing data (see the Appendix). Secondly, the gifted children are individuals, as are their teachers. The children are heterogeneous in their interaction and sociometric scores, and they are perceived as such by their peers and teachers. However, the non-statistical material has in many cases illustrated, explained and frequently supported the quantitative data.

There were two areas of exploration in this chapter which are considered to be particularly important because of the originality of the findings. The first area is that concerned with the relationships between the perceptions of the gifted children by their peers, the gifted children, and the teachers about the social status and academic ability of the gifted children. The second area is the negative relationships between the interaction and sociometric scores. These two areas will be discussed in more detail.

It appears that the specific teacher label of the term gifted was not particularly relevant for the perceptions of gifted children by their peers, in that a distinction between children who were labelled gifted or non-gifted was not made by the peers or by the gifted children. Perhaps more important was the awareness of the peers concerning the academic ability of the gifted children, which appeared to increase developmentally. Similarities appeared to exist between the gifted childrens' self-concept and peer perception of academic ability which were also developmental. Many teachers and headteachers are reluctant to go through the procedure of labelling children as gifted because of the supposed effect on the children, however it would appear that academically able children are in effect *labelled by their peers*. This may be the result of labelling by previous teachers, as the non-gifted children had been considered gifted in the past.

The self-perception of the gifted children concerning their social status, as measured by the sociometry, did not appear to be particularly discerning. There are several possible explanations for this. Previous psychological research would suggest that the children had not reached the developmental stage where they would be aware of how they were perceived socially by the other children. The children may not have acknowledged to themselves their social situation, and therefore would not be able to commit it to paper, nor reveal it in an interview. On the other hand, the understanding of how other people perceive onself is always difficult, especially when it is concealed from one. Therefore, unless the peers were openly unpleasant, hostile, or aggressive, there may have been no indication for the gifted children of how to perceive their own social status. This was clearly shown in the study of Benny, who was surrounded by his peers, but was disliked by them. The final point reveals a difficulty which is inherent to the methods of sociometry used. A child who has one or two 'good friends' could well perceive himself as well liked, and accurately so. But negative choices from other members of the class would give a negative sociometric impression.

The negative relationship between sociometric choice within the classroom and interaction scores, especially in middle schools, has implications that need to be considered seriously. If high classroom interaction affects the classroom social status of gifted children, then teachers need to be aware of the possible connection. However, as already pointed out, the one may not cause the other. There was some indication in the previous chapter that interactional sequences were not necessarily entirely controlled by the teacher, and the process may be two-way. But, if teachers understand that the presence of a particularly able child in the classroom may distort the dynamics of interactive behaviour in favour of that child, and that the child may be affected socially within the classroom environment as a consequence, then that teacher is able, and may wish to take positive steps to alter the situation (such possibilities will be discussed in the next chapter). The present research has indicated what may be the case for some children, and the possible consequences, knowledge of which may be useful for teachers to recognize similarities or differences in their own classrooms.

Notes

1. The following formula, taken from Proctor and Loomis (1951), gives the Choice Rejection Status (CRS) which gives the choice rejection pattern of individual i:

$$\text{Choice Status} = CS = \frac{C}{(N-1)}$$

$$\text{Rejection Status} = RS = \frac{R}{(N-1)}$$

Choice Rejection Status = CRS = CS − RS
where
C = number of persons choosing i
R = number of persons rejecting i
N = number of persons in the class

Using this formula it is then possible to compare individuals from different classes using the standard deviation score as follows:

$$z_x = \frac{X-M}{\sigma_x}$$

where

X = the CRS score

$$M = \frac{\Sigma X}{N}$$

$$x = X - M$$

$$\sigma_x = \sqrt{\frac{x^2}{N}}$$

$$z_x = \frac{x}{\sigma_x}$$

2. Pearson's correlation would have been inappropriate here because the data were not distributed normally. In many cases individual children deviated a great deal from the mean, so a correlation that used the figures would have been affected by individuals. Kendall's Rank Correlation, according to Kendall, measures the degree of correspondence between two rankings, or measures the intensity of rank correlation (Kendall, 1970). By using a rank correlation one is able to see the correspondence between children ranked according to their sociometric scores and their interaction scores, in other words, the likelihood of a child being top on one and top on the other.

3. The numbers for both first and middle schools were small (see the Appendix).

4. Experience using Nash's method of ability placement was that the children tended to put themselves towards the middle of the class in ability. For example, children whom the teachers considered to be at the top of the class in ability placed themselves one-quarter to one-third of the way down the class, and those at the bottom of the class put themselves up. This method was found to be so unsatisfactory that it was replaced by the 'Where Are You Game'.

5. The children in the present study moved to middle schools at the age of nine.

6. It is unfortunate that the 'Guess Who' data were not available for Robert as he had the highest number of disciplinary interactions of all the first school gifted children.

7. It was mentioned in Chapter 4 that third year teacher training students worked with groups of gifted and/or very able children one afternoon per week for several weeks.

8. The actual significance figure was 0.028, 1-tailed test, thirty-seven cases.

7   Conclusions

Many of the substantive findings of the study were discussed extensively within the context of the analysis. In the concluding chapter the focus will be on a few issues and dilemmas arising from the analysis, namely:

(a) Prescriptions developed from the analysis of classroom observation.

(b) The individual nature of the gifted children and the danger of stereotyping.

(c) One area in which the labelling approach is inadequate.

The chapter will conclude with an examination of the strengths and weaknesses of the present research, and suggest possible areas for future research.

Prescriptions

Four important problems were presented in previous chapters:

(a) The lack of knowledge by teachers concerning gifted children.

(b) The paucity of educational provision for the gifted children.

(c) The inequality of teacher-pupil contact, which tended to favour gifted children.

(d) The apparent negative relationship between teacher-gifted pupil inter-actions and the social status of the gifted children.

Knowledge about the awareness of gifted children would best be achieved within the province of initial teacher training, and through in-service courses provided for those presently teaching. Unfortunately, such courses have had, and still have low priority in the minds of many teachers and educational administrators, the reasons for which were discussed in Chapter 1. However, interest in, and provision for gifted children are developing in several parts of the country, though these developments are mainly reliant on the commitment or enthusiasm of individuals and small pressure groups.

It was demonstrated in Chapter 5 that there was a tendency for gifted children to dominate the interactions that occurred between teachers and children. It was suggested that in terms of contacts with the teacher, the presence of the gifted child may be considered to be disadvantageous for the remainder of the children in the class. Teachers should be made increasingly aware of the inequalities of teacher-pupil interactions, especially as they concern gifted children. However, the assumption cannot be made that teachers are in total control of the interactive patterns of the class. In Chapter 5 it was pointed out that interactions are dynamic, involving a two-way process of initiation and response on the part of teachers and children. Therefore, although teacher awareness of the interactive patterns are important, it may not necessarily be within the power of the teacher to counteract or change these patterns. There are a variety of possibilities that teachers might consider as suitable methods for providing for gifted children, which may also have some influence on the dominance of classroom interactions by some gifted children.

Despite the impression given in the media that primary schooling is progressive, it has been suggested that methods of teaching in primary schools are mainly didactic (Kirby, 1981; and Simon, 1981). This was generally the case in the middle school classrooms observed. In first schools, the general tendency was for children to work at their own pace, individually or in small groups. In Chapter 4 it was suggested that the methods used in first schools facilitated the incorporation of both specific and circumstantial enrichment for gifted children. It was noted that in middle school classes where schemes were used, such as SMP for mathematics, and SRA for English, circumstantial enrichment was almost inevitably available for the gifted children.

Two methods of teaching are proposed which might also help gifted children, as well as the other children in the class. The first is small group teaching, and the second is the development of projects which are created by and through the interests of the children in the class. Small group teaching methods incorporate a variety of systems of organization which would be dependent on the philosophy of the teacher concerned. The groups may be created by the teacher according to the ability of the children, and may include children of like or mixed ability; or they may develop according to friendship groups; or children who have similar interests may form a group. These groups need not necessarily be permanent. If teachers changed to small group teaching methods, where children collaborate and work together it might be advantageous for all the children, and especially the gifted children. In this type of environment the gifted children would no longer be competitors and possible academic threats to their peers, but would be fellow discoverers and researchers. The method would aid the language, work and organizational skills of all the participants, and would permit the teacher to interact with the children on a more individuated basis. If allowed to work through their own interests children, such as Hank, might be able to extend their knowledge, and develop their expertise into other areas of the curriculum. However, some teachers may not be sufficiently confident to teach in this way, or they may reject group teaching for pedagogic reasons. In the case of the latter group of teachers, it would be reasonable to take care during question and answer lessons that questions were varied in difficulty.

Social isolation within the classroom may be considered by many teachers to be detrimental for a child. In Chapter 6 it was indicated that there was a tendency for gifted children who had high interaction scores to be perceived negatively by their peers, and may therefore have been relatively isolated socially. However, it was also shown that this social isolation was not necessarily transferred to the playground environment. Bearing the latter point in mind, some teachers may not consider that social isolation within the classroom is important. In which case, there are more possibilities available for the teacher in providing for gifted children.

The first possibility would be for the gifted child to be allowed to work independently of the rest of the class, on individual projects and assignments, in other words enrichment methods may be used. This would be similar to the method of working which the children would meet later on in their educational careers, at secondary school or university, where the majority of time is spent working independently of peers. Renzulli has suggested that where it is clear that a child has mastered an area or a skill in a subject, as assessed by a pretest, then 'compacting' should occur. Compacting is where such a pupil is allowed to miss work in areas in which he is already competent, and use the time 'saved' on extension activities (Renzulli et al, 1983).

There are enrichment materials being developed at present which are designed specifically for gifted and/or very able children. If these materials alleviate the problems of differential contact with the teacher, then they may be economically justifiable. Most of the enrichment material is intended to be self-explanatory and self-teaching. It should therefore result in the teacher being able to give more attention to the other children. However, the school has to have the initial financial resources to cover the purchase of the materials, which would have to be appropriate to the needs and interests of the particular child. The cost would be mitigated if central resource areas for gifted children were developed, containing published materials, as well as those produced by individual teachers or, as described by Foster, groups of teachers (Foster, 1983). This would reduce the personal pressure on teachers, as well as provide an extension of choice of enrichment materials. However, care would have to be taken that teachers were aware of the resource centre, and that it was situated in a centre which was visited by teachers for other reasons than the presence of a gifted child in their class.

At present many primary schools are entering the *microcomputer revolution*. A microcomputer can provide enrichment for gifted children on an individual or a small group basis. Green suggested that the microcomputer can be valuable for gifted children, who enjoy using it as an enrichment tool,and provide relief for the class teacher from the pressure of occupying the child (Green, 1981). Ellingham stated that 'a computer ... has been found to be particularly useful for "stretching" the more gifted children in our unstreamed classes.' (Ellingham, 1982, page 35). The microcomputer can be used in a variety of ways with gifted children, as it can with all children. However, possibly the most beneficial for the child and the teacher, from the point of view of enrichment, would be to use it for simulation, educational game playing, as a data bank, and in combination with other materials for topic work. There is no reason why gifted children who are interested should not learn how to write programs. Microcomputers are being used with a few groups of gifted children at present, and some software is being developed for specific use with gifted children (Schools Council Newsletter, 1982).

Although there are many advantages in using microcomputers with gifted children, there are several aspects of its use which need to be considered. The assumption cannot be made that children who are gifted will necessarily enjoy working with a microcomputer. The cost of providing software which is specifically for gifted children needs to be justified. However, it is possible, and will in all probability become more so, to hire software from a central library, such as the MUSE Software Library, at minimal cost (as little as twenty pence in January 1982). This would enable the teacher to choose software according to the interests and capabilities of the particular child at that time. Further justification would be needed for the allocation of extra time on the micro-computer to the gifted child, as compared with other children. However, the cost of teachers as a resource is more expensive than that of microcomputers. It has been indicated that some gifted children do dominate the use of the teachers as a resource, and therefore the occupation of these children on the microcomputer, at times, may be beneficial for their classroom peers, as well as for themselves. At present there are insufficient microcomputers in schools for the numbers of children. Therefore, there is no possibility that gifted children will spend too much time working on the microcomputer and thereby create a danger of limiting the development of their social skills.

A further possibility of providing for gifted children is to have a peripatetic or advisory teacher in an area, who is responsible for gifted children. This system is already being used in a variety of ways in some counties. The peripatetic teacher can be used to withdraw gifted children from their normal classrooms to be taught individually. Again, from the point of view of differential interaction in the classroom, this may allow the teacher to concen-trate on the other children in the class. At the same time, the gifted children are catered for intellectually, by being permitted to work at a level commensurate with their abilities. The peripatetic teacher could develop materials suitable for the use of a particular child in the classroom. This relieves the busy teacher from the pressure of providing for one or two children individually, at the same time as developing material for the other children. The peripatetic teacher may also act as an informed advisor to the classroom teacher, which can be done in two ways. Advice can be given about classroom organization, or the handling of individual gifted children. Also, knowledge can be imparted about where to obtain curriculum materials, and subject expertise from other adults in the community. Further, the peripatetic teacher may organize in-service courses for teachers and groups, during which curriculum materials may be developed. This system has been used in Essex, where residential courses for gifted children were run to test out the materials developed, and to provide in-service experience with gifted children for teachers (Wallace, 1982a).

Gifted children are individuals, and therefore the provision for each child should be considered according to the individual personality of the child and of the teacher concerned. There is no *correct way* to provide for gifted children. Only a way for each child. The present research has indicated what has happened to some children, and the possible consequences for those children. Such information may be useful for teachers who may recognize similarities to and/or differences from what occurs within their own classroom.

The Heterogeneity of Gifted Children

Throughout this book it has been emphasized that the sample of gifted children contains a diverse group of individuals. Although overall tendencies were discussed, there were shown to be enormous divergencies between individual children. This was particularly obvious in the quantitative analysis which referred to interaction and sociometric data. This diversity might be attributed, in part at least, to the age range of eight years which was covered, but children of the same age were also shown to be very different from one another. The research on gifted children, which was considered in the initial chapters, much of which took giftedness to be objectively given, frequently proceeded to categorize gifted children homogeneously and attempted to reveal common causal factors for giftedness. There is a danger in this procedure resulting in the depersonalization of gifted children, where they become a part of their category characterizations and are no longer considered as individuals. Schur labelled this procedure as becoming *deviantized*. (Schur, 1979). The child is no longer a child, but a gifted child. This danger is increased by the use of teacher checklists, which are recommended by a variety of sources (Clarke, 1983; Devon County Council, 1977; Hoyle and Wilks, 1974; Kerry, 1981; Wallace, 1982b; and West Sussex County Council, 1974). Although the checklists are normally accompanied by admonitions that they should not be taken literally, but used as a guide, they may still contribute to some of the stereotyped images concerning gifted children which are voiced within staff rooms.

Schur has suggested that with deviancy, interest in the studies which attempt to categorize groups will decline and be replaced by studies of the process by which behaviour and individuals are defined and reacted to as deviant (Schur, 1980). This study has attempted to do just that, and in the event has also revealed the complicated and interactive nature of the process of defining and designating children in schools as gifted.

The Labelling Approach and 'Covert' Giftedness

The use of the labelling approach was considered to be valuable in that it focussed on children who were labelled and thereby treated as gifted in schools. It also provided a framework which aided the understanding of the processes by which gifted children were categorized as gifted. Of necessity the approach precluded a researcher-imposed definition of giftedness which has been inherent in many previous studies. However, it also prevents examination of *covert* gifted children (Acklaw, 1982; Bridges, 1969; Clarke, 1983; and Painter, 1977). Covert giftedness is defined as giftedness which is not apparent to the teacher because of the under-achievement of the child. Clearly the use of labelling theory precludes the discussion of children who are not labelled as gifted. However, considerable concern about these children exists, and it has often been considered that the use of IQ tests would screen for them.

There are three points which are relevant to this research. The first concerns the definition of giftedness, whether giftedness entails achievement and/or potential for achievement which can be revealed by testing. This was examined in the practical application of labels by headteachers and teachers to actual children in Chapters 2 and 3, where it was indicated that teachers tended to label children as gifted according to achievement, whereas headteachers tended to use test results. The second point is that the tendency of the children in the present sample to interact more with their teachers than the mean for their class, may indicate that they were initially labelled as a result of this tendency, and the quiet 'covert' gifted children may have been overlooked by teachers in the labelling process. Finally, Vernon suggested that 50 per cent of gifted children are 'missed', the greatest proportion of whom originate from the ranks of the working-class (Vernon, 1969). This confirms two points made in the research, that working-class children were under-represented among the children labelled as gifted; and that once labelled as gifted they were likely to be delabelled. Wood, in a small-scale survey of headteachers' attudes to giftedness, found that more than half of the sample agreed that many gifted children were unrecognized in schools (Wood, 1974).

Unfortunately, it is outside the scope of the present research to do more than draw attention to the issues, the more fitting solutions to which would need to be identified and answered by further research.

The Research

This research has embarked on an original perspective of the study of gifted children. Its particular feature is the comprehensiveness of its design, its pragmatic nature, and the combination of quantitative and qualitative methodologies. However, these features imposed an exploratory rather than a conclusive element on the research because of their time-consuming demands, and the consequently low numbers of children studied. However,

Elliott does suggest that there is a naturalistic element to the generalizability of case studies, and it is the task of the audience, rather than the researcher, to generalize through the audience's experience of classroom life (Elliott, 1978).

Further research is needed in order to confirm and/or extend some of the results. Possible suggestions are as follows:

(a) The examination of differences between, and the differential treatment of, children labelled as gifted by teachers, and those screened for giftedness using test procedures.

(b) A larger-scale study of the interactions between teachers and gifted children, similar to the present study, using a combination of qualitative and quantitative observation techniques, but incorporating a more soph-isticated observation schedule appropriate to the study of gifted children.

(c) Research into the effect of Local Education Authorities' policy on the process of labelling and the provision for gifted children.

(d) A study of the use of microcomputers in the education of gifted children, and the development of software suitable for use with gifted children.

(e) A comparison of the education of gifted children in private and state schools in terms of differences in provision, and incorporating classroom observation.

(f) An examination of the labelling process when the children who are labelled as gifted transfer to secondary school.

The aim of this book was to study the gifted children in the normal classroom with few preconceived notions on the part of the researcher. It was also intended to arrive at an understanding of the perceptions of the partici-pants by incorporating a multi-dimensional methodology. It is hardly surpris-ing that an original approach should provide new and interesting data. Only time and repetition in further research will reveal its adequacy. However, if it stimulates thought and discussion it will be valuable in itself.

Appendix

Methodology

In the Introduction several research studies were cited that claimed to show the lack of efficiency by teachers in identifying gifted children. These would appear to have been based upon a unitary conception of giftedness, which ignored or presumed the teachers' interpretation of giftedness. In the present research, the stance tends to lean towards that of the *interactionist* camp, as derived from the work of Mead (Mead, 1934). Importance is attached to the way that the participants perceive their world and the dynamics of how they interact in that world. In order for a researcher to understand what is observed, it would appear to be necessary to have some comprehension of the meanings and the viewpoints of those involved, rather than imposing the researcher's own. As stated by Blumer 'people act toward things on the basis of the meaning that these things have for them, not on the basis of the meaning that these things have for the outside scholar' (Blumer, 1976, page 15).

On the basis of the conclusions derived from the literature review in Chapter 1 and the application of interactionism to the study of gifted children in schools, there are several implications, for the research methodology which are as follows:

(a) That the children studied be those who are categorized as gifted by the teachers, not by the researchers, because these are the children who will be treated as gifted children.

(b) As suggested by Berger and Luckman, that the perceptions of all the participants be examined because of the likely variation in world view or construction of reality between groups and individuals (Berger and Luckmann, 1967). For this study the participants are the teachers, peers and the gifted children.

(c) As interaction takes place in a social context (in this study the classroom and the playground) it would appear essential that activity in both these arenas be observed especially as there is at present a paucity of reported observational studies of gifted children in *normal* classrooms.

Concurrent with the interactionist perspective is the view that a combination of *quantitative* and *qualitative* research overcomes some of the pitfalls and criticisms associated with either. It may be considered that the former provides generalizable and the latter illustrative, and at times, explanatory material. However, the synthesis of dissimilar methodologies does create problems. Quantitative data collection requires a reasonable number of subjects in order to be viable statistically, whereas qualitative data is more time-consuming to obtain and therefore limits the number of possible subjects. Qualitative data can be employed to generate hypotheses. On the other hand, the analyses of quantitative research data generally demands that the hypotheses be formulated prior to entering the research field in order that the appropriate measures be used. In this study some working hypotheses were postulated beforehand, and measuring devices were chosen to test them. At the same time it was anticipated that these hypotheses would become more complex, be amended, or modified, through the analysis of the qualitative data, especially the teacher interviews. Glaser and Strauss's constant comparative method was adapted so that the hypotheses that were generated as an ongoing part of the analysis of interview and observational material would be tested by the whole sample, and not by a separate sample (Glaser and Strauss, 1967).[1]

The research perspective of interactionism plus a combination of quantitative and qualitative methodologies can simultaneously be encompassed in the method of *triangulation*. Cohen and Manion described two uses of triangulation, the first that of 'different accounts of the same events are provided by different observers from different locations or viewpoints' (Cohen and Manion, 1981, page 51) which complies with the symbolic interactionist requirement of acquiring the perspectives of all the participants. This will be called *primary triangulation*. Their second use was 'the use of two or more methods of data collection in the study of some aspect of human behaviour' (Cohen and Manion, 1980, page 208) which can comply with the quantitative/qualitative perspective, and shall be labelled *secondary triangulation*.

Primary triangulation is provided in the present research by the perceptions of the classroom participants, teachers, peers, and gifted children, represented as three triangles in figure 36. The perceptions of non-participating influencers, such as previous teachers, headteachers, educational psychologists, parents and so on, are indicated by the dotted triangle. Primary triangulation occurs between the triangles. Secondary triangulation is the combination of methodologies within the triangles. The next section will describe the methods used in the research, which will then be applied to the concepts of primary and secondary triangulation.

Figure 36   Primary triangulation

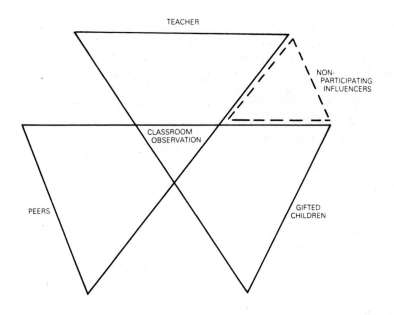

Teachers

The method used for interviewing the teachers was that of a focussed yet non-directive interview. The purpose of the interview was to elicit the deeper attitudes and perceptions of the teachers, and was therefore open-ended. There was an interview guide (figure 37) which was used to prompt the teachers, but they were encouraged to talk as much as possible about the areas that concerned and interested them with regard to the gifted children. As a consequence of this method of interviewing, not all the questions included in the interview schedule were necessarily covered during the course of an interview. The teachers were interviewed at a time convenient to them, usually during a lunch hour, in an empty classroom or staffroom. Unless otherwise requested by the teacher a tape recorder was used as it was found after the initial few interviews that note-taking was disruptive of continuity. The transcriptions of tape recorded interviews were also considered to be qualitatively superior. It was found to be very helpful to inform the teachers that the author was a qualified teacher, as they appeared to be more willing to talk once they were so informed.

   After the interview the teacher was requested to complete the Bristol Social Adjustment Guide (BSAG) for each gifted child in his or her class. Care was

Figure 37   Teacher Interview Guide

What is your definition of giftedness?
In what area is the child gifted?
What brought the child to your notice? Who first thought that he was gifted?
How does the giftedness show?
What is he like to have as a member of the class?
What is he like as a person?
Does he have any problems?
What do the other children think of him?
What are his particular interests?
How do you organize your class?
What curriculum does he follow?
What curriculum material would be useful?
Do you do anything special with him?
Is there anything that you have read or heard that has influenced your thinking about gifted children?
What are the parents like?
Would you like to have a gifted child yourself?
How do you estimate the relative academic positions of the children?
How do you distribute your time between the children in the class?
How do they sit in the class?
Are the children streamed?
Are the parents told about the child being gifted?
Would you or anyone else suggest attempting to get a scholarship or going to a private school?
What is your subject?
How many years have you taught?
What are your qualifications?

taken that this was completed subsequent to the interview so that the question of social adjustment did not distort the interview.

The BSAG is a measure of the disturbance of day school children. According to the BSAG Manual the Guides are a method of detecting and assessing behaviour disturbance in children aged five-sixteen. The teachers are requested to report factually what can be observed about the child's behaviour, not to make any interpretation. Five core syndromes form the basis of the assessment, unforthcomingness, withdrawal, depression, inconsequence, and hostility, which are polarized towards under or over-reaction (Stott, 1974).

There are several problems with the Guide. It was developed in Canada, rather than England, though it has been used extensively here. Stott used a combination of his own observations which he formed into a schedule of descriptions of maladjusted behaviour in children, which were then modified. by teachers. Thus, the Guide is a description of children classified as maladjusted. There would therefore appear to be a circularity in the development of the test, which may be considered difficult to alleviate in a categorization which is not physically measurable. However, the present study was not specifically seeking to measure disturbance objectively, but was interested in the perceptions of teachers concerning the disturbance of their gifted children. For the purpose of exploring the perceptions of teachers the Guide appeared to be appropriate. The BSAG had also been used by both Hitchfield and Freeman in their studies of gifted children (Freeman, 1979; and Hitchfield, 1973). As both studies were English, and relatively recent, it was considered to be valuable to make a comparison of the perceptions of the teachers concerning the disturbance of the gifted children between the present study and Freeman and Hitchfield's studies.

Non-Participating Influencers

Where possible headteachers and previous teachers were interviewed, usually in less depth than the class teachers, but following a similar format.

Ten out of the thirteen schools allowed access to the school records of the gifted children, which gave an historical perspective as well as, where appropriate, the opinion of the educational psychologist. Eight of the children had been part of a previous study by the author which provided more longitudinal information (Maltby, 1979).

The use of an interactionist perspective in this study means that the research is not fully comprehensive unless the parents would have also been consulted. Their perceptions of giftedness, of their children, and of the provision made for their children by the schools would have been valuable. However, there were several reasons why parents were not interviewed.

Firstly, several headteachers made it clear that they did not wish the parents to be approached. A variety of reasons were given, such as that they did not wish the parents to know that the child was part of a research study; they did not wish the parents to know that the child was considered to be gifted by the school; and they felt that the parents were antagonistic towards the school. Conversely, many of the headteachers would have been willing for the parents to be approached. Access to schools was totally dependent on the willingness of headteachers to grant it. The inclusion of a request to interview parents would have denied access to several schools, and would have considerably reduced the numbers of gifted children in the study as a consequence.

Secondly, during the field work particular care was taken to ensure that the gifted children were not made aware that they were the subjects of research. The methodology of the research was designed to disguise any interest in the gifted children. If the interviewing of parents of gifted children had been included in the research, it would have become clear to the gifted children that they were of specific interest. To disguise that interest, several parents per class could have been interviewed (in the same way that several children were interviewed) but this would have been impossible in the time available.

Finally, there had been previous research which studied parental perceptions of gifted children (Freeman, 1979; Hitchfield, 1973). There had been no previous studies of gifted children within the context of the classroom. This was one of the reasons for the original decision to concentrate on the latter area in the present research.

Bearing these points in mind, the exclusion from the research of perceptions of the gifted children by their parents was considered to be justified.

All Children

A predominant area of concern for teachers revealed in earlier research by the author was that many of the gifted children appeared to be lonely (Maltby, *op. cit.*). Other previous research in America and England has revealed contrasting viewpoints. Some have stated that gifted children were above average in popularity (Abroms et al, 1979; Killian, 1981; Parkyn, 1948 (in New Zealand); Shields, 1975; and Terman, 1925). Contrasting research had indicated that many gifted children had problems with interpersonal relationships (Freeman, 1979 and 1980; Gowan, 1972; and Scouller, 1975). These researchers frequently used teacher or parental assessments of the popularity of the gifted children. The present study also uses teacher assessment, but corroborates it with the further evidence which is about to be described.

The simplest method would have been to ask all the children in the class what they thought of the gifted child. However, this was not possible because care had to be taken throughout the research that none of the children were aware that the gifted child was the object of the study. The quantitative data described below was gained using sociometry and 'Guess Who', and the qualitative by observation in the playground, and to a lesser extent (from the point of view of social relationships) in the classroom.

Sociometry is a method of assessment and description of interpersonal attraction and rejection among the members of a group. It was invented by Moreno in the USA in the 1930s (Moreno, 1934) who defined it as dealing

> with the mathematical study of psychological properties of populations, with experiment and technique of and the results obtained by the application of quantitative methods. This is undertaken through methods which inquire into the evolution and organisation of groups and the position of individuals within them. (quoted in Lee, 1976, page 39)

Traditionally, sociometry has developed two approaches, those of whole-group processes and individual differences. Jennings suggested that sociometry revealed the structure of interrelationships but not the reasons for them, such as why particular children are isolated or unchosen (Jennings, 1973).

Roff et al and Oden and Asher have reported that the test-retest reliability of sociometric measures are satisfactory (Oden and Asher, 1977; and Roff et al, 1972). However, there would appear to be several limitations and problems with sociometry which will be explored in detail as being relevant to this research.

Sociometry as a method was developed in America in the context of what might be considered to be a materially-orientated society which emphasized numbers of friends rather than depth of relationships. Foot et al pointed out that sociometry dichotomizes between friends and non-friends without encompassing the 'continuous dimension of friendly affect' (Foot et al, 1980, page 3). They also indicated that the choices made by the children may be affected by whom they were sitting next to, or whose eye they happened to catch while completing the test. There is also the problem that the choices made may only be relevant for a particular child at that specific time, as some children may change their playmates or preferences quite frequently, which may be related to age or stage of social development. Another difficulty is that sociometry does not necessarily reveal actual friendships, but ones that the children would like to have, ideal friendships. Other methods were consequently used to compensate for this in the present study, such as classroom and playground observation.

There has been considerable controversy concerning the validity of requesting children to perform a sociometric exercise which will not be acted upon. It is difficult for a non-teaching researcher to avoid this problem, but it can be alleviated by emphasizing that the results will be used, even though not in the classroom; that what each child says is really important to the researcher; and if they know that their teacher will read what has been written they may feel that she will act accordingly (as many of the teachers in fact did).

The reliance on the cooperation of the children was partly dependent on the author having been present in the classroom for several days. The sociometry was completed towards the latter part of the stay in the classroom if possible, but this was totally dependent on the convenience of the teacher. As the younger children were interviewed individually, they had to be started earlier in the week in order not to disrupt the normal workings of the class. There is a dichotomy here between the researcher as participant observer, wishing not to be noticed, and the researcher as data gatherer having to acquire the cooperation of the children in order for the data to be valid.

The sociometric format was adapted from that used by Shaw (Shaw, 1954). It differentiated between *sitting next to, working with,* and *playing with* another child, in order to ascertain if there were differences between the environments of the classroom and the playground. It requested the children to make as many positive and/or negative choices as they wished (figure 38).

The 'Guess Who' is closely related to sociometry. It was originated by Hartshorne et al, who claimed it to be a device used 'as a means of discovering the subjects' general reputation among their classmates.' (Hartshorne et al, 1930, page 221). The test was further extended by Kelly and also by Ball (Kelly, 1955; and Ball, 1981). Hartley makes two reservations concerning 'Guess Who' as a methodology, '... the data refer to reported, not observed, behaviour.

Figure 38   Sociometry Questionnaire

Write your name.
Please fill in these questions. You can write as many names as you want, or none at all.
1.   Who do you like sitting next to the most?
2.   Who do you like sitting next to the least?
3.   Who do you like to work with most?
4.   Who do you not like to work with?
5.   Who do you most like playing with?
6.   What do you least like to play with?

Secondly, the children are responding to behavioural categories of the teachers' researchers' making rather than their own' (Hartley, 1981, pages 141–143). The first criticism is irrelevant to this study, as it was the perceptions of the children that were required, and they were observed on many occasions. The second criticism is acknowledged as valid for all questionnaires of this type. The use of Kelly's constructs to elicit the childrens' own perceptions would have been preferable, but it would have been too time consuming to use with the 682 children involved (Kelly, 1955). Also comparisons across age ranges would have been difficult because of the increase in complexity of psychological constructs with age (Brierley, 1967).

The technique of 'Guess Who' presents word or character pictures to which the children attach the name(s) of their classmates. The test (figure 39) starts with two irrelevant questions to give the children practice, and then goes on to the areas of ability in sport (question 3), academic ability (questions 4, 5, 7 and 8), discipline (questions 6 and 12), friendliness (question 9), modesty (questions 10 and 11), leadership ability (question 13), and being demanding of teacher time (question 14).

The question of how knowledgeable the gifted children were about their own academic abilities was of interest. For the purpose of assessing the accuracy of childrens' perceptions of their class positions the methodology of Nash was adapted (Nash, 1973). The names of all the children in the class were written on slips of paper. The name of the child being interviewed was put on the table. The child was asked to make two piles, one for those children who were better than, and one for those who were worse than, he at school work. The names of the children were read out by the author and the child indicated the appropriate pile. This gave an estimate of each child's self-perceived class position.

An incidental study was carried out simultaneously regarding the validity of the measure of ability placement. The teacher was asked to name two or three most able (apart from the gifted child), and two or three least able, members of the class. It was these children who were selected for interviewing and ability placement, and it was thereby hoped to establish the perceptual accuracy in self-positioning of academic ability by the gifted, most able, and least able children according to their teachers' assessment.[2]

Figure 39   'Guess Who' Questionnaire

Guess Who

Here are some word-pictures of children you may know. Read each statement carefully and see if you can guess whom it is about. It might be about yourself. There may be more than one word-picture for the same person. Several boys and girls may fit one picture or perhaps no one. Read each statement. Think about your classmates and write after each statement the names of any boys or girls who may fit it.

1. This person laughs a lot, and is always cheerful and happy.
2. This person is very sad, and looks miserable and unhappy.
3. This person is very good at PE and games, and seems to find it easy.
4. This person works hard, and seems to prefer work to play.
5. This person finishes the work very quickly, and does not have any trouble with it.
6. This person gets into trouble with the teachers a lot. It is as though he or she is always wherever the trouble is.
7. This person is good at everything he or she does, without even trying.
8. This person finds the work at school easy, and does not seem to have to make an effort.
9. This person is hard to get on with, even when one tries hard.
10. This person thinks that he knows it all, and spends a lot of time showing off.
11. This person knows it all, but does not show off, in fact is very modest.
12. This person is a goody-goody, always does what the teacher wants, and never gets into trouble.
13. This person is good at organizing, and tells us what to do in the playground, and gets games going.
14. This person gets a lot of the teacher's time, and is always demanding his or her attention.

For a sample of twenty gifted children the 'Where Are You Game' (WAYG) was used instead of the ability placement. The WAYG was considered to be more useful as it encompassed more dimensions of self-perception than purely academic ability. It was originally developed by Engel and Raine as a measure of self-regard (Engel and Raine, 1963). The psychometric properties of the test were investigated by Ellerman in Australia who concluded that it was a useful test for the full range of primary age children (five to twelve) and that it was valid and reliable as an assessment of children's self-regard in research (Ellerman, 1980). In Ellerman's version the following contrasting dimensions were used, happy versus sad, smart versus not smart, well-liked versus not well-liked, athletic versus non-athletic, attractive versus unattractive, strong versus weak, and obedient versus disobedient, all of which gave an overall score of self-regard. Some of these dimensions were inappropriate for this research and were consequently replaced. The final contrasting dimensions used included happy versus sad, clever versus not clever, well-liked versus not well-liked, attractive versus not attractive, obedient versus not obedient, like school versus do not like school, like school work versus do not like school work, friendly versus not friendly, and good organizer versus not good organizer (figure 40). The format is not used as a measure of self-concept, but

Figure 40   The Where Are You Game

	1	2	3	4	5	
Happy						Sad
Clever						Not clever
Well liked						Not well liked
Attractive						Not attractive
Obedient						Not obedient
Like school						Do not like school
Like school work						Do not like school work
Friendly						Not friendly
Good organiser						Not a good organiser

as a guide to how the children perceived themselves. The fact that it had been used previously with some level of reliability and validity over similar age ranges indicated that the children in this study would be able to cope with the Likert scaling procedure. The administration of the sociometry, 'Guess Who' and WAYG are now given.

Permission to administer the tests was requested from the headteacher first, and then from the class teacher. In only one school was there any difficulty where the headteacher made it clear that he was concerned about some of the 'Guess Who' questions, and requested the class teacher to discriminate between suitable and unsuitable ones. She did this so forcefully that the 'Guess Who' data for that class had to be discarded (see figure 43). A parent from the same school complained about question 2 on the 'Guess Who', so this question was crossed out for the remaining schools.

The teachers of the younger first school children were asked if they considered their children able to write in the names of their classmates. In those classes where they were not, the children were interviewed individually. The advantage of this was that it was possible to follow up some of the childrens' answers in more detail, and to interview the gifted child without it being apparent to the other children. The disadvantage was that the procedure was very time consuming, taking between ten and fifteen minutes per child.

The administration for group and individual administration was as follows:

> Researcher – I am doing research about children and teachers in schools, which is why I have been in your class. Does anyone know what research means? ... I would like you to fill in these sheets for me, so that I know more about you as people. It is very important that you do not talk to each other afterwards about what you have written because it is private (first schools) or confidential (middle schools). Does anyone know what private/confidential means? ... You can talk to your parents or your teacher about it, but not to each other because it could be cruel. You must not look at what other people are writing

because you might not like what you see and because I want to know what *you* think, not what your next door neighbour thinks. Write your name at the top of both sheets. Are there any children in the class with the same names?

The children and the author worked out which children had the same names, and that for those children a surname initial had to be used.

Researcher – The first part you can write lots of names, one name or no names, but you can only write the names of the children in this class. It does not matter how you spell the names so long as I can read it.

Each question was read out, and the children answered. With the younger children the questions were read one at a time, but with the older ones all six questions were read out. The whole class had to wait until everyone had finished.

Research – The next bit is Guess Who, and it is word pictures about children in your class. You have to put the names of people in the class who fit the picture. You can put one name, lots of names, no name or your own name. One person can fit lots of times (adapted from Hartshorne et al, 1930, page 221).

Each question was read out, and difficult words were explained.

Researcher – The Where Are You Game is all about you. I want you to put a tick in the square which is most like as you as a person. The first one is happy at one end and sad at the other. Square 1 is very happy, square 2 is a bit happy, square 3 is in the middle, square 4 is a bit sad, and square 5 is very sad. Put a tick in the box which best fits you as a person.

All the boxes for each dimension were explained in this way.

Researcher – At the end it says I am ... I want you to put anything there which you think describes you.

The sheets were collected in by the author.

Selected Children

All the gifted children were interviewed. A small number of other children in each class were also interviewed in order to disguise particular interest in the gifted children. It was found necessary to be more structured in the interviews with the children than with the teachers especially with the younger children, because of the difficulty of overcoming some of the children's reluctance to talk. The questions were as follows:

Figure 41   Child Interview Guide

Do you have any brothers or sisters? How old are they?
What do you like doing best in school?
Who do you like playing with in school?
Who would you like to be if you could change places with someone in the class?
Why?
What do you like doing best out of school?
What TV do you watch?
What sort of books do you read?
How much do you read?
Do you belong to the library? How often do you go?
(Younger children) Do you read to your mother? Does your mother read to you?
What time do you go to bed?
What do you do at weekends?
Do you belong to any clubs?
Do you have any hobbies?
What hobbies would you like to be able to do?
What instruments do you play?
Who do you play with outside school?
What to do you want to do when you leave school?

Observation in the Classroom

As already stated, in studying the gifted child in the classroom it was considered desirable to obtain as comprehensive a perspective as possible, and not be limited to the methodology of one particular research paradigm. In particular, systematic observation schedules were not used because of their restrictive and preconceived categories (Delamont, 1976a; Delamont and Hamilton, 1976; and Hargreaves, 1972). Fortunately the initial research school was extremely cooperative, and permitted the author to remain several weeks in one classroom. This gave the opportunity to establish areas which might merit attention, and experiment with methods of collecting data. Both Delamont and Morrison recommend the collection of a combination of data (Delamont, 1976b; and Morrison, 1975) which was a policy that was used in this study. Systematic observation was developed in a manner which was considered to be appropriate from observations made within the classroom. The procedures finally used for classroom observation, measurement of interactions between teachers and children, and assessment of concentration will be discussed.

Classroom observation involved writing *full field notes*, about what occurred in the classroom with specific reference to the gifted child. First and middle school classrooms are extremely busy and active places, and there are enormous differences between classes according to the teaching styles employed. There are also variations within a class according to the activity (ies) taking place at that particular moment. Poppleton referred to these activity (ies) as the setting, and suggested that they define the kinds of interactions which are likely to occur (Poppleton, 1975). Even though the focus of attention was on the gifted child it was necessary to remain aware of what occurred elsewhere. The observation transcripts were incomplete as regards the other children, but care was taken to transcribe verbatim conversations between the gifted child and the teacher, and the other children.

Perhaps the ideal method would have been to have had the teacher and the gifted child wearing a microphone, with the other children wearing dummy microphones. This would have allowed for the collection of much greater detail. However, these resources were not available, especially as classroom observation was only one part of the research. It might also have discouraged some teachers from participating, and would have been difficult to organize without altering what occurred naturally in the classroom.

It is inevitable that the presence of the researcher will, to some extent, affect what occurs in the classroom. Participant observers are fortunate in that they are able to acclimatize their subjects to their presence over a long period of time (Becker et al, 1961; Cohen, 1955; and Wolcott, 1971). These researchers became fairly secure that what occurred in their presence was not dramatically affected by their presence. The fact that the author was in a classroom for fairly short periods of approximately one week, meant that precautions had to be taken to make the presence of the researcher less noticeable to the teacher and the children. It was discovered that it was best to sit to one side of the classroom so that the teacher's attention was not caught when she was standing or sitting in the front. It was also found advantageous to be behind and to one side of the gifted children so that they did not observe the author looking at them too frequently. Serious observation notes were not made for the first morning or day. This was an attempt to counter the Hawthorne effect (Mayo, 1939)[3] as far as possible, and to allow the children to become familiarized to the researcher's presence. McIntyre has suggested that the presence of an observer is not usually of major importance if the above types of precautions are observed (McIntyre, 1978).

Children were discouraged from speaking to the author, or asking for help during lesson time. The antithesis to this was that it was considered necessary to allow the teachers some free time in exchange for the lunch hour that was occupied with the interview. The author therefore usually took a lesson, though this was normally used for the sociometry and similar activities. In these circumstances a more dominant role had to be taken as opposed to attempting to appear to be part of the furniture. Where possible the lesson occurred towards the end of the week.

It quickly became apparent that the gifted child observed in the first classroom was interacting with the teacher more frequently than the other children did. It was therefore decided to see if this pattern would be repeated in all the classrooms. The concern was primarily with quantitative data to assess the number of times the teacher interacted with the gifted child as compared with the number of times she interacted with the rest of the children in the class. This excluded the length and assessment of the quality of the interactions. There were two methods used for the collection of this data. A record was made of all the interactions that took place between the teacher and any individual child, specifically whether they were teacher-initiated, child-initiated, or disciplinary interactions, with a special note when such interactions occurred with the gifted child (22 classrooms).

The second method was adapted from that used by Lacey (Lacey, 1970). A piece of paper was sectioned, each section being allocated to a specific child according to the seating arrangements in the class. As each interaction with the teacher occurred an appropriate sign was placed in the child's box. This method was developed at a later stage of the research, but was only appropriate when the children had allocated seats, and consequently it was used in a smaller number of classrooms (7 classrooms).

There were found to be advantages and disadvantages with both these methods of data collection. The former provided greater detail concerning the interactions between the teachers and the children, such as actual transcripts of questions, answers, conversations and so on. However, it excluded details concerning the pupil participants, apart from the gifted child. The latter method gave numerical details of teacher/child interactions for all the children in the class including the gifted, but could not provide details concerning the subject matter. In the seven classes where the named box method was used, it was combined with the use of the alternative method in order to give more substance to the otherwise somewhat bald numerical information.

The settings allocated to the compilation of this data were when the interactions were frequent, such as question and answer lessons, and when the children were queueing at the teacher's desk. In other words, times when the opportunity for teachers and children to initiate interactions were greatest. The interactions were classified into three main areas of teacher-initiated, child-initiated, and disciplinary as follows:

(a) Teacher initiated – when a teacher started a conversation with a child by question, remark, command, compliment, telling off and so on. In the case of a child with his hand up the interaction was classed as teacher initiated if it was in response to a question by the teacher which the child was nominated to answer.

(b) Child initiated – when a child started an interaction with the teacher such as by raising his hand at a time when the class was not responding to questions, (for example a request to go to the toilet); going up to the teacher to speak to her; queueing at her desk; calling out remarks or statements; or when a child called out the answer to a teacher question, unchosen or uninvited to do so by the teacher.

(c) Disciplinary – although this was included in the teacher initiated category, it is treated separately in the analysis and therefore requires definition. A disciplinary interaction was recorded when a teacher rebuked a child for doing something wrong, which included telling a child to move as a result of misbehaviour; requesting the child to stop talking; telling the child to get on with work; and included the commonly-used expression 'Sssh' as it was taken as a form of teacher defined discipline.

Evans and Wragg, when researching verbal interaction between teachers and severely subnormal children, suggested

that teachers tend to have set interaction patterns with individual children, patterns which are likely to be repeated with little variation over a number of visits (Evans and Wragg, 1969, page 318).

Evens and Wragg also observed the interactions between teachers and individual children. Their views are supported by Kutnick who found there to be similarities in teacher and child behaviour for different sessions of observation (Kutnick, 1980). The fact that these studies found interactive patterns to be repetitive suggest that the present data may have some reliability.

There was a tradition of enquiries into the assessment of attentiveness in America in the 1920s and 1930s which is fully described by Jackson. These studies attempted to establish relationships between the level of attention of children and subsequent learning (Jackson, 1968). More recently, research in this area has reoccurred (Bennett, 1978, and Bennett et al, 1981 and 1982; Galton et al, 1980), which may be partially attributed to the use of observational categories of children which record involvement or non-involvement.

The concentration span of the gifted children in the present study was measured with the use of a stop watch, totalling the time that the child was distracted within the total concentration period observed. This was always done during a period when the child, together with the rest of the class, was involved in a written task, preferably English or mathematics, or both (many of the children were observed on more than one occasion), and at a time when it was intended by the teacher that the whole class be relatively silent. The older children were expected to do work of this kind for lengthier periods of time, therefore the total amounts of time spent on observation of this type was greater in middle schools.

There are several difficulties with the assessment of concentration, some of which are discussed by Bennett (Bennett et al, 1981, page 119). There are judgmental difficulties in interpretation of the attention or non-attention of a child; the appearance of dreaming may disguise attentiveness, whereas a child who gives an impression of intense concentration may be contemplating other things. Attentive and non-attentive is a crude categorization which excludes shades of partial attentiveness. Thirdly, there is the question of the reliability of the interpretation of a single observer, but the presence of more than one observer could be disruptive in a classroom. Finally, discussion with another child may be concerned with the work in hand. Teachers vary in their attitudes towards children helping each other, or talking generally. However, the last mentioned problem was partially avoided by timing during activities which were intended by the teachers to be completed individually. It should, nevertheless, be emphasized that the majority of cases were straightforward despite the apparent profusion of difficulties.

In this study the child was timed as distracted when talking to other children unless it was clearly obvious that the talk was task related, such as when the children were pointing at a page, or looking up a word in a dictionary. Discussions concerning how many lines had been written (which were frequent) were counted as distractions. The timing of concentration ceased temporarily when the child joined a queue to see the teacher, or went to sharpen a pencil, which Boydell and Galton coded as task related (Boydell, 1975a; and Galton et al, 1980).

The gifted children were observed in the playground environment where it was noted with which children they played, and what activities took place.

Access to Schools

The field work was carried out from January 1980 to July 1981. Permission was granted by the Chief Primary Advisor to approach all the first and middle schools in a specific LEA in South-East England to discover the presence of gifted children in the schools.[4] The representativeness of social class distribution in the chosen LEA was almost identical to that of the total population as given in the 1971 Census (G.B. Census, 1975).[5] There were fifty schools in the LEA representing a school population of 12,500. All the schools were telephoned, and the purpose of the research was explained to the headteachers with a summary of the author's credentials.[6] The headteachers were asked if they had any gifted children and sixty-five children were acknowledged as being gifted. An appointment was then made with the headteacher in order to negotiate access to the school and relevant class. It was made clear that the full cooperation of the class teacher was essential, and this was established before the research in that class was started.

Access was not granted by the headteachers to study all the gifted children in the LEA. Reasons for exclusion included the presence of a student; teacher difficulties; smallness of the staff room; the child being already a subject in an ongoing study; maladjustment of the child; and reluctance of the teachers to participate. The final sample consisted of thirty-nine gifted children in twenty-four classes in thirteen schools. The number of children in each age range is given in figure 42. There were fifteen girls and twenty-four boys in the sample of gifted children. The tendency for there to be more gifted boys than gifted girls has been well documented in the research concerning giftedness, and Hopkinson has detailed several possible explanations for it (Hopkinson, 1978).

The execution of the research was totally dependent on the assent of the teachers and the headteachers, some of whom placed restrictions on specific aspects of the methodology. Methodologies were also developed as the research progressed. Figure 43 shows the information that was available for each child.

Figure 42   Distribution of sample gifted children by age among classes in first and middle schools.

First school class	No. of gifted	Middle school class	No. of gifted
1	1	1	9
2	5	2	0
3	3	3	12
4	8	4	2
Total	17*		23*

* One child Benny, was observed twice, once in the first and once in the middle school where there was another gifted child in the class.

The following is a description of the thirteen schools involved in the research, together with the names of the gifted pupils who attended.

School A, First school, 140 pupils
Arthur, Benny

The school is an inner town school with a predominantly upper working-class catchment area. It has a small playground, no playing fields, and the architecture is from the 1930s.

School B, First school, 111 pupils
Alexandra, David, Don, Vi

The school is on the edge of a large council estate, but has a small intake of children from prosperous homes. The school is modern, and at the time had a great deal of space with playing field facilities and two large playgrounds.

School C, First school, 103 pupils
Ricky

The school has only four classes in an old building, and is an inner town school with few facilities. The playground is small and there is no greenery. The children come from predominantly working-class homes.

School D, First school, 179 pupils
Hugh, Jim, Keith, Liz, Maggy, Mary, Rita, Rosemarie

The school is in a fairly prosperous area, and has many middle class children. The school has a good reputation in the town. The younger children are grouped vertically, and work areas are shared between classes. The building is modern and there are good facilities both inside and outside.

Figure 43   Availability of data for individual gifted children

Name of child	Teacher interview	Child interview	School records	BSAG	Classroom observation	Playground observation	Sociometric questionnaires	'Guess Who' questions 1–12	'Guess Who' questions 13–14	Where Are You Game	Social Class
First School											
Arthur	A	A	A	A	A	A	A	A	U	U	A
Ricky	A	A	A	A	A	A	A	A	A	A	U
David	A	A	A	A	A	A	A	A	A	A	A
Don	A	A	A	A	A	A	A	A	A	A	A
Karl	A	A	A	A	A	A	A	A	U	U	A
Rita	A	A	A	A	A	A	A	A	A	A	A
Robert	A	A	A	A	A	A	A	U	U	A	A
Mary	A	A	A	U	A	A	A	A	A	A	A
Jim	A	A	A	A	A	A	A	A	A	A	A
Maggy	A	A	A	A	A	A	A	A	A	A	A
Hugh	A	A	A	A	A	A	A	A	A	A	A
Rosemarie	A	A	A	A	A	A	A	A	A	A	A
Keith	A	A	A	A	A	A	A	A	A	A	A
Liz	A	A	A	A	A	A	A	A	A	A	A
Benny	A	A	A	A	A	A	A	A	U	U	A
Vi	U	A	A	U	U	A	A	A	A	A	A
Alexandra	U	A	A	U	U	A	A	A	A	A	A
Middle School											
Sandy	A	A	A	A	A	A	A	A	U	U	A
Vicky	A	A	A	A	A	A	A	A	U	U	A
Peter	A	A	U	A	A	A	A	A	A	A	A
Ann	A	A	A	A	A	A	A	U	U	A	A
Ken	A	A	A	A	A	A	A	U	U	A	A
Lilo	A	A	A	A	A	A	A	A	A	U	A
Kathy	A	A	A	A	A	A	A	A	A	U	A
Benny	A	A	A	A	A	A	A	A	A	A	A
Hank	A	A	A	A	A	A	A	A	A	A	A
Laurence	A	A	A	A	A	A	A	A	A	U	A
Les	A	A	A	A	A	A	A	A	A	U	A
George	A	A	A	A	A	A	A	A	A	U	A
Sylvia	A	A	A	A	A	A	A	A	A	U	A
Adrian	A	A	A	U	I	A	A	A	A	U	A
Jo	A	A	A	A	A	A	A	A	A	U	A
Nicholas	A	A	A	A	A	A	A	A	A	U	A
Mandy	A	A	A	A	A	A	A	A	A	A	A
Tony	A	A	A	A	A	A	A	A	A	A	A
Pat	A	A	A	A	A	A	A	A	U	U	A
Geoff	A	A	A	A	I	A	A	A	A	U	A
Christopher	A	A	U	A	A	A	A	A	A	A	A
Angela	A	A	A	A	A	A	A	A	U	U	A
Dennis	A	A	U	A	A	A	A	A	A	A	A

Key
A   Available
U   Unavailable
I   Inappropriate

School E, First/Middle school, 199 pupils
Karl, Sandy, Vicky

This school is situated in the centre of the town behind one of the large shopping areas. It has mainly working-class children. The building is modern, and was designed to be open plan with work and quiet areas shared between every two classes. The school has three playgrounds, the larger of which is only used at lunchtime. However, there is no green area available.

School F, First/Middle school, 218 pupils
Angela, Pat

The school is situated on the outskirts of the town in an area which has a village atmosphere. It has a large middle-class intake of children. Uniform is worn by the majority of the children. The building is modern, but conditions are cramped and classes large as the school has a good reputation. Many children from this school go on to private schools. The playing fields are large, and are surrounded by countryside.

School G, First/Middle school, 359 pupils
Geoff (music)

This school is situated in the town and has many working-class pupils. The school is on the border of a large council estate which has its own Educational Priority Area school. Some of the children from the estate go to school G. The school was built in the 1930s and has no playing fields. The headteacher is particularly keen on music.

School H, First/Middle school, 289 pupils
Ann, Ken, Mandy, Robert, Tony

The school is in a suburban area with a large number of middle-class pupils. The school building is modern with extra classrooms for science, French and so on. The school is surrounded by playing fields.

School I, First/Middle school, 225 pupils
Christopher, Peter

The school has a large and varied catchment area. The building is old, but there are some prefabricated classrooms, one of which is for science and art. The school has a small playing field.

School J, Middle school, 230 pupils
Dennis

The school is an inner town school with a predominantly upper working-class catchment area. The building is modern and surrounded by playing fields. School J is the middle school for school A.

School K, Middle school, 232 pupils
Jo, Nicholas

The school is situated in the centre of a council estate but has a small middle-class intake. The building is modern with many facilities including a science laboratory, French room and swimming pool. It also has large playing fields.

School L, Middle school, 318 pupils
Adrian (football), George, Kathy, Laurence, Les, Lilo, Sylvia

The school is in a suburban area with an intake of children from all social classes and quite a number of middle-class children. The building is reasonably modern and there are several prefabricated classrooms. The school is surrounded by greenery, and has large playing fields.

School M, Middle school, 421 pupils
Benny, Hank

The school is in a suburban area and has a large number of middle-class children. The architecture of the building is from the 1930s and conditions are cramped. The playing fields are large.

Expansion of the Concept of Triangulation

The research methods described above will now be applied to the concept of primary and secondary triangulation. Primary triangulation was described as the perceptions of the participants triangulated between groups. For example, teachers were asked what the children thought about the gifted child; the peers filled in a sociometric and 'Guess Who' questionnaire which could give their opinion of the gifted child; and the gifted children completed the 'Guess Who' (where they were able to nominate themselves), the WAYG which was about themselves, and were also interviewed; a previous teacher or headteacher may also have given an opinion. The primary triangulation is, in this case, between the three or four groups consisting of teachers, children, gifted child, and possibly non-participating influencers.

Secondary triangulation was defined as the use of two or more methods of data collection. A model of primary and secondary triangulation is given in figure 44 where the particular methods used in the research are given. It can be seen that in the above example secondary triangulation also occurred. In the triangle representing the peer group the children completed the sociometry and 'Guess Who', and they were also observed in the playground if they played with the gifted child. In the gifted child group the gifted child was interviewed, completed the 'Guess Who' and WAYG, and was observed in the playground. The analysis of data using a combination of methods can verify or refute the data collected using one method alone.

Figure 44   Model of primary and secondary triangulation

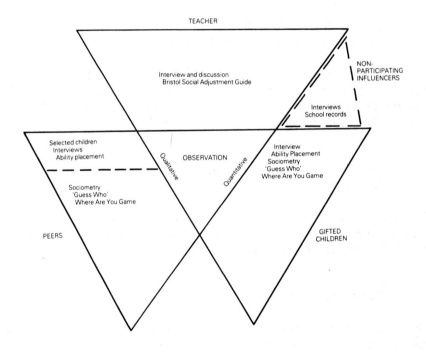

Notes

1. It is argued that this permits the use of one-tailed testing of hypotheses which have been formulated at a later stage, providing that the direction was predicted before the analysis of the data.
2. This method, which was originally suggested by the work of Nash (Nash, 1973),

was not found to be satisfactory because there was a general tendency for the children to place themselves towards the middle of the ability continuum. The method was eventually replaced with the WAYG.

3. The Hawthorne effect refers to research which took place in the 1930s where it was noted that the presence of the researcher had an effect on the behaviour of the subjects. Thereafter, researchers have usually attempted to alleviate this problem, especially those researchers who use the method of participant observation.

4. Obtaining access to schools was extremely time-consuming. Headteachers were frequently unavailable when telephoned, necessitating many calls. The appointments with the headteachers also interrupted the fieldwork. A system was therefore developed of spending one week organizing the school research timetable for the following half term. The first and last weeks of any term were not considered desirable weeks for observation because they were regarded as untypical. All field notes and interview materials were subsequently typed, which was time-consuming but considered to be essential. For every two weeks spent in schools at least one week of transcription was involved.

5. The 1981 Census indicated a total increase in population for the whole county concerned of just over 5000. A comparison of the social class distribution in the county and the total population indicates a close similarity in all social classes except 111N, which is slightly over, and 111M which is slightly under-represented in the county. The minimal increase in population between 1971 and 1981 indicates a probable similarity in social class distribution. Detailed results of social class composition from the 1981 Census were not available at the time of writing.

6. Many of the headteachers requested a definition of giftedness when they were telephoned. It was made clear that it was the intention to study those children who were categorized by their teachers as gifted. Frequently, there followed a discussion concerning definitions of giftedness in which it became apparent that definitions held by headteachers were extremely diverse. Headteachers also varied in their approach to the question of giftedness. Some knew which children were considered to be gifted in their schools and arranged for the author to meet the relevant teacher(s) immediately. Others needed to find out from their teachers which children they categorized as gifted. One headteacher arranged for the author to explain to the whole staff of the school the purpose of the research from which they made their decision concerning whether to proceed with the research in their school. The fact that the author was a qualified teacher facilitated the process of gaining access.

Bibliography

ABROMS K.I., MOELY B.E., COLLIN J.B. and KENNED M. (1979) *A Developmental Study of Intellectually Gifted Pre-School Children and their Relationships to Measures of Psychosocial Giftedness,* Presented at the Third World Conference for Gifted and Talented Children, Jerusalem, July.

ACKLAW J. and WALLACE B. (1982) *Identifying Bright Pupils: A Teacher's Guide and Handbook,* Essex County Council.

ALBERT T. (1982) 'The cheapest way to help the brightest and the best', *The Guardian,* 23 November.

AXON J. (1979) 'The Schools Council Curriculum Enrichment Project for gifted children', *Journal of Applied Educational Studies,* Vol 8, No. 1, Spring.

AXON J. (1982) 'The Schools Council Curriculum Enrichment Project for Gifted Children' in GRUBB D.H.W. (Ed) *The Gifted Child at School,* Oxford Society for Applied Studies in Education.

BALDWIN J.W. (1962) 'The relationship between teacher-judged giftedness, a group intelligence test and an individual test with possible gifted kindergarten pupils', *The Gifted Child Quarterly* (Winter).

BALDWIN R.W. (1966) *Social Justice,* Pergamon Press.

BALL S.J. (1981) *Beachside Comprehensive: A Case-Study of Secondary Schooling,* Cambridge University Press.

BARRON F. (1969) *Creative Person and Creative Process,* N.Y. Holt, Rinehart and Winston.

BECHER T., ERAUT M. and KNIGHT J. (1981) *Policies for Educational Accountability,* Heinemann.

BECKER H.S. (1963) *Outsiders, Studies in the Sociology of Deviance,* Free Press.

BECKER H.S., GEER B., HUGHES E.C. and STRAUSS A.L. (1961) *Boys in White: Student Culture in Medical School,* Chicago, University of Chicago Press.

BENN, C. (1982a) 'The myth of giftedness' (Part I), *Forum,* Vol. 24, No. 2, Spring.

BENN C. (1982b) 'The myth of giftedness' (Part II), *Forum,* Vol 24, No. 3, Summer.

BENNETT N. (1976) *Teaching Styles and Pupil Progress,* Open Books

BENNETT, S.N. (1978) 'Recent research on teaching: A dream, a belief a model', *British Journal of Educational Psychology,* 48, pp. 127–147.

BENNETT N. and DESFORGES C. (1982) *New Directions in Research on Teaching and Learning,* Paper presented at the Annual Conference of the BPS, York, April.

BENNETT N., DESFORGES C., COCKBURN A., and WILKINSON B. (1981) *The Quality of Pupil Learning Experiences,* Interim Report, August, Centre for Educational Research and Development, University of Lancaster.

BERGER P.L. and LUCKMANN T. (1967) *The Social Construction of Reality: A Treatise in* the Sociology of Knowledge, Allen Lane.

BERLAK A. and BERLAK H. (1981) *Dilemmas of Schooling, Teaching and Social Change*, London, Methuen.

BERNSTEIN B. (1971) *Class, Codes and Control, Theoretical Studies towards a Sociology of Language*, Routledge and Kegan Paul.

BLUMER H. (1976) 'The methodological position of symbolic interactionism', in HAMMERSLEY M. and WOODS P. (Eds) *The Process of Schooling: A Sociological Reader*, Routledge and Kegan Paul.

BOYDELL D. (1974) 'Teacher-pupil contact in junior classrooms', *British Journal of Educational Psychology*, 44, 313–8.

BOYDELL D. (1975a) 'Pupil Behaviour in junior classrooms', *British Journal of Educational Psychology*, 45, pp. 122–9.

BOYDELL D. (1975b) 'Individual attention: the child's view', *Education 3–13*, Vol 3.

BOYDELL D. (1978) *The Primary Teacher in Action*, Open Books.

BOYDELL D. (1981) 'Classroom organisation 1970–7', in SIMON B. and WILLCOCKS J. (Eds) *Research and Practice in the Primary Classroom*, Routledge and Kegan Paul.

BRIDGES S.A. (1969) *Gifted children and the Brentwood Experiment*, Pitman.

BRIDGES S.A. (1975) *Gifted children and the Millfield Experiment*, Pitman.

BRIERLEY D.W. (1967) *The use of personality constructs by children of three different ages*, Unpublished PhD thesis, London Birkbeck College.

BROOKS R. (1972) *Bright Delinquents: the story of a unique school*, NFER.

BROOKS R. (1980) *Gifted Delinquents*, Brighton Polytechnic.

BURT C. (1921) *Burt Reading Tests 1–5*, St. Albans, Herts, Staples Press.

BURT C. (1962) 'The gifted child', in BEREDAY G.Z.P. and LAUWERYS J.S. (Eds) *The Gifted Child, The Yearbook of Education*, Evans.

BURT C. (1963) 'Is intelligence distributed normally?' *The Brit. Jnl. of Stat. Psych.*, November, Vol XVI, Part 2, pp 175–190.

BURT C. (1975) *The Gifted Child*, Unibooks.

CALLOW R.W. (1982) 'The Southport Inquiry and After' in GRUBB D.H.W. (Ed.) *The Gifted Child at School*, Oxford Society for Applied Studies in Education.

CHAPPELL C. (1982) *Social and Emotional Development*, Seminar at Third Teachers' Conference on Gifted Children, Leonardo Trust, London, July.

CITY OF BIRMINGHAM EDUCATION COMMITTEE (1979) *Report of the Chief Education Officers Study Group on Gifted and Outstanding Children 1976–8*, City of Birmingham Education Committee.

CLARKE G. (1983) *Guidelines for the recognition of gifted pupils*, Schools Council Programme 4, Individual Pupils, Longman for Schools Council.

COHEN A.K. (1955) *Delinquent Boys: The Culture of the Gang*, Glencoe, Illinois, The Free Press.

COHEN L. and MANION H. (1980) *Research Methods in Education*, Croom Helm.

COHEN L. and MANION M. (1981) *Perspectives on Classrooms and Schools*, Holt, Rinehart and Winston.

CORNISH R.C. (1968) 'Parents, teachers and pupils' perceptions of the gifted child's ability' *Gifted Child Quarterly*, 12, pp 14–17.

CROLL P. (1981) 'Social class, pupil achievement and classroom interaction' in SIMON B. and WILLCOCKS J. (Eds) *Research and Practice in the Primary Classroom*, Routledge and Kegan Paul.

DAVIE R., BUTLER N. and GOLDSTEIN H. (1972) *From Birth to Seven. A Report of the National Child Development Study*, Longman and National Children's Bureau.

DELAMONT S. (1976a) *Interaction in the Classroom*, London, Methuen.

DELAMONT S. (1976b) 'Beyond Flanders' Fields: The relationship of subject-matter and individuality to classroom style', in STUBBS M. and DELAMONT S. (Eds) *Exploration in Classroom Observation*, Chichester, Wiley.

DELAMONT S. and HAMILTON D. (1976) 'Classroom research: A critique and new approach' in Stubbs M. and Delamont S. (Eds) *Exploration in Classroom Observation*, Chichester, Wiley.

Delisle J. (1982) *Counselling: The Non-Productive Gifted Child: A contradicition of Terms?* Paper given at Third Teachers' Conference on Gifted Children, Leonardo Trust, London, July.

Desforges C. and Cockburn A. (1982) *Matching Tasks to Children*, Paper presented to the Annual Conference of the BPS, York, April.

Devon County Council (1977) *Find the Gifted Child, A Paper for Guidance*, Devon County Council.

Douglas J.W.B. (1964) *The Home and the School: A Study of Ability and Attainment in the Primary School*, London, MacGibbon and Kee.

Douglas J.W.B., Ross J.M. and Simpson H.R. (1968) *All our Future: a longitudinal study of secondary education*, Peter Davies.

Ellerman D.A. (1980) 'Self-regard of primary school children: Some Australian data', *British Journal of Educational Psychology*, 50, pp 114–122.

Ellingham D. (1982) 'Marcliffe Primary School', in Garland R. (Ed.) *Microcomputers and Children in the Primary School*, Lewes, Falmer Press.

Elliott J. (1978) 'Classroom research: Science or commonsense?' in McAleese R. and Hamilton D. (Eds) *Understanding Classroom Life*, Windsor, NFER.

Engel M. and Raine W.J. (1963) 'A method for the measurement of the self-concept of children in the third grade', *Jnl. Gen. Psych.*, 102, pp. 125–137.

Erikson K.T. (1973) 'Deviant Behaviour: An interactionist approach' in Rubington E. and Winbert M. (Eds) *Deviance the Interactionist Perspective, Text and Readings in the Sociology of Deviance*, 2nd edition, Macmillan Co.

Evans D. and Wragg E.C. (1969) 'The use of a verbal interaction analysis technique with severely subnormal children' in Wolfson J. (Ed.) *Personality and Learning 2*, Open University, Hodder and Stoughton.

Floud J.E., Halsey A.H. and Martin F.M. (1957) *Social Class and Educational Opportunity*, Heinemann.

Foot H.C., Chapman A.J. and Smith J.R. (1980) (Eds) *Friendship and Social Relations in Children*, John Wiley and Sons Ltd.

Foster L. (1983) 'Building materials for gifted children', *Gifted Education International* Vol. 1, No. 2, pp. 107–109.

Frazer E. (1959) *Home Environment and the School*, University of London Press.

Freeman J. (1979) *Gifted Children – Their Identification and Development in a Social Context*, MTP Press Ltd.

Freeman J. (1980) *The Influence of the Educational Environment on Gifted Children*, PhD thesis, Manchester University.

Freeman J. (1981) 'The intellectually gifted', in Abroms K. and Bennett J. (Eds) *New Directions for Exceptional Children: Genetics and Exceptional Children*, No. 7 San Francisco, Jossey-Bass, September pp. 75–86.

Freeman J. (1982) 'Some emotional aspects of giftedness', in Grubb D.H.W. (Ed.) *The Gifted Child at School*, Oxford Society for Applied Studies in Education.

Gage N.L. (1978) *The Scientific Basis of the Art of Teaching*, NY, Teachers College Press.

Gallagher J.J. (1958a) 'Peer acceptance of highly gifted children in elementary school', *Elementary School Journal*, 58, pp. 465–570.

Gallagher J.J. (1958b) 'Social status of children related to intelligence, propinquity and social perception', *Elementary School Journal*, 58, pp. 225–231.

Gallagher J.J. (1964) *Teaching the Gifted Child*, Boston, Allyn and Bacon.

Gallagher J.J. (1975) 'Characteristics of gifted children: a research summary' in Barbe W.B. and Renzulli S. (Eds) *Psychology and Education of the Gifted*, N.Y. John Wiley.

Gallagher J.J. and Crowder T. (1957) 'The adjustment of gifted children in the regular classroom' *Exceptional children*, Vol. 23, pp. 306–319.

GALTON M., SIMON B., and CROLL P., (1980) *Inside the Primary Classroom*, Routledge and Kegan Paul.

GARNER J. and BING M. (1973) 'Inequalities of teacher-pupil contacts', *British Journal of Educational Psychology*, 43, pp. 234–43.

GEAR, G.H. (1975) *Effects of the Training Program, "Identification of the Potentially Gifted" on Teachers' Accuracy in the Identification of Intellectually Gifted Children*, Unpublished PhD. thesis, University of Connecticut.

GEAR G.H. (1978) 'Effects of training on teachers' accuracy in the identification of gifted children', *The Gifted Child Quarterly*, Spring, Vol XXII, No. 1, pp. 90–97.

GERMAN J.K. (1979) *The Selection of and Provision for Physically Gifted Children in one LEA*, Unpublished M.Ed Thesis, University of Liverpool.

GETZELS J.W. and JACKSON P.W. (1962) *Creativity and Intelligence, Explorations with Gifted Students*, N.Y. John Wiley and Sons.

GETZELS W. and DILLON J.T. (1973) 'The nature of giftedness and the education of the gifted child', in TRAVERS R.W.M. (Ed) *Second Handbook of Research on Teaching*, Chicago, Rand McNally.

GIBBS J.P. (1966) 'Conceptions of deviant behaviour: the old and the new', in LEFTON M., SKIPPER J.K. and McCAGHY C.H. (Eds) *Approaches to Deviance: theories, concepts and research findings*, N.Y. Appleton – Century – Crofts.

GLASER F.G. and STRAUSS A.L. (1967) *The Discovery of Grounded Theory, Strategies for Qualitative Research*, Weidenfeld and Nicolson.

GOOD T.L., SIKES J.M. and BROPHY J.E. (1973) 'The effects of teacher sex and student sex on classroom interaction', *Journal of Educational Psychology*, Vol 65, No. 1 pp. 74–78.

GOODE E. (1978) *Deviant Behaviour: An Interactionist Approach*, N.J., Prentice-Hall Inc.

GOODACRE E.J. (1968) *Teachers and their Pupils' Home Background*, NFER.

GOWAN J.C. (1972) 'Improving the mental health and performance of gifted children', in *Emotional Disturbance and the Gifted Child: Implications for School People*, Greensburg, Pa. Westmoreland Intermediate Unit.

GREAT BRITAIN, DES (1963) *Half our Future: A Report of the Central Advisory Council for Education* (England), Chairman Sir J. Newsom, HMSO.

GREAT BRITAIN, DES (1967) *Children and their Primary Schools: A report of the Central Advisory Council for Education* (England), Chairman Lady B. Plowden, HMSO (2 vols.).

GREAT BRITAIN, DES, HOYLE E. and WILKS J. (1974) *Gifted Children and their Education*, HMSO.

GREAT BRITAIN, DES, HMI (1977) *Gifted Children in Middle and Comprehensive Secondary Schools, A discussion paper by a working party of Her Majesty's Inspectorate*, HMSO.

GREAT BRITAIN, DES (1982) *Mathematics Counts: report of the Committee of Inquiry into the Teaching of Mathematics in Schools*, Chairmanship D.H. Cockcroft, HMSO.

GREAT BRITAIN, HMSO (1980) *Classification of Occupation and Coding Index*

GREAT BRITAIN OFFICE OF CENSUS AND SURVEYS Census (1971) Great Britain, Economic Activity, Part IV (10% sample), Table 29, HMSO (Pub. 1975). Census (1971) England and Wales 1971, Economic Activity County Leaflet, HMSO (Pub. 1975). Census (1981) Population Census, 1981 HMSO.

GREEN E. (1980) *The Role of the Microprocessor in the Education of Gifted Children*, Unpublished MA dissertation, University of Sussex.

HALSEY A.H., FLOUD J. and MARTIN F.M. (1956) *Social Class and Educational Opportunity*, London, Heinemann.

HARGREAVES D.H. (1967) *Social Relations in a Secondary School*, Routledge and Kegan Paul.

HARGREAVES D.H. (1972) *Interpersonal Relations and Education*, Routledge and Kegan Paul.

HARGREAVES D.H. (1976) 'Learning to be deviant in schools, aspects of the hidden curriculum', in ROBERTS T. (Ed) *The Circumstance of Learning*, University of Manchester.

HARGREAVES D.H. (1977) 'The process of typification in classroom interaction: models and methods', *British Journal Educational Psychology*, 47, pp. 274–284.

HARGREAVES D.H., HESTER S.K. and MELLOR F.J. (1975) *Deviance in Classrooms*, Routledge and Kegan Paul.

HARTLEY D. (1981) 'Infant-school children's perceptions of the behaviour of same and opposite sex classmates', *British Journal of Social Psychology*, 20, pp. 141–143.

HARTSHORNE H., MAY M.A. and SHUTTLEWORTH F.K. (1930) *Studies in the Nature of Character* Vol III, Studies in the Organisation of Character, N.Y., The Macmillan Co.

HARTUP W.W. (1970) 'Peer interaction and social organisation', in MUSSEN P.H. (Ed) *Carmichael's Manual of Child Psychology* (Vol 2), N.Y., Wiley.

HAVIGHURST R.J. (1965) *A Survey of the Education of Gifted Children*, Chicago, Chicago University Press.

HAWKINS R. and TIEDMAN G. (1975) *The Creation of Deviance, Interpersonal and Organisational Determinants*, Columbus, Bell and and Howell Co.

HAZNEDAR B.S.K. (1981) *Using the D-48 Test in the Identification of the Disadvantaged Gifted*, Unpublished PhD thesis, Univerity of Alabama.

HEBER R.F. (1956) 'The relation of intelligence and physical maturity to social status of children', *Journal of Educational Psychology*, 47, pp. 158–162.

HENDERSON L.B. (1981) *The Influences of Gender and Structure of Intellect Ability Factors on Teacher Perception of Gifted Children*, Unpublished PhD thesis, Oregon State University.

HITCHFIELD E.M. (1973) *In Search of Promise – a Longterm National Study of Able Children and their Families*, Longman (plus Appendix 1974).

HOLLINGWORTH L.S. (1942) *Children Above 180 IQ*, NY World Book Co.

HOPKINSON D. (1978) *The Education of Gifted Children*, The Woburn Press.

HOYLE E. and WILKS J. (1974) *Gifted Children and their Education*, HMSO.

JACKSON B. (1964) *Streaming: an education system in miniature*, Routledge and Kegan Paul.

JACKSON B. and MARSDEN D. (1962) *Education and the Working Class*, Harmondsworth, Penguin Books.

JACKSON P.W. (1968) *Life in Classrooms*, Holt, Rinehart and Winston Inc.

JACKSON P.W. and LAHADERNE H.M. (1967) 'Inequalities of Teacher-pupil contacts', in MORRISON A. and MCINTYRE D. (Eds) *The Social Psychology of Teaching: Selected readings*, Harmondsworth, Penguin.

JACOBS J.C. (1971) 'Effectiveness of teacher and parent identification of gifted children as a function of school level', *Psychology in the Schools*, 8, pp. 140–142.

JENCKS C. (1972) *Inequality: A Reassessment of the Effect of Family and Schooling in America*, Harmondsworth, Penguin.

JENNINGS, H.H. (1973) *Sociometry in Group Relations: A Manual for Teachers*, (original 1948), Greenwood Press.

JORDAN J. (1974) *The Organisation of Perspectives in Teacher-Pupil Relations: an Interactionist Approach*, Unpublished M.Ed. thesis, University of Manchester.

KEDDIE N. (1971) 'Classroom knowledge', in YOUNG M.F.D. (Ed) *Knowledge and Control: New Directions for the Sociology of Education*, Collier Macmillan.

KELLY G.A. (1955) *The Psychology of Personal Constructs*, Vol 1, A Theory of Personality, New York, Norton.

KENDALL M.G. (1970) *Rank Correlation Methods* (4th edition), Charles Griffin and Co.

Ltd.

KENT MATHEMATICS PROJECT (1978) *Kent Mathematics Project,* Ward Lock Educational.

KERRY T. (1981) *Teaching Bright Pupils in Mixed Ability Classes: A self-instructional handbook of strategies and suggestions for teachers,* Macmillan Education Ltd.

KILLIAN J.E. (1981) *Personality Characteristics and Attitudes of Intellectually Gifted Secondary School Students,* Unpublished PhD thesis, Kansas State University.

KIRBY N. (1981) *Personal Values in Primary Education,* Harper and Row.

KOGAN M. (1975) *Educational Policy-Making, A Study of Interest Groups and Parliament,* Allen and Unwin.

KOGAN M. (1979) *The Plowden Committee and Primary School Policy,* Seminar at Sussex University.

KUTNICK P. (1980) 'The inception of school authority: The socialisation of the primary school child', *Genetic Psychology Monographs,* 101, pp. 35–70.

LACEY C. (1970) *Hightown Grammar,* Manchester University Press.

LACEY C. (1977) *The Socialization of Teachers,* Methuen.

LAWRENCE D. (1980) 'The role of the Local Education Authority', in POVEY R. *Educating the Gifted Child,* Harper and Row.

LAWTON D. (1968) *Social Class, Language and Education,* Routledge and Kegan Paul.

LEVI P. (1975) 'What to do with the Gifted', *Times Educational Supplement,* 29.8.75.

LEVI P. (1982) 'Stretching the poor', *Times Educational Supplement,* 5.11.82.

LIVESLEY W.J. and BROMLEY D.B. (1973) *Person Perception in Childhood and Adolescence,* John Wiley and Sons Ltd.

LOWENSTEIN L.F. (1981) *The Psychological Problems of Gifted Children,* Pullen Publications.

LOWENSTEIN L.F. (1982) 'Teachers' effectiveness in identifying gifted children', *Gifted Education International,* Vol. 1, No. 1, pp. 33–35.

LUTZ S.B. and LUTZ F.B. (1981) 'Gifted pupils in the elementary school setting', *The Creative Child and Adult Quarterly,* Vol. VI, No. 2.

MACKINNON D.W. (1962) 'The personality correlates of creativity: A study of American architects', in VERNON P.E. (Ed) (1970) *Creativity,* Penguin.

MAKER J. (1982) *Keynote Address,* presented at Third Teachers' Conference on Gifted Children, Leonardo Trust, London, July.

MALLET M.A. (1970) *A Study of Some 10–11 year old Intellectually Gifted Children,* Unpublished MA. Dissertation, University of Sussex.

MALTBY F. (1979) *Perceptions of Giftedness,* Unpublished MA Dissertation, University of Sussex.

MALTBY F. and BRADLEY G.C. (1983) 'A report on the third teachers' conference on gifted education, July 1982'. *Gifted Education International,* Vol. 1. No. 2.

MANNING P.K. (1975) 'Deviance and dogma, some comments on the labelling perspective', *British Journal of Criminology,* January.

MAYO E. (1939) 'Western Electric Studies', in ROETHLISBERGER F.J. and DICKSON W.J., *Management and the Worker,* Cambridge, Mass, Harvard University Press.

MAYS J.B. (1965) *Education and the Urban Child,* Liverpool University Press.

McINTYRE D. (1978) 'The characteristics and uses of systematic observation', in McALEESE R. and HAMILTON D. (Eds) *Understanding Classroom Life,* Windsor, NFER Publishing Co. Ltd.

MEAD G.H. (1934) 'Mind Self and Society', in STRAUSS A. (Ed) (1964) *On Social Psychology,* Chicago, University of Chicago Press.

MILLER R.V. (1956) 'Social Status and Socioempathic differences among mentally superior, mentally typical and mentally retarded children', *Exceptional Children,* 23, pp. 114–119.

MORENO J.L. (1934) 'Who shall survive? A new approach to the problem of human interrelationships', quoted in LEE V., WEBBERLEY R. and LITT L. (1976) Social

Relationships, Block 7, E201, *Personality and Learning*, The Open University.

MORRISON A. (1975) 'Teacher-centred strategies in interaction research', in CHANAN G. and DELAMONT S., *Frontiers of Classroom Research*, Windsor, NFER.

MORRISON A. and McINTYRE D (1971) *Schools and Socialisation*, Harmondsworth, Penguin.

MONAHAN P.W. (1980) *A Study of the Predictive Value of the Stanford-Binet Intelligence Scale, Form L-M, in the Identification of Mentally Gifted Minors at the Kindergarten and First Grade Levels*, Unpublished Ed. D. thesis, Pepperdine University.

MUNDAY L.A. and DAVIS J.C. (1974) *Varieties of Accomplishment after College: Perspectives on the Meaning of Academic Talent*, Iowa City, Research and Development Division of the American College Testing Program.

NASH R. (1973) *Classrooms Observed: The Teachers' Perception and the Pupils' Performance*, Routledge and Kegan Paul.

NEWLAND T.E. (1976) *The Gifted in Socioeducational Perspective*, Englewood Cliffs, Prentice-Hall, Inc. N.J.

ODEN S. and ASHER S.R. (1977) 'Coaching children in social skills for friendship making', *Child Development*, 48, pp. 495–506.

OGILVIE E. (1973) *Gifted Children in Primary Schools*, Schools Council Research Council.

OGILVIE E. (1975) 'Teaching Gifted Children', in WHITEHEAD J.M. (Ed.) *Personality and Learning*, Vol. 1, The Open University, Hodder.

OGILVIE E. (1980) 'The Schools Council's Curriculum Enrichment Project', in POVEY R. (Ed.) *Educating the Gifted Child*, Harper and Row.

PAINTER F. (1977) *Gifted Children – Their Relative Levels of Scholastic Achievements and Interests: Teachers' Views on their Educational Needs*, Knebworth, Herts, Pullen Publications.

PAINTER F. (1980) *Who are the Gifted? Definitions and Identification*, Knebworth, Herts, Pullen Publications.

PAINTER F. (1982) 'Gifted pupils in secondary schools' in *Looking to their Future*, NAGC Newsletter, April.

PARKYN G.W. (1948) *Children of High Intelligence*, Wellington, New Zealand Council for Educational Research.

PEAKER G.F. (1967) 'The Regression Analysis of the National Survey', Vol. II, Appendix 4, in *Children and their Primary Schools*, Report of the Central Advisory Council for Education, HMSO.

PEGNATO C.W. and BIRCH J.W. (1959) 'Locating gifted children in junior high schools – A comparison of methods', *Exceptional Children*, Vol. 25., pp. 300–304.

PIDGEON D. (1976) 'Teacher Expectation and Pupil Performance', in ROBERTS T. (Ed) *The Circumstance of Learning*, University of Manchester.

POHL R. (1970) *Teacher Nomination of Intellectually Gifted Children in the Primary Grades*, Unpublished PhD. Thesis, University of Illinois at Urbana.

POLLARD A. (1980) 'Teacher interests and changing situations of survival threat in primary classrooms', in WOODS P. (Ed.) *Teacher Strategies Explorations in the Sociology of the School*, Croom Helm.

POPPLETON P.K. (1975) 'The classroom setting as a unit of analysis in observation studies', in CHANAN G. and DELAMONT S. (Eds) *Frontiers of Classroom Research*, Windsor, NFER.

POST E.V. (1980) *The Effects of Increasing Amounts of Information and Training on Elementary Teachers' Ability to Identify Verbally Gifted Children*, Unpublished PhD thesis, the University of Texas at Austin.

POVEY R. (1980) 'Educating the gifted child: an overview', in POVEY R. (Ed.) *Educating the Gifted Child*, Harper and Row.

PRINGLE M.L.K. (1970) *Able Misfits, A Study of Educational and Behaviour Difficulties of*

103 very Intelligent Children (IQ's 120–200), National Bureau for Co-operation in Child Care, Studies in Child Development, Longman.

PROCTOR C.H. and LOOMIS C.P. (1951) 'Analysis of sociometric data', in JAHODA M., DEUTSCH M. and COOK S.W. (Eds) *Research Methods in Social Relations*, part 2, N.Y. Dryden.

RAWLS J. (1972) *A Theory of Justice*, Oxford.

RENZULLI J.S. (1977) *The Enrichment Triad Model: A Guide for Developing Defensible Programs for the Gifted and Talented*, Conn., Creative Learning Press Inc.

RENZULLI J.S. (1978) *What makes giftedness? Re-examining a definition*, Phi Delta Kappan, November.

RENZULLI J.S. (1981) Seminar presented to the Leonardo Trust at the DES.

RENZULLI J.S. and SMITH L.H. (1983) 'Curriculum compacting: an essential strategy for working with gifted students, *Gifted Education International*, Vol. 1, No. 2, pp. 97–102.

ROBB G. (1974) 'The education of gifted children', in PRINGLE M.K. and VARMA V.P. (Eds) *Advances in Educational Psychology*, Vol. 2, University of London Press.

ROBERTS S. and WALLACE B. (1980) 'The development of teaching materials: principles and practice', in POVEY R. (Ed.) *Educating the Gifted Child*, Harper and Row.

ROE A. (1952) 'A psychologist examines sixty-four eminent scientists' in VERNON P.E. (Ed.) (1970) *Creativity*, Harmondsworth, Penguin.

ROEDELL W.C. and ROBINSON H.B. (1977) *Programming for Intellectually Advanced Children: A Program Development Guide*, Child Development Research Group, University of Washington.

ROFF M., SELLS S.B. and GOLDEN M.M. (1972) *Social adjustment and personality development in children*, Minneapolis, University of Minnesota Press.

ROSENTHAL R. and JACOBSON J. (1968) *Pygmalion in the Classroom*, Holt, Rinehart and Winston.

RUBINGTON E. and WINBERG M. (1973) *Deviance the Interactionist Perspective, Text and Readings in the Sociology of Deviance*, 2nd edition, Macmillan Co.

SALMON-COX L. (1981) 'Teachers and standardised achievement tests: What's really happening?', *Phi Delta Kappan*, May, pp. 631–633.

SCHONELL F.J. and SCHONELL F.E. (rev. 1972) *Schonell Graded Word Reading Test*, Edinburgh, Oliver and Boyd.

SCHOOL MATHEMATICS PROJECT (1964) *The School Mathematics Project*, Director B. Thwaites, Cambridge University Press.

SCHOOLS COUNCIL CURRICULUM (1980) *Schools Council Curriculum Enrichment for Gifted Children Project* (1980 onwards) Globe Education.

SCHOOLS COUNCIL PROGRAMME 4: INDIVIDUAL PUPILS (1982) *Groups and their Activities*, Newsletter 5, Summer.

SCHUR E.M. (1979) *Interpreting Deviance, A Sociological Introduction*, Harper and Row.

SCHUR E.M. (1980) *The Politics of Deviance, Stigma Contests and the Uses of Power*, N.J., Prentice Hall Inc.

SCIENCE RESEARCH ASSOCIATES (1961) *Reading Laboratory*, Chicago Science Research Associates.

SCOULLER J.D. (1975) *Guidance Needs of Middle School Educable Mentally Retarded and Gifted Children*, Unpublished Ed. D. thesis, University of Florida.

SHARP R. and GREEN A. (1975) *Education and Social Control, A Study in Progressive Primary Education*, Routledge and Kegan Paul.

SHAW H. (1954) 'A study of popular and unpopular children', *Educational Review*, 6, pp. 208–20.

SHERTZER B. (1960) *Working with Superior Children*, Chicago, Science Research Associates.

SHERWOOD F. (1983) 'Teaching Able and Gifted Children (A study of initial and in-service teacher training in England, Scotland and Wales, 1981–1982), *Gifted Education International*, Vol. 1, No. 2.

SHIELDS J.B. (1975) *The Gifted Child*, Slough, NFER.

SIEGEL S. (1956) *Nonparametric Statistics for the Behavioural Sciences*, McGraw-Hill Book Co. Inc.

SIMON, B. (1981) 'The primary school revolution: myth or reality?', in SIMON B. and WILLCOCKS J. (Eds) *Research and Practice in the Primary Classroom*, Routledge and Kegan Paul.

SMITH G.J. (1980) *Teacher-judged-giftedness: the Effects of Inservice Attitude and Teaching Experience on Identification Accuracy*, Unpublished Ed. D. thesis, Arizona State University.

STEADMAN S.D. and GOLDSTEIN H. (1982) *Testing in Schools: the teachers view of testing*, Presented at BERA Annual Conference, St. Andrews, September.

STEADMAN S.D., PARSONS C. and SALTER B.G. (1978) *A First Interim Report to the Programme Committee of the Schools Council*, Mimeo, Schools Council.

STEVENS A. (1980) *Bright Children in Comprehensive Schools*, Harmondsworth, Penguin.

STOTT D.H. (1974) *The Social Adjustment of Children – Manual of the Bristol-Social Adjustment Guides*, Hodder and Stoughton.

STRAKER A. (1982) *Mathematics for Gifted Pupils*, Schools Council Programme 4, Individual Pupils, Longman for Schools Council.

TAYLOR E.A. (1952) 'Some factors relating to social acceptance in eighth-grade classrooms', *Journal of Educational Psychology*, 43, pp. 257–72.

TAYLOR G. and AYRES N. (1969) *Born and Bred Unequal*, Longman, Sociology of Education.

TEMPEST N.R. (1974) *Teaching Clever Children 7–11*, Routledge and Kegan Paul.

TERMAN L.M. (1925) *Genetic Studies of Genius, Vol. 1, Mental and Physical Traits of a Thousand Gifted Children*, California, Stanford University Press.

TERMAN M. and ODEN M.N. (1947) *Genetic Studies of Genius, Vol. 4, The gifted child grows up: Twenty five years follow-up of a superior group*, Vol. 4, Stanford, Calif., Stanford University Press.

TORRANCE E.P. (1962) *Guiding Creative Talent*, Englewood Cliffs, N.J. Prentice Hall.

VERNON P.E. (1969) *Intelligence and Cultural Environment*, Methuen.

VERNON P.E., ADAMSON G. and VERNON D.F. (1977) *The Psychology and Education of Gifted Children*, Methuen.

WADDINGTON M. and O'BRIEN G. (1979) *Promise Unfolding – A Study of Able Adolescents*, National Association of Gifted Children.

WALLACE B. (1982a) *Provision for Gifted Children in Essex*, Paper presented at Third Teachers' Conference on Gifted Children, The Leonardo Trust, London, July.

WALLACE B. (1982b) *Identifying Bright Pupils: A Teacher's Guide and Handbook*, Paper presented at Third Teachers' Conference on Gifted Children, The Leonardo Trust, London, July.

WALLACH M.A. and KOGAN N. (1965) *Modes of Thinking in Young Children*, N.Y., Holt, Rinehart and Winston.

WALTON G. (1961) *Identification of Intellectually Gifted Children in the Public School Kindergarten*, Unpublished PhD thesis, University of California at Los Angeles.

WARNOCK M. (1977) *Schools of Thought*, Faber.

WARREN C.A.B. and JOHNSON J.M. (1972) 'A Critique of labelling theory from the phenomenological perspective', in SCOTT R.A. and DOUGLAS J.D. (Eds) *Theoretical Perspectives on Deviance*, N.Y. Basic Books.

WEBER M. (1948) *Essays in Sociology*, Routledge and Kegan Paul.

WEST SUSSEX COUNTY COUNCIL (1974) *Gifted Children*, West Sussex County Council.

WHITSON B.L. (1981) *Relationships among Measures of Intelligence and Reading Achievement in Young Gifted Children*, Unpublished PhD thesis, University of

Washington.

WILLIS P. (1977) *Learning to Labour*, Saxon House.

WILSON C. (1963) 'Using test results and teacher evaluation in identifying gifted pupils', *Personnel and Guidance*, 41, pp. 720–721.

WISEMAN S. (1964) *Education and Environment*, Manchester University Press.

WISEMAN S. (1967) The Manchester Survey, Vol. II. Appendix 9 in *Children and their Primary Schools, Report of the Central Advisory Council for Education*, HMSO.

WITHALL J. (1956) 'An objective measurement of a teacher's classroom interactions', *Journal of Educational Psychology*, 47, 203–212.

WOLCOTT H.F. (1971) 'An ethnographic approach to the study of school administrators', in YEE A.H. (Ed.) *Social Interaction in Educational Settings*, Englewood Cliffs, N.Y., Prentice-Hall Inc.

WOOD N.D. (1973) *Teaching Gifted Children*, Francis Gerrard.

WOODS P. (1974) 'Problems of giftedness', *Contemporary Review*, Vol. 225, Nov., pp. 249–54.

Subject Index

acceleration
  and educational provision for gifted
    children, 87, 89–92, 102–9
access
  to schools, 228–32, 234
Assisted Places Scheme, 10, 42, 51, 88,
  95, 98, 101–2
Australia, 221

Bristol Social Adjustment Guide
  (BSAG), 172–3, 189, 193, 195–200,
  215–17, 233
Britain, *passim*
British Ability Scales, 15
Burt Reading Tests, 35, 51

Canada, 216
Cockcroft Report, 127–8
compensatory education, 9–12
creativity
  and giftedness, 1, 2, 5, 6, 53
curriculum materials, 12, 88, 91, 94,
  109–32, 208

discipline
  and gifted children, 157–61, 185–95,
  226–7

educational equality
  and giftedness, 8–13
Educational Priority Areas, 8–9
educational provision
  and acceleration, 87, 89–92, 102–9
  and differential grouping, 87–92,
    92–102
  and enrichment, 87, 89–92, 109–32,
    205–9

for gifted children, 87–133, 169,
  205–9, 211
  and segregation, 87–92, 92–102
enrichment
  and educational provision for gifted
    children, 87, 89–92, 109–32, 205–9

gender, 200–1
gifted children, *passim*
  academic ability of, 183–5, 201, 220
  categorization of, 5, 17–51
  classroom performance of, 58–60,
    103–4, 109–32, 135–70, 171–203
  and concentration, 161–9, 227
  and discipline, 157–61, 185–95,
    226–7
  and distraction, 161–9, 228
  educational provision for, 87–133,
    169, 205–9, 211
  and gender, 200–1
  and interactions with teachers,
    135–61, 169, 181–3, 201–2, 205–9,
    210–11, 226–7
  labelling of, 53–85, 87, 201, 210, 211
  and maladjustment, 195–200, 216
  peer perceptions of, 171–203
  as percentage of total population,
    17–18
  self-perceptions of, 171–203, 220–3
  social relations of, 171–203, 205–9
  and under-achievement, 11
  see also giftedness
giftedness, *passim*
  and creativity, 1, 2, 5, 6, 53
  criteria for, 5–15, 17–51, 53
  definitions of, 5–15, 17–51
  and educational equality, 8–13

and historical context, 5–15
and home environment, 73–80, 96–7, 101–2, 200
and justice, 8–13
as a national asset, 9–10
and philosophical context, 8–13
and political context, 8–13
polymathic definitions of, 20–33
and psychological context, 5–7, 8
and social class, 56, 69–85, 94–102
see also gifted children
Guess Who questions, 81, 105, 172–3, 177, 183–4, 188–95, 203, 218, 219–21, 232–3

Head Start programme, 9
headteachers
and educational provision, 90–132
and labelling of gifted children, 56, 68–9
and perceptions of gifted children, 17, 18, 19–22, 42–50, 53, 210, 234
home environment
and giftedness, 73–80, 96–7, 101–2, 200

Intelligence Quotient (IQ), 1–3, 5, 8, 11, 13, 15, 17–20, 21, 32, 33–42, 45, 46, 48, 49–50, 51, 53, 62, 63, 68, 69, 75, 97, 210
intelligence tests, 1–3, 6, 7, 15, 33–42, 50, 51
see also Intelligence Quotient
interactions
of teachers and gifted children, 135–61, 169, 181–3, 201–2, 205–9, 210–11, 226–7
interactive labelling theory, 54
see also labelling

justice
and giftedness, 8–13

Kent Mathematics Scheme, 32, 51, 126

labelling
and giftedness, 53–85, 87, 201, 210, 211
local education authorities (LEAs), 9–10, 15, 17, 65, 66, 67, 68–9, 71, 88–9, 90, 91, 92, 102, 132, 211, 228

maladjustment
and gifted children, 195–200, 216

mathematics
and gifted children, 25–6, 32, 51, 126–8, 198–200
methodology, 213–34
microcomputers, 207–8, 211

National Association of Gifted Children (NAGC), 11–12, 13, 66, 172, 191, 195
National Child Development Study, 12
National Foundation of Educational Research (NFER), 31, 50, 61, 63, 83
New Zealand, 218
Newsom Report, 70

ORACLE study, 140–1

participant observation, 224–8
Peabody test, 33–4
Plowden Report, 8–9, 70, 89
primary schools, *passim*
project work
and enrichment, 125–6, 133, 206

Schonell Graded Word Reading Test, 35, 51
School Mathematics Project, 25–6, 51, 126, 206
Schools Council Curriculum Enrichment Packs (SCCEPs), 12, 115
Science Research Associations Reading Laboratory (SRA), 41, 51, 111, 123, 128–9, 206
segregation
and educational provision for gifted children, 87–92, 92–102
social class
and giftedness, 56, 69–85, 94–102
see also social relations; social status
social relations
of gifted children, 171–203, 205–9
see also social class; social status
social status
of gifted children, 171–203
see also social class; social relations
sociometry, 171–203, 218–20, 233
Stanford Binet Intelligence Test, 1, 3, 6, 15, 33–4
streaming, 107–8

teachers
and assessment of children's academic position, 80–4
and discipline of gifted children, 157–61, 185–95, 226–7

and distribution of time in the
classroom, 135, 142–50
and educational provision for gifted
children, 92–133, 169, 205–9
and identification of giftedness, 1–2,
17–51, 53
and interactions with gifted children,
135–61, 169, 181–3, 201–2, 205–9,
210–11, 226–7
and labelling of gifted children, 55–7,
65–9, 201, 210, 211
and methodology, 215–17
and perceptions of gifted children,
22–50, 69–84, 171–203, 205–9
and social class in relation to
giftedness, 69–84
topic work
see project work

United States of America (USA), 1, 3, 5,
6, 8, 9, 42, 64, 66, 172, 218–19, 227

Where Are You Game (WAYG), 150,
172–3, 221–3, 232–4
Wechsler Intelligence Score for Children
(WISC), 2, 6, 7, 15, 33–5, 38